D1235114

IN THE STARS THE GLORY OF HIS EYES

K. TROY

In the Stars the Glory of His Eyes

Tales of an Irish Tour Guide in Rome

IGNATIUS PRESS   SAN FRANCISCO

Except where noted, the Scripture citations used in this work are taken from the Revised Standard Version of the Bible—Second Catholic Edition (Ignatius Edition), copyright © 2006 National Council of the Churches of Christ in the United States of America. Used with permission. All rights reserved.

Cover art:
"On Pilgrimage"
Mixed media digital collage
Art and cover design by Enrique J. Aguilar
Individual photos from
Wikimedia Commons and unsplash.com

© 2022 by Ignatius Press, San Francisco
All rights reserved
ISBN 978-1-62164-520-7 (PB)
ISBN 978-1-64229-211-4 (eBook)
Library of Congress Control Number 2022934003
Printed in the United States of America ∞

To Lolek . . .

I see his blood upon the rose
And in the stars the glory of his eyes,
His body gleams amid eternal snows,
His tears fall from the skies.

I see his face in every flower;
The thunder and the singing of the birds
Are but his voice—and carven by his power
Rocks are his written words.

All pathways by his feet are worn,
His strong heart stirs the ever-beating sea,
His crown of thorns is twined with every thorn,
His cross is every tree.

—J. M. Plunkett

Contents

PROLOGUE

Invoking the Madonna

The mother of Jesus said to him, "They have no wine."

—John 2:3

Any choir likes to sing in front of a packed audience, but how were we going to get a crowd to come to our concert in the basement of an obscure church in July, when virtually everyone had left Rome on account of the stifling heat? The choir was really good, a group of schoolgirls from a prestigious Catholic school in the south of England. Their director was passionate and energetic, with a real streak of perfectionism. There was no doubt that the event was going to be entertaining, but would anyone be there? If no one turned up, it would be considered a disaster—and it would be my fault, since I had booked the cheapest venue I could find in Rome.

The parish priest of Santa Lucia del Gonfalone used the basement under his church to feed the poor and the homeless in the locality during the day. The basement could hold more than one hundred people, and it had a grand piano. Visiting choirs were welcome to use the venue for concerts for a very modest fee. The church is located in Via dei Banchi Vecchi just a short distance from the Tiber. It would be difficult to find a more centrally located venue in Rome. In the evening, however, precious few people walk in that area. The street doesn't lead directly anywhere, unlike the busy thoroughfares between Campo dei Fiori, Piazza Navona, and the Pantheon. We couldn't hope to fill the concert with people who happened to be passing by, because, after a certain hour, virtually no one passed by at all.

It was three days until the concert, and we needed to do some effective publicity fast. How could we convince people to come, I wondered? There were concerts going on every night in some church or another at the city centre, and many of the choirs seemed awesome. Why would anyone choose to come to ours? Then an idea struck me. If Irish groups were in town and heard that there was going to be free wine and food after the concert, then they would show up in their droves, regardless of the quality of the music. So I asked the parish priest if we could do a little wine and cheese reception after the concert in the room next door to the hall. He readily agreed, once I promised that we would leave the room exactly as we found it. My wife, Laura, was in Ireland with the kids, but she managed to e-mail me a poster for the concert with the all-important words "Wine reception afterwards. Free admission. All welcome." These posters were printed in copious numbers and put on display at the reception desks of every hotel that I passed in the following days.

The day before the concert, I took the choir to the church basement, where they had an extended rehearsal. While they were rehearsing, I went out on the street to locate the nearest supermarket. It wasn't too far away, on the other side of a small square. Twenty minutes later, I was crossing the square in the opposite direction, gingerly pushing a shopping trolley loaded with wine bottles, potato crisps, and cheese. There was a wino lying on a mat not far from the entrance to the supermarket. When he heard the clinking of bottles and spotted the wine in the trolley, his eyes lit up at once.

"*Ti serve aiuto* [Do you need help]?" he called over to me. I had a momentary image of me chasing after him and the trolley around the streets of Rome while our choir performed to an empty hall.

"*No, grazie!*" I replied and kept moving as fast as I could, jealously guarding my precious load. On the contents of this trolley the success of the concert hung—of that I had no doubt. A short time later, all the wine and snacks were stored in the adjoining room. The choir finished their rehearsal, and we began arranging the seats for the audience.

The evening of the concert came, and the girls had an early dinner to make sure they were ready to sing at 9:00 P.M. We arrived at the basement at about 8:30, and I was very pleased to see that about a quarter of the seats were already taken. This surely boded well. I would have been more than happy if the venue was even half full for the concert. The girls were excited and nervous as they waited in the adjoining room while people continued to trickle into the basement. By 8:50, to my amazement, the place was completely full, and there were now people standing at the back. At this point, I was getting a little bit worried. Why were there so many people here? Had they come just for the free wine? What would they think once they discovered that they were being poured the most economical wine I could find at the supermarket? I cringed inwardly. Why had I bought such cheap fare?

I peeped out from the room to have a look at the audience. They appeared a motley group. All ages were represented, from twenty-somethings to old-age pensioners. There seemed to be various nationalities. Was I just imagining it, or did many of them have an edgy look, as if they were already wondering where the booze was?

There was no air conditioning in the basement, and

the temperature was starting to rise considerably. Someone knocked on the door of the adjoining room, where we were waiting, and asked for a glass of water. With horror I realised that I had bought only wine, plus a few bottles of soft drinks for the girls: there was no water of any sort! The parish priest was sitting in the crowd, and I went out to him to ask if he had any bottles of water in his office. He disappeared and came back a few minutes later.

"The water in the taps down here is not drinkable. These two bottles are all I have. Sorry."

We distributed the water in plastic cups for those near the entrance who spotted what we were doing and had asked for a drink. Within a few minutes, the bottles were empty. Was it just the heat, or did this audience have an inordinate level of thirst?

Nine o'clock had already arrived, and it was time to begin. I resolved to nip out once the girls started singing and buy as much water as I could carry from one of the bars in the locality, but the choir director turned to me just then and said, "Kieran, I am going to give a little presentation on each piece before we sing it. Seeing that a lot of the people here seem Italian, do you mind standing up beside us and giving a short translation each time after I speak?"

My heart sank, but it was one of those cases where the tour guide has no option but to agree. I nodded dolefully. The girls trooped out and took their positions behind the grand piano. They received a warm round of applause, but I couldn't help wondering how warm the reaction would be once the crowd went in next door for the reception afterwards.

The girls began singing their first piece. The acoustics were surprisingly good, and in ordinary circumstances, I would have enjoyed listening to them. But the water situation was now critical. By the time this concert was over, I knew that people would be parched, and that was not a reference to those individuals who had come along just for the alcohol. I slunk down the side aisle and towards the exit, tore up the stairs into the alleyway outside, and then dashed along Via dei Banchi Vecchi. I hoped to find a bar where I could quickly buy a few bottles of water and then get back to the concert before the choir began its next piece, but there wasn't an open establishment anywhere in sight! I ran back down into the basement just as the audience was finishing applauding at the end of the first piece. The choir director was looking around anxiously to see where I had disappeared to, but she gave me a smile as I strode to the front to translate the next introduction.

The choir began singing again, and I stood over to the side against the wall, despondent. The audience looked happy and stimulated, but I had no doubt that part of this was due to the happy thought of the free drinks they expected to be soon enjoying. What would I do? Soon I would have a riot on my hands! And some of these people were Germans! I knew only a few Germans personally, but I had heard that theirs was a nation that liked their alcohol—lots of it. What a rude awakening was in store for them!

Typically for me, I turned to prayer at that moment, only because there seemed no other way out. It came to mind that at the wedding feast at Cana, when the young couple ran out of wine, Mary turned to Jesus and said simply, "They have no wine." I addressed a simple prayer to the Mother of God: "Mary, they have no water!"—but it was a cry from the heart.

It was natural for me at that moment to address my plea to the Madonna. One of our group leaders had recently been saying that the natural recourse for pilgrims seeking protection in this day of air travel was the Blessed Virgin, whom he called "Our Lady of the Skies."

After translating the introduction to the third song, I sidled my way to the back of the basement to see if I could judge the mood of the house. There was a young man of uncertain nationality leaning against the back wall near the door. He didn't look all that interested in the concert, nor did he seem particularly well dressed, but the light was low and I couldn't see very well. On impulse, I whispered to him, "Do you understand Italian?"

"Yes."

I beckoned to him, and he followed me out the exit and halfway up the stairs from the basement.

"Do you know any bars or cafés around here that are still open?" I whispered.

"Yes," he replied.

I held up a fifty-euro note. "Can you get me twelve large bottles of water?"

Without a word, he took the note and disappeared.

I translated the next introduction and took my position leaning against the wall. Even though the choir were singing their hearts out, I couldn't help shaking my head gloomily.

"I'll never see that guy, the water, or my fifty-euro note again!" I thought miserably. "What was I thinking of! He hadn't even asked if I wanted sparkling water or still!"

I had to stop myself from throwing my hands up in the air in exasperation. "How could I expect otherwise?" I thought. "A guy like that only comes along for the free drinks, and then he is presented with a fifty-euro note on top? He must have thought all his Christmases had come at once!"

Forty minutes later, the concert ended to rapturous applause. "I know why they're rapturous," I thought cynically. "They think they can finally get their hands on the wine!"

Strangely, though, the audience gave a standing ovation and refused to stop until the choir did an encore. I had expected a stampede for the drinks as soon as the concert was over. While the choir performed their encore, I headed towards the adjacent room to begin opening the bottles of wine. I had considered announcing to everyone that we would have to cancel the reception because of a lack of water, and maybe it would be better if everyone just made his own way out of the building as soon as possible? But then I reconsidered. Better to give this horde of barbarians bad wine than no wine at all, even if there was no water. The words of Marie Antoinette—"Let them eat cake"—seemed strangely apt: I would soon be facing the guillotine myself once this mob tasted the fare that I had prepared for them. I shuddered when I considered my lack of judgement. What had possessed me to put posters up around Rome advertising free alcohol?

I opened the door quietly and slipped into the room. To my great surprise, the young man was placing bottles of water and plastic cups along the tables.

He turned around when I entered. "I saw that you were busy, so I took the liberty of setting up. Oh, and by the way, here is your change," he said, handing me the money before resuming what he had been doing.

I was flabbergasted but didn't have much time to dwell on my errors of discernment. A few minutes later, he and I were flat out pouring drinks and distributing snacks to a far-from-angry "mob." The concert had been so enjoyable, I came to realise, that even bad wine tasted acceptable afterwards. And among the crowd were some cultured Germans who seemed to have little interest in alcohol and entered into an animated discussion with our choir director on her unique technique of conducting.

The concert, it transpired, was an unqualified success. Many of the audience lingered on long after every drop had been drunk, discussing the various pieces and complimenting the choir with great enthusiasm. The girls and their conductor were in high spirits an hour later as we climbed the steps out of the basement while the parish priest locked up. It was only when we were well down the street that it struck me that I had omitted to do something. It had slipped my mind completely. My prayer had been answered—even what had been left unsaid had been granted in abundance —but I had forgotten to say thank you to Our Lady of the Skies.

I

Lady of the Skies

We have this treasure in earthen vessels, to show that the transcendent power belongs to God and not to us.

—2 Corinthians 4:7

It was July 12, 2005, and I was on a night train travelling northward along the Mediterranean coast, a slow train that would not arrive in Rome until the early hours. There was a tiny sliver of moon in a starry sky above the still water. Though today I can still recollect the beauty of that scene, my attention then was not on moon, stars, or sea. It was a series of events that had unfolded in the previous months that captured my attention, all of them coming to a climax on that very evening.

I remember the first time I saw Father Higgins. We had a group of more than fifty people lined up in front of the check-in desk in Dublin for a flight to Milan. The airport was busy, and I was ushering a couple of our group towards the desk when someone with a luggage trolley passed in front of us. A suitcase fell off, and our passage was blocked. I glared impatiently at the man pushing the offending trolley. The man looked back at me seriously. He was of slight stature with a thin face and a thick mop of white hair.

"Kieran?" he said tentatively.

"Yes?" I replied, taken by surprise.

"It's me, Father Higgins!" he said with a beaming smile. He had seen that I had a sign tucked under my arm and had guessed my identity correctly.

About five months before, I had had my first contact with Father Higgins. Laura and I were advertising a trip to Rome, Florence, and Bobbio. Bobbio is a small town in the valley between Genoa and Piacenza, an obscure enough place, were it not for the fact that Ireland's greatest missionary, Saint Columban, ended his incredible journeys there. The phone rang in the office, and for the first time, I heard the soft western accent of Father Higgins. He spoke in short bursts of rapid words.

"I've seen your ad in the paper," he said. "So you're taking a group to the tomb of Saint Columban? Isn't that something!"

As we discussed the proposed trip, he was amazed to discover that the itinerary included virtually all of the places that he most wanted to visit or revisit in Italy. Many of the places he knew already, such as Rome's Irish College and the principal sights in Florence, but the tomb of Saint Columban at Bobbio was a place where he had always dreamed of going but had never had the opportunity. He was thrilled to find out that our programme included all of his favourite spots in Rome, even the restaurant that he and his classmates used to frequent during their student days in the city.

And so Father Higgins booked himself on the trip. But he would phone back regularly before the departure date to ask questions about the journey and to say that a couple more of his friends wanted to join us, if we had any more space for them. In the end, Father Higgins took a party of fourteen people along with himself on the trip. His phone manner was always the same—courteous, timid even—but with boyish good humour and an infectious enthusiasm about the forthcoming journey.

Finally, we met on that occasion when his trolley crossed my path in Dublin Airport. The trip itself registers in my memory like so many other pilgrimages of a similar sort, a blur of monuments and events in which only a few happenings stand out, but all of those happenings involved Father Higgins. We landed in Milan and drove to Bobbio, where we spent two nights, paying our respects at the tomb of the Irish saint. From there, we drove all the way to Florence, where we spent another two nights and trekked from the tombs of Galileo and Michelangelo in Santa Croce to the Palazzo Vecchio, and from there on to the Duomo, finishing our tour looking in weary awe at Michelangelo's *David* in the Accademia. The last four nights were spent in the Irish College in Rome and included an audience with Pope John Paul II.

During the journeys, Father Higgins would usually sit with his group towards the back of the coach, but fairly often he would make his way to the front while the bus was still moving and sit on the front step beside me. Often I would know he was coming in advance, for I would hear the driver groan as he caught sight of Father Higgins' approach in the rearview mirror. Sometimes the visit to the front of the coach would be to reminisce about an event that he recalled from his student days and that had come back to him now on account of something we had just seen. Other times, he would offer a suggestion or piece of advice on something that could be done in the best interests of the group, a little change to the order of the itinerary, or an extra visit that could be squeezed in while we were in a particular area. The curious thing was that never once did his suggestions irritate or annoy. Never did they sound like an implicit criticism of the way that things had been originally planned. They were always offered in the same way: with a mixture of timidity and good humour, humility and enthusiasm. It was clear that he was offering them only because he felt they would be of benefit to everyone. But apart from the humility and the courtesy, the self-effacing stories and humorous anecdotes, other things soon began to become apparent about Father Higgins: he had a quick wit and a warm sense of humour, a remarkable memory and a good intellect; it also became clear that he had a natural sensitivity towards problems and difficulties that might be facing others.

The first suggestion from the amiable priest that I can recall was made as our coach was pulling out of Bobbio on the second day. Father Higgins ambled down to the front and perched himself on the step almost as soon as we were on our way.

"Kieran, there's a statue of Columban on the outskirts of town, isn't there? I think we saw it on the way in from Milan."

"That's right. We'll be passing it in a minute."

"Wouldn't it be good if we could have a group photo there, right in front of the statue—Saint Columban with all of us modern-day wanderers, exiles like himself from the old Emerald Isle!"

And so we stopped the coach at a junction and held up the traffic while we disembarked and gathered around the statue for a photo, with Father Higgins at the centre smiling broadly towards the camera.

I do not remember the journey from Bobbio to Florence at all, but in Piazzale Michelangelo, which is situated on a hill overlooking Florence, we disembarked and gazed at the city spread out before us. Father Higgins was delighted with the scene.

"Look, there's the Duomo, and Giotto's campanile beside it! You can see the polychrome marble from here! Isn't it remarkable! Look, that must be Santa Croce off to the right with the scaffolding on it! Oh my! Isn't it all just wonderful!"

When we finally began our tour proper the next day, we found that there were many weary legs in the group. In Florence in those years, private coaches had to drop passengers off along the Arno River, quite a distance from the principal sights. By the time we had seen the tombs of Galileo and Michelangelo in Santa Croce and admired the works of Giotto, people were already faltering. Our guide, whose name was Elvio, began marching the group in the direction of Palazzo Vecchio, the next stop on our tour.

"Elvio," I said tentatively, "these people are not so young anymore. Maybe we could stop somewhere for a tea break and let everyone sit down for a while?"

"What?" the guide asked incredulously, looking at his watch. "We haven't even started our real tour of Florence yet, and you want to stop for tea?"

"Just look at the group, Elvio," I replied. "Can you see them even making it as far as the centre?"

"Maybe you're right," he reluctantly conceded.

And so we descended on a café close to Santa Croce, taking up all of the seats, inside and out. It took a good half hour for everyone to be served, which gave the group a welcome rest.

"Don't worry, Elvio," I said. "We'll reduce the tour by half an hour to make up for this delay, and, you know, their capacity to absorb what is being said goes way up once they've had their tea!"

Our guide had noticed how animated everyone had become while they were having their drinks and recalled how lethargic they had been previously during the tour. "This tea break is a great idea!" he commented. "I'm going to try it with all my tours from now on!"

All the time, Father Higgins was sitting on a high stool inside at the bar, chattering away in animated Italian with the barmen. "This pause for tea is inspired, Kieran," he confided to me. "The tour is great, but people need time to absorb the scene, to take it all in. And for us Irish, tea is required to do that. We imbibe the atmosphere along with the tea. But I prefer an espresso myself!"

My clearest memory of that trip is a scene that unfolded a few days later, when we arrived in Rome and had already immersed ourselves in the chaos and magic of the Eternal City. There is a restaurant called Scoglio di Frisio on the Via Merulana near the Basilica of Saint Mary Major. During their student days in the 1950s, Father Higgins and his friends used to come to this restaurant whenever they had managed to scrape some cash together or when a visitor to the college had given one or another of them some money to go out for a meal. The restaurant is laid out so as to represent a cave in the Bay of Naples. The main dining area is like a large cavern on the edge of the sea, but there is also a smaller cave partially divided off from the main area. In the mid-1950s, the young Sean Higgins and his friends often used to sit at a table in this more secluded part. That area of the restaurant had been given the name "the Sacristy" by the seminarians of the college.

For the group of June 2004, we had dinner booked in Scoglio di Frisio for one of the nights. Father Higgins' excitement was palpable as we walked down Via Merulana and neared the restaurant. He was overjoyed to find that the place was still being run by the same family of half a century earlier, and I saw him talking animatedly with Eugenio, the owner, while we were sorting out seating for the group. When everyone was seated and the noise and confusion had abated, the pianist struck up a tune and a soprano began singing. As I looked around to see where Father Higgins had gone, I was amused to discover that he had managed to seat himself and his entire party of fourteen in the Sacristy! The rest of us were seated in the main area. Through one of the cavernous openings into the Sacristy I could see Father Higgins standing to raise a glass at me with an impish smile. Later I went over to see how things were going. To this day, I can still see the look of contentment on his face as he sat around the table with his friends, helping others with the menu, calling out cheerful instructions to Eugenio and his staff—the same family who had served him so many times at the same table an incredible fifty years earlier.

The trip was no sooner over and the group had returned to Ireland when we received a call from Father Higgins. He wanted to lead his own pilgrimage to Italy the following summer, and this time he had very definite ideas for the itinerary. The group would stay again in the Irish College in Rome, but this time, along with the essential sights of the city, we would visit various places that had historical associations with Ireland. Then we would leave Rome and stay the last few nights in Gaeta on the coast road towards Naples. Here was situated the old villa that had once been owned by the Irish bishops and was used by the students and staff of the Irish College to escape the terrible heat of Rome during those summers when they were compelled to remain in Italy. Many of the other pontifical colleges in Rome also had places outside the city that were used for the same purpose. The Irish villa was always referred to as "Formia" by

the students and staff of the Irish College, though the building was up the coast from Formia and properly located in
Gaeta. Father Higgins had spent a very memorable summer
here as a student in the late 1950s and longed to relive those
days.

The villa was on the bay in sight of an old fortress in Gaeta
that was used as a prison. In those years when Father Higgins was a student, the prison held the notorious Gestapo
colonel Herbert Kappler, who was responsible for carrying
out Hitler's orders to the letter in the Ardeatine Massacre
in Rome in 1944. Under the villa were ancient archaeological remains from the first century B.C. These would become
a source of controversy later when the Italian Ministry of
Fine Arts took a case against the Irish College.

When the Irish seminarians arrived in Formia in late June,
they would spend hours each day swimming, hiking, and going on excursions. In the evenings, they read, improved their
Italian, and learned to type. Each summer, the *trampolino*, a
wooden structure mounted on four airtight barrels, would
be repaired and recommissioned as a board from which the
students would dive into the warm, crystal-clear water of
the bay. After 1963, the rules at the college changed, and
students began to return to Ireland in the summer, prompting the sale of the villa in 1971 to a local family. A couple of
decades later, it was transformed into a fine hotel. This was
where Father Higgins wished to take his group. He wanted
to step once again into the water of the bay and be filled
with the memories and inspirations that were so precious
to him. Yes, it would be a journey into the past, but only
because he wished to be nourished with the same cultural
and spiritual influences that had nourished him so well when
he was little more than a boy. And he wanted his friends

and family to experience the same influences by seeing the places in the locality that he would have visited as a student.

Every Wednesday, the students would make a *gita*—an excursion—to a place such as the Benedictine monastery of Montecassino or the sanctuary of the Blessed Trinity on nearby Monte Spaccato. They would sometimes walk along the route of an ancient Roman road—the Via Flacca—that lay between Formia and Sperlonga and once provided the only access to some of the bathing areas along the coast. On the last Wednesday of July, the students climbed to the statue of Christ the Redeemer on Monte Redentore, almost thirteen hundred metres above the coast of Formia. This was a way of paying their respects to the annual tradition of climbing Croagh Patrick (located in Father Higgins' native diocese of Tuam, on the west coast of Ireland) on the last Sunday of July. Between the villa and the town of Gaeta there was a parish run by a local priest called Don Chinappi. He liked to have the students from the villa play a role in his annual procession with the Blessed Sacrament along the waterfront for the feast of the Assumption. These things made the summer spent in Formia all the more meaningful and had a deep and lasting impression on Father Higgins.

The new trip was penned in for the following July, when the Irish College would become available to be used as a guesthouse at the end of the academic year. A provisional date was set, but this ended up being changed slightly when the airlines eventually released their schedules for 2005. We still had the pilgrimage season of 2004 to complete, so we remained in Italy, travelling around with groups, until November. Regular phone calls would come from Father Higgins at often inopportune times as he worked out his itinerary in detail.

"I'm just about to enter Saint Peter's for a tour now, Father Sean. Maybe we could speak later?"

"Sure, Kieran. I'm just talking aloud. Nothing urgent. I'll get you another time."

When we returned to the office in Ireland for the winter, Father Higgins' calls would come a couple of times a week. The programme was tweaked and retweaked. Each time a change was made, he asked us if we wouldn't mind printing out the new version and posting it to him. He was of the old school and didn't use e-mail. There was always the same politeness and humility, the apologies for being a nuisance. And the curious thing, once again, was that these extended phone calls never caused annoyance, no matter how busy things were in the office that winter.

On one occasion, he asked if Laura and I would be able to meet him halfway for lunch, at a hotel in County Roscommon overlooking Lough Ree, to discuss the programme. It was here that we became aware for the first time that Father Higgins was unwell. He looked much the same as he had done during the trip earlier that year, but even thinner maybe, and with a certain air of tiredness. He still looked himself, though, and had the same infectious cheerfulness, so we didn't pay much attention to it at first.

"You know I've been on chemotherapy?" he said at one point.

"No!" we replied together.

"Yes, it's been going on quite a while now." He stopped and gave a nervous chuckle. "I'm not sure if I'll even still be around next July." Then he became more serious. "But I'd like the trip to go on ahead, you know, regardless of whether I'm around or not. There's no point in worrying. All my travel plans are in the hands of Mary our Mother, Lady of the Skies!"

The phone calls continued into the spring of 2005. New visits were added to the itinerary, and the order of things was frequently changed and improved. An excursion would be made to the monastery at Montecassino. This would evoke the summer Father Higgins had spent in Gaeta as a student, during which he had visited Montecassino a number of times. We would visit the tomb of Saint Maria Goretti in Nettuno on our journey between Rome and Gaeta. This courageous young girl, who forgave her attacker before she died, was an inspirational figure for Father Higgins. When she was made a saint in 1950, the ceremony of canonisation was held in Saint Peter's Square for the first time ever because the basilica itself could not contain the crowds that wished to attend. The reverberations caused by that canonisation event were still palpable in the city when Sean Higgins arrived as a teenager to begin his studies just two years later.

"Alessandro Serenelli—yes, that was the name of the man who killed her—he was present at her canonisation, a changed man, and all because of Maria and the way she forgave him."

Father Higgins wanted, in particular, to visit a number of places associated with Saint Oliver Plunkett, a man who had lived in relative comfort for twenty-two years in Rome but gave it all up to become a tireless reformer, reconciler, and evangelizer in an Ireland ravaged by war and conquest. Oliver Plunkett was a beacon of integrity and goodness amid the darkness of seventeenth-century Ireland. It seemed that he had become a sort of role model for Father Higgins. During our phone conversations, Father Higgins would recount fascinating snippets from the story of Plunkett, linking a chapter of his life to one place or another in Rome. "We could visit the Propaganda Fide College on our way

to the Spanish Steps, you see. Saint Oliver taught in there
for many years and was named Archbishop of Armagh in
the chapel. It would be good to see that while we're passing,
wouldn't it? We're in the area anyway, Kieran. What do you
think? Or would it be too much trouble?''

In this way, over dozens of phone conversations, the
itinerary grew and changed, and then was adjusted some
more. Bookings came in from Father Higgins' friends, family, and parishioners. By early April 2005, the group had
reached its target size of fifty, and soon afterwards, the details of the trip were settled to the priest's satisfaction. The
first draft of the itinerary had been made on July 21, 2004.
The last version was drawn up a full ten months later, on
May 17, 2005. On this occasion, Father Higgins asked that
the night tour by coach should include a mention of the
former locations of the Irish College in Rome. These could
be pointed out as we drove in the vicinity. In particular,
he wanted us to indicate the location of the college in the
mid-1600s when Saint Oliver Plunkett was a student there.

The programme was finally in place. It would be a trip to
celebrate our Catholic faith, exploring its enduring link with
the successors of Peter, recalling the connection of heroic
Irish figures such as Saint Oliver Plunkett with Rome during
the times of persecution, and reflecting on Italian heroes of
the faith, such as Saints Benedict and Maria Goretti.

"It's something that wouldn't have been done too often,
you see; that's why it's worth trying. And we'll take in my
old restaurant in Rome to see if they still know how to make
spaghetti alle vongole. You know, I can't wait for the group
to dip their feet in the ocean off the Villa Irlanda, but I don't
think too many of us would be able for the *trampolino* at this
stage!''

Everything seemed just right, and the phone calls became

less frequent. At this point we were already in Italy, working with other pilgrimages, and there was little time to reflect on anything else. But whenever I did have time to remember the imminent arrival of Father Higgins' group, I had to admit to myself that I felt a thrill at the prospect. It is easy and uplifting to take a group on a tour when they have enthusiasm for the place that you are visiting, and Father Higgins had enough enthusiasm by himself to energise any group completely. And then there was the intriguing prospect of pursuing an itinerary as unique as this one, not to mention the novelty of the stay in Formia. Laura and I had called to see the Villa Irlanda that spring when we were driving up from Naples. As it turned out, it happened to be just two days before the death of Pope John Paul II. At one point on the journey, we parked the car and began walking down a tree-lined road in sight of the sea, struck by the natural beauty of the area. We knew that it would be even better to see it through Father Higgins' eyes and to have the places brought alive with stories from his student days.

In late June, the plane tickets, flight itineraries, and baggage labels were posted to everyone individually. The group was due to travel from Dublin to Rome on July 7. Everything was in order, and there appeared to be no further worries about Father Higgins' health. Any concerns we had had about his fitness to travel had gradually dissipated as the day of travel approached. It had been agreed that if he had not been well enough to travel, he would have let us know in good time, but no word of any sort had come. We were busy with other pilgrims and the days were passing quickly. On July 1, I was on my way out of the house to take a group to the catacombs when Laura remarked, "You know whose feast it is? Saint Oliver Plunkett's!"

"Father Higgins will be sure to celebrate today," I replied.

We were completely unprepared for the sad events that were about to unfold. The feast of Saint Oliver Plunkett would be Father Higgins' last full day on earth. On July 2, a phone call came to say that he had died suddenly that morning.

When I received the phone call with the news of Father Higgins' death, I was on a coach in Rome with a group from the Mater Dei Institute of Dublin. We were heading to the Church of Saint Lawrence outside the Walls. Behind the church there is the great monumental cemetery of Campo Verano, a burial place that originally developed around the tomb of Saint Lawrence, one of the most revered martyrs of the city. During a quiet moment, I took the chance to walk to the Irish College tomb, not far inside the entrance. This tomb contains the remains of some students and staff of the college who died in Rome down the years. On the feast of All Souls, the Irish College students used to come here for a short but reverential ceremony in remembrance of the dead, a tradition that would also have been in place in the time of Father Higgins.

But on this day, July 2, 2005, I just stared blankly at the Irish College vault, not registering the names of those who were buried beneath. Why couldn't God let Father Higgins have this final trip with his friends and family, I wondered? Father Higgins had put such energy into preparing the pilgrimage. Why allow him to do all of that and yet take his life just days before departure? Rome meant so much to him! Surely it would have done him and his family good to have made that final trip together? His six years in the Irish College were among the most memorable in Father Higgins' life. He had immersed himself in the city and all it had to offer in terms of Catholic history, culture, and faith. The other students called him by the nickname "Cuttings" because he had the habit of cutting interesting articles from newspapers and magazines and storing them in a scrapbook for future perusal. Everything he had done in his student days here was done with a sense of enthusiasm and openness. He loved to attend the papal liturgies in Rome, enjoying their solemnity, particularly the Holy Week ceremonies at Saint Peter's. The celebration of the Stations of the Cross by the Holy Father at the Colosseum on Good Friday was a favourite event. During his free time, Father Higgins would walk everywhere and had anecdotes to relate about every street in the city. Could he not have been allowed to enjoy it one last time?

As I stood in Campo Verano, however, other questions were also beginning to form in the back of my mind, the questions that arise when your business is small and frequently skating not too far above insolvency: Will the trip be cancelled? Surely his friends and family won't want to travel now in their condition of grief? Even if some of them do travel, what about the rest? Will they expect refunds? The airline certainly won't refund us a penny, but will the hotels give something back?

That evening, I spoke to Father Higgins' great friend Margaret. She did secretarial work in the parish and had been heavily involved in the planning of the trip and in gathering up the bookings. "I don't know how many will want to travel, Kieran," she said. "We have the funeral to think about now, but I will contact everyone and see how they feel. We'll get back to you as soon as possible."

I often think about how Margaret went about contacting everyone to find out if they still wished to travel to Rome. She was in a state of grief herself and involved in the arrangement of a very emotional funeral. The easiest thing would have been to say, "Maybe we should just cancel the whole thing. It's not the right time for a trip.'' Many people would have done that, but Margaret had a sense that Father Higgins wanted the group to travel no matter what, in whatever state of grief, even a couple of days after his own funeral.

The next day, she phoned again.

"How did you get on, Margaret? I'm sure it can't have been easy to get in touch with everyone."

"Well, it wasn't too difficult, actually. They were all about in the area, not too far away."

"I can't imagine that many of them are in the mood for travelling to Rome."

"Oh no, actually, they all want to travel."

"*All* of them?"

"Every last one."

When I put down the phone, I began the process of re-wording all of the things I had intended to say about the various places we would be visiting. Originally the idea had been simply to attempt to describe them as they were in themselves. But now it seemed right to portray them as Father Higgins' had portrayed them to me over those multiple phone calls in which he had worked out his itinerary, telling the stories from his perspective and using his anecdotes. Although I began this process with a feeling of melancholy and sadness, the drama and tension seemed over. The group would be travelling as planned, and some sense of normality seemed to return. Little did we know that the drama was only beginning.

On July 6, the day before the group was due to travel, Alitalia announced that all its flights would be cancelled the following day as a result of a strike. The airline still had a legal duty to look for alternative flights for its passengers. By the early afternoon of July 6, alternative flights had been found for only about half of Father Higgins' group.

And these "solutions" were far from satisfactory. None of these flights was direct from Dublin to Rome. All involved stopovers in London, Paris, or Amsterdam. Some required taking off from Dublin at dawn and waiting for hours for the connecting flight in the intermediate airport. Some members of the group would have such a long stopover that they would not arrive in Rome until the following day. And half of the group had no alternative "solution" at all. They would have to wait until July 8 before making their way to Rome. It was a completely unacceptable situation for a group of this sort. Many of them were quite elderly and would have found travel arrangements of this sort impossible at worst, traumatic and exhausting at best.

That morning, I had been with the group from the Mater Dei Institute, visiting the Trastevere area of the city, Tiber Island and the Jewish Ghetto. I still had not heard the news about the strike and the cancellation of flights. Someone had pointed out to me during the morning that today, July 6, was the feast of Saint Maria Goretti. How appropriate that seemed! This saint who meant so much to Father Higgins would be busy today praying for his group as they prepared themselves for an emotional journey that would include a visit to her very tomb. But Maria Goretti was far from my mind a couple of hours later, when the girl in the Alitalia office gave me details of the flight arrangements that were being made for the group. Within twenty-four hours they would be dispersed all over Europe, some of them needing to change terminals in daunting places such as Heathrow and wait hours for connecting flights. They would then arrive at different times over an interval of eighteen hours at a Rome airport that had been thrown into chaos by the impending strike.

I put down the phone after speaking to the Alitalia office

in Dublin and looked at Laura in despair. "How can we tell the group that they have no alternative but to accept travel arrangements of this sort? After all they've gone through already!"

"Maybe the wisest thing to do is just cancel everything?" Laura replied. "Isn't it strange, though, that they haven't offered us any seats on the direct Aer Lingus flight from Dublin to Rome?"

"That's because Alitalia doesn't have any kind of partnership with Aer Lingus, whilst they do have arrangements in place with other airlines like Air France, apparently. Do you think we should try contacting Aer Lingus ourselves?"

She lifted the phone and dialled the international number for the Aer Lingus reservation desk. When the operator finally answered, Laura asked for forty-nine seats from Dublin to Rome on the following day. "You must be joking!" the agent replied with a laugh. "You'll never find that number of seats still available for tomorrow!"

But when he looked at the system, he was amazed to find that there was indeed that number of seats still available.

"They have enough seats," Laura whispered over to me. "But they want seven and a half thousand euro for them —one way! What will we do? Will Alitalia refund it to us eventually?"

"I have no idea. Will we go for it?"

"Yes!"

And so, using a variety of credit cards, Laura began the process of buying seats for the entire group, not knowing if we were even entitled to a refund from Alitalia, but with a feeling of absolute certainty that we were doing the right thing. The strange unfolding of events had somehow impressed upon us that Father Higgins' trip was simply different. The usual considerations of profit and loss didn't seem to apply anymore.

We phoned Margaret and told her the good news about the flight. She had remained in contact with us and was aware that the entire trip was in jeopardy, but never once had she uttered a pessimistic word or suggested cancelling the whole idea. She had stood firm like a gentle rock in a seemingly ever more chaotic stream of events. When we delivered the good news, she took it upon herself to contact the entire group and to change the timing of the coach departure from the west of Ireland to Dublin. She was relieved to hear that everyone would be able to travel together. The other group we were working with that week from the Mater Dei Institute was not so fortunate. After spending hours in Fiumicino Airport on the morning of July 7, many of them ended up having to return to the accommodation in Rome for a further night. The rest were placed on flights to different airports around Europe with connections to Dublin some hours later.

It was the evening of July 7, and we had only just sorted out the alternative arrangements for the Mater Dei group in a desperately chaotic Rome airport, when the Aer Lingus flight from Dublin landed. Nervous and uptight, I met the group in arrivals and took them to the Irish College. What can you say to family and friends in these circumstances? The easiest thing to do was to behave as normal, giving a commentary on the city as we drove in from the airport, catching sight of the Baths of Caracalla after we had passed under the ancient city walls, skirting the end of the Circus Maximus, glimpsing the dome of Saint Peter's in the distance, up past the Colosseum and on towards the Irish College. But I didn't describe Rome exactly as I would have done to one of our usual groups. Now I was trying to present it as Father Higgins would have done.

The itinerary was followed exactly as it had been planned, to the letter, but a couple of surprises occurred along the way that made me wonder if Father Higgins was not very much present with us still. The first evening included dinner at Scoglio di Frisio, followed by a night tour of the city by coach. Eugenio had been told of the death of Father Higgins and met us with great dignity at the entrance to his restaurant. During the night tour, I did not omit to point out the former locations of the Irish College, in particular the one attended by Saint Oliver Plunkett. The next day, Friday, we visited Saint Peter's, the tomb of the apostle and those of the other popes, as well as the Pantheon and Piazza Navona, pointing out the hotel where the Irish bishops stayed for the First Vatican Council in 1870. In the evening, we visited the famous fountains at Villa d'Este in Tivoli, showing the group the location of a former summer villa owned by the Irish College. Dinner was in one of Father Higgins' favourite restaurants, Monteripoli, above Tivoli, with impressive views over Rome.

On Saturday morning, we had Mass in the cathedral of Rome, Saint John Lateran Basilica, where Father Higgins had been ordained in 1958. Across the road is the highly venerated Holy Stairs, an ancient staircase taken from Jerusalem by Saint Helen in the fourth century. According to tradition, Jesus stood on top of these steps after he had been scourged. Pilate shouted to the crowd, "Whom shall I release, Barabbas or the king of the Jews?" (cf. Mt 27:17, Mk 15:9). The crowd shouted the name of Barabbas, and Jesus descended the steps to take up his cross. After our visit to the Holy Stairs, Father Higgins felt it would be appropriate to go directly to the nearby Basilica of the Holy Cross to see the relics of the Passion of Jesus.

As often happened in those busy days, I would take the opportunity to read my notes during lunchtime to prepare for the afternoon tour. Work usually finished late, and there was generally little or no time at night to prepare for the following day. After visiting the Basilica of the Holy Cross, just as Father Higgins suggested, we intended to call in to see the chapel of the old Propaganda Fide College, where Saint Oliver Plunkett had studied before becoming a member of the staff there. But there was free time for lunch first, and many of the group went towards the café close to the gate of the Irish College. I needed to go over my notes, so I discreetly nipped into a bar on the other side of the square where I could read without disturbance. I had a photocopy of the *Catholic Encyclopaedia*'s article on Plunkett in front of me as I ate my sandwich, scouring it for anything that linked Saint Oliver to the chapel in Propaganda Fide College. It was the chapel that Father Higgins had wanted to visit, after all, and that was the only reason for discussing the life of Saint Oliver on that day. To my amazement, the article stated that Oliver Plunkett was named archbishop of Armagh in that place on July 9, 1669! It was the event that sealed the fate of Plunkett, and we were about to enter the chapel on the very anniversary!

This chapel is not usually open to the public at that time, so we had arranged to be met by a staff member who would let us in. A couple of hours later, I stood with the group in the chapel and told them the story of Saint Oliver Plunkett and his appointment as archbishop of Armagh, an appointment that led directly to the most heroic period of his life and his eventual martyrdom. People were struck by the fact that we had unknowingly timed our visit to this chapel to coincide with such an important anniversary.

Something similar happened a few days later. We had left Rome after having an intimate Angelus with the new pope, Benedict XVI, in Castel Gandolfo. Our first stop was in Nettuno, by the sea, to pay our respects at the tomb of Saint Maria Goretti, that noble young girl whose blood was shed at the dawn of the twentieth century, almost as a sign of the terrible events to come. Then we went on south to visit the Abbey of Montecassino, "the cradle of Western monasticism" and the location of the tomb of Saint Benedict, patron of Europe. Father Higgins had visited the tomb of Saint Benedict a number of times during his summer in Formia. As we drove up the hairpin bends to the abbey, I was surprised to see an unusually large number of coaches in the parking area. What could possibly be happening here on a Sunday in July, the very time of year when most Italians would normally escape to the beach and avoid visits of a monumental sort? When we disembarked, we soon discovered that that very day, July 11, was the feast of Saint Benedict. It was the perfect day to be there.

The long process of planning the itinerary with Father Higgins had not taken anniversaries or feast days into account. The dates were imposed on us by brute considerations of airfares and availability of rooms at the places of accommodation. It was hard not to think that Providence had been involved in influencing the planning of the trip, as well as the unfolding of the sequence of events. There is no doubt that these coincidences had great value in comforting the group and making them feel that there was something "right" about the fact that they had travelled. The most significant coincidence, however, was one that had already occurred on the day of departure, but I would not discover it until a couple of days later.

The group had been informed in advance that they would have a change of courier before the end of the trip. Laura and I had business to attend to in Ireland, so a courier had been employed for the last few days in the Villa Irlanda— a far-from-ideal situation, even though we were entrusting the group to a good courier. It was something that left us with little choice, however, and so I crept out of the Villa Irlanda well before dawn, while everyone was still sleeping. The station was nearby, and I boarded a night train to Rome.

To this day, Laura and I have not had the good fortune to meet again any member of the group of Father Higgins. Towards the end of 2005, we went to remove all of the files from our cabinet for the clients who had travelled with us that season. It was time to prepare for the next season and to begin inserting the files for the 2006 groups. I could not bring myself to remove the file for Father Higgins' group, so we left it there in the cabinet for another year. The same thing happened when the time came to clear away the old files for 2006. Now, many years later, Father Higgins' file is still in our cabinet, occupying the leftmost slot that would once have been reserved for the first group of the year. When we visit the site of the old Irish College in Via degli Ibernesi in Rome or give a tour at Propaganda Fide, Father Higgins is travelling with us still.

On that final evening in the Villa Irlanda, before I boarded the night train for Rome, the group had gathered around the outdoor pool of the Villa after dinner. South of Rome, the Italian twilight is famously short, but on this evening, the light over the western sea seemed to last much longer than usual. The cicadas were noisy in the palm trees around us, and the air was balmy. A sense of relaxation and peace was tangible among the group.

I was sitting with Margaret, and we were discussing the way things had gone.

"I'm sorry that you and Laura had to fork out all that money for our flight from Dublin," Margaret said. "The people in this group would have no problem reimbursing you, you know that."

But Laura and I had already foreseen this situation, and I told Margaret that we had agreed between us that we wouldn't accept offers of reimbursement of any sort. If anyone was to refund us, it would have to be Alitalia (as it turned out, after a frank exchange of correspondence, and without legal action of any sort on our part, the Italian airline refunded every penny in January of the following year).

"The evening before he died," Margaret told me, "one of the last things Father Higgins said was that he needed to go now and pack his bags for the journey to Rome."

"He really wanted to make this pilgrimage, didn't he?"

"Yes," said Margaret, "and you know, I have felt from the first day that he is making the pilgrimage with us."

"Really?"

"Yes. And the way you described all of the places that we have visited, it was just like he was here with us describing them to us himself."

Margaret probably didn't realize it, but that was the greatest compliment she could have given me.

"We were devastated when he died," Margaret continued. "And, of course, we still are, you know. If you knew the good he did in the parishes in which he was stationed! And then for him to be deprived of his one last trip to Rome seemed so hard to comprehend. He loved Rome so much!

It had entered into so much of his character and spirituality. I asked myself 'Why couldn't he have been given just a couple of more weeks?'"

"I have been having trouble comprehending it too."

"But I think I understand it better now. This whole trip has been for us, for *our* benefit. It was never for him! The good Lord planned it this way from the very beginning. It was going to be our way of learning to say goodbye to Father Higgins, a time for his friends and family to be together for the first time without him and celebrate the things and places that he loved. And that is exactly how it has been for all of us."

When Margaret described it like that, with the light fading over the sea, a light was finally lit in my mind. How slow I had been to comprehend! The events of the previous ten days began to take on a different significance entirely. But Margaret had not finished yet.

"I have had the notion that he was here with us during the trip, and even before we took off in Dublin Airport. That was when the first of those little surprises happened."

I felt a slight shiver down my spine and sat forward in the chair. "Really? What was that?"

"We went through the departure gate and got on the shuttle bus to take us to the plane. All of us were on the same bus. As it drove around the front of the plane before stopping, we clearly saw the name on the nose of the aircraft."

"The name on the aircraft?" I repeated mechanically, unable to guess what Margaret might be referring to. "What was it?"

"Oh, that was what I wanted to ask you," she replied, not seeming to register my question. "Do all the Aer Lingus planes have their own names? Or can the same name appear on more than one aircraft?"

"They all have a unique name, Margaret," I said. "Like ships. I think the company has over fifty aircraft, and each one has its own name. As far as I can tell, they're all called after Irish saints."

"That's what I thought," she replied, looking into the distance.

"But, Margaret, you still haven't told me the name on your plane!"

"As soon as I saw it, I felt that everything was going to be all right," she went on. "We all saw it together from the shuttle. The plane was the *Saint Oliver Plunkett*."

To this day, more than fifteen years later, on every occasion that one of our groups boards an Aer Lingus flight to Italy, I look at the nose of the plane and read its name. We have travelled with every obscure Irish saint under the sun, but I have never since seen the *Saint Oliver Plunkett*.

A few hours after Margaret had made this revelation, the slow night train to Rome was following the coast under a moonlit sky. It crawled through station after station, shuddering to a halt each time and then starting off with a jolt again. Everyone else in the carriage was asleep, but I was wide awake, wondering at the things that had happened. A poem came to mind, written by one of the leaders of the 1916 rebellion in Dublin, Joseph Plunkett, a man of deep faith. Very appropriately, or so it seemed to me now, he was descended from the same family as Saint Oliver. After the failed rebellion, and a few hours before his execution by firing squad, he married his sweetheart, Grace Gifford, in the prison chapel.

I see his blood upon the rose
And in the stars the glory of his eyes.
His body gleams amid eternal snows,
His tears fall from the skies.

If Joseph Plunkett could not avoid seeing God in such everyday things, then how could we deny the presence of the Lord in the events of the previous days? I was sure now that Father Higgins had been living by trust in the grace of such providence all along. Some months earlier, he had spoken on the phone about God's being "behind the surface of things."

"There is a lot of rejection of the Church in Ireland now. Many people have turned away from the faith and replaced it with themselves. Once, people were more concerned about having a right relationship with God and neighbour. Now the emphasis is all on physical and mental well-being. But often they turn back to the faith when tragedy or death comes. Only God can deal with the big issues in life.

"People are rejecting the Lord, Kieran, but he's just behind the surface of things, leading people to himself, if only they will follow. It's true, the Church is taking a battering —and maybe we deserve a lot of it. Yet we know from his promise to Saint Peter that God is always with us, even if we are not with him." Father Higgins then gave one of his trademark chuckles. "We might look like the old fighter in the ring who is on the ropes, but we're a Church still standing!"

2

A Church Still Standing

You are the light of the world. . . . Let your light so shine
before men, that they may see your good works and give
glory to your Father who is in heaven.

—Matthew 5:14, 16

Rome was a dangerous place to be during the Nazi occupation of 1943–1944. The city was under the command of an
ambitious SS officer, Herbert Kappler, aided by the Italian
Fascist police, run by the notoriously cruel Pietro Caruso.
Gangs of thugs were employed by Kappler and Caruso to
roam the streets, rounding up Jews and those suspected of
opposing the Fascist regime. The thugs were paid a hand-
some bounty for every fugitive handed over, creating an atmosphere of tension and distrust throughout the city.

Kappler would be sentenced to life imprisonment after
the war for the Ardeatine Massacre. The story of the massacre is still engraved in the minds of many Romans. More
than thirty German soldiers had been killed in an ambush
near the Trevi Fountain by the Italian resistance. To appease
Hitler, Kappler callously organised the killing of ten Italians
for every German soldier killed. It would stand as the worst
atrocity in Rome of the Second World War.

But in the midst of the terror and suspicion, the hench-
men and thugs, there were also many heroes and heroines.
Thousands of Jews were being silently hidden in convents

and monasteries, despite the "anti-racial laws" that made the harbouring of Jews a capital crime punishable by death. Ordinary people were also sheltering many hundreds of escaped Allied soldiers. One of the most notable was a Maltese widow named Henrietta Chevalier. She and her family took enormous risks to hide and feed escaped prisoners of war.

Perhaps the most remarkable of all of these heroes was also one of the most unlikely. Monsignor Hugh O'Flaherty of County Kerry was working in the Vatican at the outbreak of the war. An avid sportsman, he had won the Italian golfing championship in the 1930s. Growing up in Ireland during the time of the War of Independence, he had already seen the horrific excesses of a cruel occupational army. The Black and Tans were a group of about ten thousand constables recruited in Britain and sent to Ireland as reinforcements during the conflict. They soon gained a reputation for extrajudicial killings, brutality, attacks on civilians and property, arson, and looting. It would be an understatement to say that Monsignor O'Flaherty, having grown up in these conditions, had a natural antipathy for the British. Yet he would risk life and limb during the Nazi occupation to hide, feed, and clothe soldiers who were, for the most part, subjects of His Majesty's government.

In 2014, the Monsignor Hugh O'Flaherty Memorial Society of Killarney made a trip to Rome to commemorate the achievements of their fellow Kerryman and his clandestine network. The "Rome Escape Line," as it came to be called, had saved the lives of more than six thousand people, between Allied soldiers and Jews. For a previous trip in 2012, Laura and I had put together an itinerary that took in all the principal places associated with Monsignor O'Flaherty's life and work in Rome. The 2014 programme would revisit some of these places but would also have to offer something different. The first group visited the Irish ambassador, so, for the second trip, we thought it would be appropriate to call to the British Embassy. The British ambassador, after all, was the successor of D'Arcy Osborne, who had been the British minister to the Holy See during the war. Sir D'Arcy and his butler, John May, were among O'Flaherty's closest collaborators in the early days of the escape organisation. The minister did not wish to compromise his position by taking an active part in the running of the organisation, but his butler was fully involved in hiding prisoners, locating food and clothing for them, and obtaining false documents, among innumerable other tasks. His resourcefulness and quick-mindedness would make him a legendary part of the Rome Escape Line.

The British ambassador in 2014 was Nigel Baker, and he readily agreed to meet us. We were invited to his residence on the Quirinal Hill. Before the meeting, we entered into correspondence with the embassy regarding the difficult position of the residence. It was on the fifth floor, accessible either by ten flights of stairs or by using a small lift that could hold only three people. In addition, there was a narrow metal staircase that had to be tackled afterwards because the lift didn't go all the way to the top!

I went to visit the residence a few days before the arrival of the group, taking with me our son, Stephen. Ambassador Baker had informed me that we would be met by a man called Rolando and shown around the building. When we arrived on the Quirinal Hill, we presented ourselves to the guard at the security kiosk and were told to wait a moment. Sure enough, Rolando appeared punctually and took us across the courtyard to the beautiful staircase leading up to the residence. He apologized that he did not speak English and introduced himself as the *maggiordomo*—the butler—of the British ambassador. "Gosh," I whispered to Stephen. "This is the modern-day equivalent of the legendary John May!"

After examining with concern the size of the lift, we followed Rolando up the many flights of stairs, mindful of the impending arrival of sixty Irish people. The residence had wonderful character with old wooden rafters and a fine, spacious drawing room. The view from the terrace above was surely one of the best I had experienced in Rome. We could see the Pantheon, Saint Peter's, and even the Olympic Stadium. The issue of getting sixty people into that attic was discussed, and Rolando assured us that he would be there on the day to ensure that everything went smoothly. Furthermore, there was the question of how we would get the coach to drop off and pick up outside on the street. The residence was across the road from the Quirinal Palace, home of the president of Italy. Police were everywhere, and there was a ban on private coaches stopping in the area. Our coaches had already been fined on two occasions in the previous year. According to the regulations, coaches are allowed to drop off and pick up at hotels but not to stand idle. Dropping off and picking up at hotels is tricky enough in Rome, but stops at unauthorised locations is a risky business for coach and driver. The vehicle can be impounded for the day and the driver punished with penalty points on his license.

"I'm not so concerned about the drop-off," I told Rolando. "There's an official drop-off point at the Traforo, which is not so far away. But the weird thing is that it is illegal to pick up a group at that point! The nearest official place is Via Ludovisi, which is an awful distance away and involves climbing a steep hill."

Rolando looked out on the street thoughtfully. Down below we could see police standing in conversation across the street from the ambassador's residence. Across the square, on the other side of the obelisk, four tall carabinieri were standing outside the presidential palace. "Look," he said. "You just worry about getting the group here. Once they're here, we'll find a solution for getting them back to the hotel."

A few days later, we found ourselves upstairs in the diplomatic residence. Ambassador Baker put on a great reception for the group, all the cakes and biscuits made that very day by his wife. He gave an interesting and stirring talk on the work of O'Flaherty during the war. You could sense that he had a sincere admiration for the Irish monsignor. He also furnished the group leaders with historical information from the British war archives that they had never seen before, including a detailed breakdown by nationality of the thousands of soldiers hidden by O'Flaherty and his network.

Rolando was dressed immaculately in his butler's uniform and seemed like a figure from a stately house of a previous century. During the reception, he was everywhere, putting guests' coats in the locker room, pouring coffee, encouraging people to try this or that cake, getting everyone to sign the register, showing people to the terrace. As I watched him scurry around, I kept thinking of the stories I had read of John May in the classic books on the Monsignor written by J. P. Gallagher and Brian Fleming. "Does the British Ambassador to the Holy See always have a butler of this kind?" I wondered to myself. "Is resourcefulness and energy part of the job description?"

It was time to go, and we had to figure out a way of getting back to our coach without excessive walking. This group was elderly and, like many Kerrymen, fiercely nationalistic, but that hadn't stopped them enjoying a little too much

of the wine generously supplied by Her Majesty's government. I went to Rolando. "How will we get the group to
the coach?" I asked wistfully.

"Contact your driver," he replied. "Ask him to drive by
the Quirinal Palace. We will be waiting for him."

Our driver, Salvatore, was none too pleased to hear that
we were expecting to be picked up directly outside the entrance to the residence.

"Stop the coach in front of the presidential palace?" he
roared into his mobile phone. "Do you want to send me
into early retirement?"

"Look," I replied. "You know I wouldn't normally ask
you to do anything like that. But the *maggiordomo* of the
ambassador says to do it. I think we can trust him."

"The coach will be here in about fifteen minutes," I told
Rolando. "Let's take the group downstairs."

It took a while to get everyone out of the residence and
down to the ground floor. Just as we crossed the courtyard
towards the exit, I saw our coach fly by outside without
stopping. I phoned him immediately.

"Salvatore! Where the heck are you going?"

"There's a whole minibus of carabinieri directly across
the road from the residence!" he said in a panicky voice.
"They have machine guns! And just down the road, there's
a dozen police patrolling the area outside the presidential
palace! I couldn't stop there!"

"What will we do?" I asked Rolando.

"Come with me," he replied.

We left the group standing in the courtyard, and he took
me out a back door to a side street that connects Via Venti
Settembre to Via Nazionale. As I followed him, I had visions
of John May leading fugitives to safety during the war while
vans of trigger-happy Gestapo with machine guns patrolled

the streets. I had drunk a couple of glasses of Her Majesty's wine too many myself, and my imagination was beginning to take hold of me. How would we get these sixty fugitives from Kerry out of the area without our driver being arrested or maybe shot? Should we try to create some sort of diversion to distract the carabinieri while we bungled the group onto the bus?

Rolando had a look at the street behind the residence but then shook his head. "It's too narrow for the coach, I'm afraid."

We went back to where the group was waiting. "Call your driver," he said. "We'll load them in front of the main entrance."

"In front of the main *entrance*?" I exclaimed, conscious that I probably had a woozy grin on my face. "Okay, Rolando! If you insist!"

I called the driver. "Come back around by the Quirinal Hill," I said, supressing a hiccup. "This time go more slowly. The prisoners—sorry, I mean the passengers—will be waiting for you. The *maggiordomo* is taking care of everything."

Salvatore was the vociferous kind of driver, but, like many Romans, he was naturally obliging and hated to see elderly people struggle to reach his bus. He could have refused to come back for us. He could have rightfully insisted that we walk for miles to the official pickup point. But back around by the Quirinal Hill he came.

I expected Rolando to ask permission of the carabinieri for us to stop the coach and pick up the group—that is what I would have done, and probably would have received an emphatic no!—but the butler did nothing of the sort. He didn't appear to notice the officers at all nor the host of presidential guards looking suspiciously at us from the other side of the square. He simply asked us all to gather on the sidewalk directly across the street from the obelisk that stands in front of the Quirinal Palace. Then we saw our coach coming into view, approaching the obelisk at a slow speed, our driver's nervous face all too apparent. Rolando stepped out in front of the coach and directed it to stop about twenty metres in front of the obelisk, almost straight in front of the minibus with the carabinieri. Then the butler stepped into the street and blocked the traffic in both directions until all sixty of us were across. His smart butler outfit with the tails flapping in the wind gave him an official air, but it was not exactly suited to the part of directing traffic, especially when the entire area was milling with real police in a variety of uniforms.

It took a while to get the group across the road, and then there was a queue to mount the steps into the coach. Some drivers started blowing their horns impatiently, which made me feel that our number was up. I tried to hurry people on, avoiding all eye contact with our driver, who could not have been a happy sight at that moment. At one point, the noise rose into a crescendo as multiple cars blew their horns in unison—a telltale sign that Roman drivers have reached their limit—but Rolando didn't bat an eyelid until we were all safely on the coach. During this time, the carabinieri continued to stand around their minibus, smoking cigarettes and chatting to one another, studiously looking in the other direction as only Italian policemen can do.

Once we had the coach loaded, I asked Rolando to step on board for a moment.

"Rolando, before you go, I want to say something to the group. You remember who John May was, don't you?"

He smiled. "Yes, of course!"

I switched on the microphone and called everyone to attention for a moment.

"We all owe a great debt of gratitude to Rolando, butler to the British ambassador, successor to John May, the man who could get anything done in Rome, even under the noses of the police!" There was a loud cheer. Rolando gave a wave and then crossed the road back to the residence. As the coach pulled away, the driver and I exchanged glances. He had a look of delirious relief on his face. We had just made an escape in Rome worthy of the Kerry monsignor.

Other things happened during that trip in 2014 that made me feel as if we were reliving, albeit in a slightly comical way, some of the events of the O'Flaherty story in Rome. This was especially true of our experience at the Rome golf club. Hugh O'Flaherty was a first-class golfer, having grown up at the entrance to the Killarney golf course, of which his father was caretaker. Playing golf was banned for diocesan priests in Rome, but O'Flaherty was not a priest of the Rome Diocese, so he played golf at every opportunity. Providentially, the time he spent golfing was enormously beneficial for his future efforts to aid refugees in Rome, for he met a whole host of influential people in Roman high society while playing golf. Some of these contacts would become central figures in the Rome Escape Line.

Our job was to organise a visit to the golf club for the group. This would surely be a simple task. All we had to do was contact the club, ask if we could make our visit, look at the course, and perhaps see some of the archival material mentioning O'Flaherty's membership and victories. There would be none of the usual hassle with parking and unpredictable police once we were outside the centre of Rome.

"Laura, can you get me an e-mail address for the golf

course at Ciampino, outside Rome?" I asked officiously. "We need to organise our visit."

Laura was on the Internet and was just about to give me the address when she stopped. "Wait a minute," she said. "There's something wrong here. The home page of the golf course at Ciampino says that the club was only founded in 1979. Hugh O'Flaherty couldn't have played golf there!"

"That *is* strange," I replied. "The books by Fleming and Gallagher both state that he played golf at Ciampino, or near Ciampino, at least. Everyone says it's that one we pass just before we arrive at Ciampino Airport. When the O'Flaherty group came to Rome two years ago, they asked me to point out the course where the Monsignor played, and I showed them that one as we went past in the coach!" (Fleming and Gallagher are the authors of the two main works on the Monsignor's life, and some of the information contained in this chapter is drawn from them.)

A little investigation revealed that the oldest golf club in Rome, founded in 1903, is in Acquasanta, significantly closer to the city than the one in Ciampino. In fact, from the old city walls at Saint John Lateran Basilica, the golf club in Acquasanta is only half the distance to the town of Ciampino. When we consulted the list of former presidents, we discovered with a thrill that Prince Doria Pamphilj was president in 1911! Pamphilj was one of the main benefactors of O'Flaherty, giving him significant sums for the feeding and clothing of escapees. Evidently this was where O'Flaherty had begun his initial friendship with the prince. We also noticed that, until the outbreak of the Second World War, the presidents of the club were all members of the Italian nobility. This helped to account for the number of aristocracy who played a key part in the Monsignor's escape organisation.

We wrote to the Acquasanta Golf Club, reminding them who O'Flaherty was and how his time at the club was so central in forming the relationships that helped to save an enormous number of lives. Surely the club would want to meet O'Flaherty's relatives and supporters, we thought. They would really want to celebrate the heroic achievements of their former illustrious member. But a couple of weeks after we wrote our passionate e-mail, no reply had come, so I phoned the club and asked to speak to a senior member of staff. I explained the story about the O'Flaherty group and our wish to visit the club.

"Yes, I have seen your letter," the official replied curtly. "How many people did you say you wanted to bring?"

"Oh, at least sixty!" I exclaimed enthusiastically. "Some of them are relatives of the Monsignor. They really want to see this place where he spent so much time and met all the people who would later help him save so many lives!"

"I see," replied the official. His tone was sullen, and I suddenly realised that he did not share our enthusiasm about the proposed visit. "But we are running a private club here. People come to play golf, and they like to sit for a drink afterwards in a relaxed atmosphere. Our club is known for its tranquillity. Sixty people would be very invasive. Group visits and tours of the sort are never allowed at Acquasanta."

I had a sinking feeling. We had already informed the O'Flaherty group that we intended to take them to the golf club. I needed to think of something to say fast before the official ended this conversation and our chance of a visit was gone. "Look, we can come at any time specified by you, even at an hour when the club is normally closed. We just want to see the building and stand there for a moment while we recount a brief history of O'Flaherty's link with the place. The visit can be as short and simple as you want it to be."

There was no reply from the official, but I took his silence as an indication that he was at least thinking the matter over. I still didn't want to give him the opportunity to make a negative response, so I quickly added, "I'll be in Rome in a few weeks' time. Do you mind if I drive out to the club and talk to you for a moment in person?"

"Okay," he replied slowly in a reluctant tone. "I don't have much time, but I can show you the kind of place we have here. Sixty people would represent an invasion of the club, and I am not sure if it will be possible. I think you will understand better when you come here and see for yourself."

After I put the phone down, Laura asked, "Would you really drive the group all the way out to the golf club just to stand in the place and say a few words about the Monsignor? There are so many other things you could do in Rome!"

"The golf club is important," I replied, "not just for what happened before the war but for what happened afterwards."

J. P. Gallagher's book on O'Flaherty (*The Scarlet Pimpernel of the Vatican*) contains a brief but fascinating description of the remarkable events that happened at the golf club immediately after the war. The hostilities had ended, and the Monsignor dusted off his clubs to reignite his love affair with golf. Sometime during a game in 1946, one of the golf balls flew off the course, and Hugh went in search of it. He found himself in the middle of a few ramshackle houses and a ruined church just off the fairway. There were refugees living in the houses. They were not Italian and seemed half starved and miserable. O'Flaherty got into his car, drove back to Rome, and then returned to the golf course with food for everyone. While the people were eating, they looked on in astonishment as the Monsignor removed his collar, rolled up his sleeves, and began cleaning the interior of the church. After they had eaten, the refugees joined in. O'Flaherty returned day after day, bringing food and clothing, renovating the church—including replacing the bell—and generally treating this "village" as if it were his own parish. He began to instruct the refugees in the Catholic faith and eventually baptised them. Appeals were made to international aid agencies for food and monetary assistance. The men were placed in employment.

"What happened at the golf club shows that O'Flaherty's work in hiding fugitives from the fascists wasn't just a one-off," I said to Laura. "The war had brought out the extraordinary in him. After the war, it looked as though he would return to normality, but then the plight of these people brought a remarkable response from him again. He just couldn't stop himself from looking out for those in need. And you know, this whole golf-club affair really reveals a lot of things about his character. I'm sure some people at the Vatican probably thought to themselves, 'Look, there goes that golf fanatic in his car again! Doesn't he have anything better to do than play golf?' As usual, he kept his work to himself. For more than ten years, he went to work in that community at the times he would normally have spent on the course, but virtually nobody knew about it until years after he died."

"Let's try to find that church then," replied Laura. "Maybe some of the people he looked after are still around."

I phoned the golf club again and asked for the same official whom I had spoken to previously.

"Oh, yes," he said drily when he picked up the phone. "The person who wants to bring sixty Irish people to visit our club."

I told him the story of O'Flaherty taking care of the little community in Acquasanta for more than ten years.

"I can't imagine where that might have been," he replied. "I know this golf course, every inch of it. There's no chapel here."

Laura and I had no alternative but to resort to the old reliable satellite photographs of the area. We spent a while poring over the area, zooming in on buildings at the edge of the golf course and then zooming out again.

"Look! That seems to be a little church!" I exclaimed. It was across the road from the entrance to the golf course.

"Isn't that a bit far away from the actual course?" replied Laura. "And it's the other side of the Via Appia Nuova. Hard to imagine O'Flaherty crossing that big road in search of a golf ball."

"Well," I said. "There was probably less traffic on it then. And the Monsignor was a big, strong fellow. He'd have no trouble sending a ball that far."

But it also occurred to me that the Kerryman was renowned for his golfing abilities. Would he really have sent a ball that much astray? Or was he just looking for a ball belonging to a less proficient partner?

We discovered that the church was called Santo Stefano Protomartire at Acquasanta. The Rome diocesan website revealed that it was founded in 1954.

"It all fits perfectly, Laura!" I said in excitement. "There were no parish churches at all in this area before the war because the area had a low population until all the high-rise apartments were built in the fifties and the population expanded enormously. O'Flaherty fixed up an old church and was probably a sort of pioneer in introducing pastoral services of that sort in the locality. But at some point, the diocese wanted to formalise that into a proper parish, so they

founded Santo Stefano Protomartire in 1954. They probably just took over what O'Flaherty had already begun, and
the Monsignor was able to withdraw and leave it all in the
hands of the new diocesan clergy."

I was enthusiastic about my theory and held to it stead-
fastly for another six weeks until we arrived in Rome and visited the area. In the meantime, we had contacted the parish
priest of Santo Stefano to ask him to post an announcement
in his church regarding the work that we believed O'Flaherty
had done in the parish at the time it came into existence.
Don Vincenzo was very accommodating, but he came back
to us a few weeks later to say that no one he had spoken to
in the parish remembered O'Flaherty.

"Very few people come to Mass anymore," he said.
"There are no parish archives here. I'm afraid I can tell
you nothing about O'Flaherty."

That was a blow, for I had envisioned taking the Kerry
group to this church and having a meeting with the very
people O'Flaherty had fed, clothed, and baptised.

"Don't worry, Don Vincenzo!" I had replied. "I'll call
next week to see the place. The group would still like to
visit the church that O'Flaherty worked in, even if nobody
remembers him anymore!"

A week later, Laura, the kids, and I were standing in the
tiny church of Santo Stefano Protomartire on the outskirts
of Rome, trying to imagine how it had been in O'Flaherty's
time.

"Gallagher's book says that he fixed up the old, ruined
church and even put a new bell in it," I said, looking around
blankly.

"This can't be it!" replied Laura. "Apart from the fact
that there's no bell, the building is entirely modern. It looks
like it was built from scratch in the 1950s. Look, even the

parish priest's house adjoined to it is made in the very same brick!''

"Maybe they just demolished the old church and started afresh?" I said unconvincingly. It seemed doubtful that a church that had been given a new bell by O'Flaherty a few years previously would have been demolished so quickly, but I was still clinging to my theory.

"We'll bring the group here anyway," I went on. "We have no other candidate for the church where Hugh did his work, so we'll have to make this one do. You know how it is, Laura. The travel brochure must be followed. The show must go on."

We drove back out on the main road and into the entrance of the Rome golf club. Laura and the kids stayed in the car while I went into the building to meet the official. If the golf club didn't welcome "invasions," then maybe it was better to leave the children in the car.

I stood for a good fifteen minutes in the lobby before the official came down from upstairs to meet me. He was cordial but very serious.

"We don't have any of those records you asked me to look for regarding membership and victories won by O'Flaherty. The club's archive doesn't go back before the war. There's nothing here, I'm afraid."

More worryingly, he still couldn't see how a group of this size could be permitted to visit the club.

"Look around you," he said, motioning to people sitting inside in the very elegant lounge, sipping drinks and reading newspapers. It was a picture of peace and calm—no music, no loud conversations. "We simply do not cater to tour groups."

"This isn't an ordinary tour group," I said, aware that I had already repeated this sentiment a number of times.

"They're here to remember a man who made a heroic stand against fascism. And an essential part of the network he developed was formed from contacts he made in this club."

I could see that this line was getting me nowhere. "How about," I said in desperation, "if we simply park our coach at the entrance? Then we will walk in the driveway and gather outside the clubhouse. We don't need to come inside the building at all. It will be November, but hopefully the weather will be dry."

We walked outside the door, where there were flower beds and a couple of outdoor seats. "Okay," said the official with his usual serious expression. "You can speak to your group out here for a few moments."

I looked around. There was little space, and it was far from ideal, but it was a case of taking whatever we could get. "If it were possible to meet a couple of people from the club who remember O'Flaherty, we could simply introduce them to the group and ask them to recount a few things they remember. Then we'll be on our way. We need twenty minutes maximum."

The official sighed with an air of resignation. "All right. But I can't be sure how many people here at the club still remember O'Flaherty. I think Roberto Bernardini is the only one. He's here today actually, giving lessons down on the course."

"Could I have a quick word with him?" I asked. "I'd like to hear what he remembers of O'Flaherty. That way, I'll know how to introduce him to the group when we arrive."

The official looked at his watch with impatience. "I don't have much time. We must go quickly."

As were leaving the building, I asked again if he knew

of any church, or even an old ramshackle building in the area, where O'Flaherty had said Masses regularly after the war.

He shook his head with an air of finality. "There is no church around this golf course."

We hopped on a golf buggy directly at the entrance. It was my first time on one of those vehicles, and I was surprised at the speed that they were capable of. As we flew across the car park, I waved across to Laura and the kids sitting in the car, and they waved back at me with surprised expressions. A minute later, we were crossing a grassy open field to where a white-haired gentleman was giving instructions to two golfers.

I discovered this only later, but Roberto Bernardini was one of the foremost golfers in Italy in the late sixties and seventies. To this day, he still holds the amateur course record in Acquasanta. He had come in second in the World Cup in 1967.

He shook my hand warmly. "Of course I remember O'Flaherty!" he said.

"Aren't you a bit young to remember back that far?" I asked incredulously. He looked well under seventy years of age, which meant he would have been born after 1945. How could he remember the Monsignor?

"I'm older than I look!" he replied. Then he told me how, as a teenager, he had caddied for the Kerryman in the 1950s. We spoke for a few minutes about the things he remembered, and he agreed to repeat everything for the group in November.

"Is there anyone else at the club who remembers the Monsignor?" I asked.

The club official had been listening to our conversation, and he cut in at this point. "There's only Roberto," he said, shaking his head.

"Oh, no," Roberto said. "There is also Bianca, and she remembers him even better than me!"

"Could you ask Bianca to meet us as well?" I asked.

"I think she would love to meet your group," Roberto replied.

The official was shifting his weight from one foot to the other in a nervous fashion beside us. "Is that all settled then?" he interjected.

"Just one last thing," I said. Then, turning back to Roberto, I asked, "Do you know of a church where the Monsignor used to celebrate Mass regularly?"

"Ah, yes," he replied slowly, as if dragging an ancient recollection up from his memory. "Yes, of course. I used to know the church very well. The Monsignor would come on Sundays and get all the caddies and golfers on the course to come to Mass with him. Sometimes there were seventy of us in there at a time."

I was stunned at this revelation. "Does the church still exist?" I asked.

"Oh yes, the church is still standing."

"The church is still standing!" I could hardly believe my ears. "Can you tell me where it is?"

"Yes. I saw it the other day, but it's in bad repair." Roberto pointed over to a clump of trees in the distance beyond the end of the field where we were standing. "It's down there," he said.

This was news indeed! The mysterious building existed after all! I turned to the official. "Can you take me down there?" I was surprised at the thick skin that I was developing, but when someone has been consistently unhelpful, there is little to be lost by demanding more.

He threw his hands wide with an exasperated gesture and looked up to heaven. "*Santo cielo!*" he said. "Oh, all right! Get on the buggy then!"

We drove back to the entrance of the field where we had come in, and I was surprised to see that there was a gravel avenue down around the perimeter of the field towards the clump of trees.

"Those buildings down there are not on the golf club's property," he said as we drove. "Over this high hedge on our left is the golf course. We use the first field on the right for some of our lessons. But down further, the property on the right-hand side of the road is owned by a number of different businesses."

The road curved around to the left, and the buildings came into sight through the clump of trees on the right. There was a netted wire fence, and everything looked abandoned and overgrown. Was this really the place where O'Flaherty had done so much work after the war, I wondered? The location seemed perfect. Through the thick hedge on the left, I could just about make out the smooth manicured surface of one of the greens. It was easy to see how a ball could have overshot the course and landed in front of these buildings.

The official brought the buggy to a halt, and I got out. He remained aboard, but he seemed to have relaxed a little, probably resigned to the fact that this group was going to visit the club and there was little he could do to prevent it.

He started to light a cigarette. "This place is so derelict that I had forgotten it existed," he said, perhaps wishing to justify his earlier "lapse" of memory. Through the brush I could just about make out either a bell tower or a chimney covered in ivy. There was certainly a church here surrounded by other buildings in a dilapidated state. Everything fitted the scant information we already had about the Monsignor's little "parish." But how were we going to get in there? I left the golf buggy behind me parked on the grass margin and followed the road as it curved to the left and then back to the right. The front of the church now came into view through the trees, but the entrance courtyard was behind gates that were tied with a heavy chain. I peered with interest through the gates at the church. It seemed extremely run-down. Surely no one had used it in at least thirty or forty years. But this simply had to be the place where O'Flaherty had being doing his good deeds while everyone thought he was playing golf!

There were buildings in front of the church with horses tied in them. A sign revealed that the place was being used as an equestrian centre. I walked around to the back of one of the sheds and found a young man carrying a bucket of cereal to the horses.

He seemed interested in the story of the unusual Irishman who had adopted a community of refugees here in the 1940s.

"We are renting the property from the Salesians," he said. "But no one has permission to enter the church. It is *pericolante*—precarious."

"Can we stand in the courtyard in November and recount the story of the Monsignor and maybe take some photographs?" I asked.

"Yes, but no one must go near the building. We're not permitted."

As we drove back on the buggy towards the clubhouse, it was agreed that the group would first visit the church, walking down the gravel avenue. Then we would return to the entrance of the clubhouse and meet Roberto Bernardini and Bianca for a few moments, standing outside the entrance to the building. For the umpteenth time, I assured the official there would be no "invasion."

Wednesday, November 5, 2014, dawned cloudy and threatened rain. In the morning, we had an audience with Pope

Francis in Saint Peter's Square. But the day held, and conditions were still dry in the midafternoon as we made our
way on foot down the gravel avenue towards the dilapidated
church. We stood at the gateway and recounted the scant
details we knew of O'Flaherty's work there: the discovery of the refugees when he was searching for a ball; the
renovation of the church; the replacement of the bell; the
building of houses for the people; the Baptisms and Masses;
years of soliciting aid from different sources. Some of the
O'Flaherty family members present recalled how the Monsignor had collected money and clothes for the project in
Ireland and the United States, though they had not been
fully aware of how much he had invested himself personally in it. We also recounted how one day he had loaded
the entire community into two coaches and drove them
to Saint Peter's Basilica, where they all received the Sacrament of Confirmation. There wasn't much to see, and not
even a lot to say, but there was a feeling of satisfaction that,
for the first time in many years, the Monsignor had been
paid some small tribute for the work he had done in this
place.

Speeches made and photographs taken, we made our way
back to the clubhouse. I didn't know what to expect but was
delighted to see Roberto Bernardini and an extremely thin
and fit-looking lady with white hair waiting for us outside
with beaming smiles. The club official was also there, deadly
serious, as always. We gathered somewhat uncomfortably in
a huddle on the pathway between the flower beds, and I had
barely begun to introduce Roberto and Bianca to the group
when Bianca turned to the club official and said to him in
Italian, "What do you think? Will we all go inside for a
while? Look, we can use the seats that have been set up for
the press conference."

Sure enough, through the enormous glass window we could see that about seventy seats had been set up in orderly rows before a table set with a white cloth and a couple of microphones positioned on it. Beyond, there was a large lounge with tables that had been set out with a buffet lunch. Lunchtime was over, and there were only about five or six people in the lounge at that moment.

The official hesitated grimly, then nodded stiffly to Bianca without saying anything and led the way in. I couldn't believe our luck! Evidently this lady had some influence in the place. We all sat in the rows of chairs while Roberto and Bianca sat at the tables in front of the microphones. The official disappeared towards the offices while we had a very entertaining twenty minutes or so in which Roberto and Bianca—who spoke excellent English—recounted some of their memories of O'Flaherty: his remarkable proficiency at golf despite his wholly unconventional way of holding the golf club; the fact that he tended to play many of the different strokes using a single club; anecdotes of some of the colourful characters who had challenged the Monsignor to a game of golf and promptly lost, including the future Archbishop Marcinkus of Vatican bank infamy. The male and female captains of the Killarney golf club were part of the group, and presentations were made.

At one point, a member of our group showed us a golf ball he had found a half hour earlier, hidden in the grass directly in front of the ruined church. This seemed to rubberstamp the general conviction, if anything more was needed, that O'Flaherty had indeed happened upon that community of refugees while searching for a lost ball.

The club official had reappeared at the back of the group at this point, as if to remind us that our time was up. I was conscious of my promise that we would be finished in

twenty minutes, so I stood up quickly and thanked Roberto
and Bianca. They were given a warm round of applause.

"Right, everyone!" I said loudly, rubbing my hands together. "The coach is waiting! Let's be on our way!"

Bianca was still sitting at the front of the group, and the
official was standing at the back. She raised her hand for attention and addressed him directly in Italian, saying, "The
club can offer this wonderful group tea or coffee, surely?
What do you say?"

Again, the official seemed to have difficulty speaking. He
shot me a quick, cold glance, then assented to Bianca with
an emotionless nod of the head. She gave a huge smile and
made a general announcement in English: "Tea and coffee
for everyone over at the bar!"

There was another round of applause, louder than the
first, and the entire group moved as one into the lounge
area. Not only did they get their choice of tea, coffee, or
soft drinks, but there was also a generous supply of biscuits
for everyone. Ten minutes later, all the tables in the lounge
area were occupied by Kerry people chattering merrily. It is
remarkable the way that a cup of tea can loosen the tongues
of Irish people. This group had been together for a number
of days, sitting beside each other on long plane and coach
journeys, sharing breakfast in the mornings and passing the
entire waking days together. But now that they had a cup
of tea in front of them, it was like meeting long-lost friends
whom they hadn't seen in years.

I looked around the scene, hoping that the official had
returned to his office so that he would not see the general
chaos that had enveloped the clubhouse. There were china
cups and saucers balanced precariously on coffee tables and
knees, splashes of milk and scattered biscuit crumbs all over
the thickly carpeted floor. The noise of happy conversation

had reached a raucous pitch. It was necessary to shout now if you wanted to be heard. This wasn't just an invasion; it was a total conquest, with looting and pillaging for good measure. Attila the Hun in his prime could hardly have generated such chaos. None of the regular club patrons was anywhere in sight. Evidently they had made a run for it. What would Hugh O'Flaherty think, I wondered, if he saw the racket that his fellow Kerrymen were raising in the hallowed confines of the golf club that he loved so well?

Despite the fact that scenes of this sort could not have been very common in the lounge, the immaculately dressed bar staff remained extremely polite, poker-faced, and patient the entire time. I had been standing a bit aloof from the proceedings, aware that the club official disapproved of our presence. Of course, it was impossible not to be secretly delighted at the treatment the group was being given and to see the way they had made themselves at home. But it didn't seem proper for me to join in. It felt better to stand on the fringe with a sombre look on my face as if I disapproved of all this merriment in the golf club. When things had settled down a bit and most people had been served, I went over to the bar to thank the staff for the service they were providing. Inevitably, as I approached the bar, I got myself sucked into the business of helping with the supplementary orders.

"Kieran, while you're up there, will you see if there's any chance of more biscuits? That nip in the air outside has given me an almighty appetite."

"Kieran, do you mind asking if I can have a refill of tea? My cup was very small altogether."

"While you're up there at the bar, any chance of another drop of milk? This tea is boiling! The first decent hot cup of tea we got since arriving in this country!"

Once these and a few other requests had been satisfied, I

thanked the principal barman for the courteous service. He was dressed in an elegant white suit and dickie bow and had maintained an air of professional detachment throughout. "What would you like to drink yourself, sir?" he asked.

I hesitated and looked around. There was no sign of the club official anywhere. I couldn't very well join in this bedlam myself, could I?

"Oh, go on then!" I said. "I'll have a cappuccino, thank you!"

A minute later, armed with my cappuccino and munching into a biscuit, I turned away from the bar and almost crashed into the official, who was standing silently behind me.

"Ah," he said. "Having coffee too?" He still had the same serious face, but now, for the first time, there was the ghost of a smile playing on his lips.

My mouth was full of biscuit, but I still managed, "Sure, why not?" Then, raising my cappuccino, I said, "Long live Hugh O'Flaherty!"

A couple of years later, Laura and I were exiting the Villa Borghese with the kids after a walk. The Villa Borghese Gardens is a large public park close to the centre of Rome. Once the property of the powerful Borghese family of Pope Paul V, it is now owned by the city of Rome and has one of the finest art galleries in the city. Just outside the gates of the gardens was parked an old Fiat 500, which surely dated from the 1960s. I had stood the children in front of it for a photo when an elderly lady emerged from the gardens with a large dog on a lead.

"So you like my car!" she said with a bright smile. It was Bianca. We exchanged phone numbers, something I had regretted not having done on our previous meeting at the golf course.

"Next time we visit Acquasanta, we'll phone you first!" I said.

A few years later, we would return to the golf club at Acquasanta with another large group of O'Flaherty family and friends. Sadly, in the meantime, Bianca had died unexpectedly after a short illness. We had learned our lesson and did not bother writing to the club official but instead contacted Roberto directly. We also contacted the Salesians who owned the church. A protracted court case regarding the ownership of the property had been resolved, and they finally agreed to give us permission to access the site. But would they open the church for us? In my e-mails, I had repeatedly asked if they could at least open the doors so that we could peek inside. The man working at the equestrian centre, however, had told me the building was "*pericolante*" and strictly off-limits, so it seemed a long shot, especially in the country that more or less invented red tape. Father Tullio, the Salesian priest who responded to my e-mails, though, seemed inclined to help us. "If it is possible, we'll do it," he wrote. "Let's wait and see."

We got off the coach at the entrance to the golf club to find Roberto Bernardini waiting for us. The great golfer had twisted his knee and could get around only with the use of a golf cart. Judge Hugh O'Flaherty, nephew of the Monsignor, sat beside Roberto on the buggy, and we all followed them on foot down the winding road towards the church. When we got there, just on cue, Father Tullio of the Salesians arrived in a small Fiat with the congregation's engineer. As we all peered through the iron gate, we saw that a tree had fallen in front of the entrance of the church.

"Just our luck!" I thought ruefully. "They'll never let us in there now!"

It seemed, though, that Father Tullio was determined to

keep his word and do what was possible. We were led around the other side of the property to a sort of gate in a high mesh fence. The engineer produced an impossibly large bunch of keys from inside his coat and opened the padlock. The gate was dragged open. More than fifty Irish people, some not the most mobile, followed Father Tullio over a winding, uneven path, overgrown with weeds and long grass. We emerged on the other side of the building and discovered that we were standing between the fallen tree and the door of the church.

The enormous bunch of keys was produced again. After some rummaging, the chains were removed from the entrance, the old wooden doors were swung open, and we were allowed to look in! It was dirty and dusty and evidently hadn't been opened in years, but what an immense satisfaction to see members of the O'Flaherty family gazing into that church where the Monsignor had done such good. Because the church was dedicated to Mary, we gathered around the entrance and sang the Salve Regina.

Just a few minutes later, the doors were closed again and the chains were back in their place.

"Your group has waited a long time to gain access to this church, isn't that so?" Father Tullio remarked a while later as we arrived back at the coach.

I did a quick calculation of the time that had passed since Laura and I had driven here with the children on that first occasion. "Five years!" I replied.

He shook my hand and waved to the group as they boarded the coach. Then he said simply, "I think O'Flaherty was a good man."

I couldn't but agree. Looking at the character of O'Flaherty from the outside, everything seemed to point to an ordinary person: his love of sport, his quick temper, his sense of humour, his basic humanity. Yet he responded in an extraordinary way to the events of the Nazi occupation. There were many on the continent during the Second World War who took risks to save people from the Nazis, but only a few can be ranked with O'Flaherty for energy, commitment, zeal, altruism, and courage. In his last tribute to O'Flaherty, Major Sam Derry, coarchitect of the Rome Escape Line, recalled how the Monsignor, once he had decided on the right course of action, would follow it through with determination and without any regard for his own safety or comfort. They would walk miles around Rome together, the Irish priest and the British army officer, bringing supplies to soldiers in hiding and moving soldiers from one safe house to the next. When they would return, exhausted, to O'Flaherty's room, Sam Derry would sleep on the couch while O'Flaherty continued to work into the early hours of the morning, completing his duties as an official of the Vatican. What needed attention needed attention that same day. Duties could not be shirked. Promises could not be broken. When the war was over, O'Flaherty wanted to hear no more about what he had done. If there was glory to be given for the good that had been achieved, then let it be given to God. He declined to draw a penny of the pension the British government awarded to him.

After the liberation of Rome, the political situation in Rome was reversed. Those who had once been the hunted were now seeking, justifiably, to round up anyone who had supported the fascists. O'Flaherty began to help some Italians and Austrians who had fought under the German flag. He publicly testified on behalf of two double agents who had done serious damage to his escape organisation. On this occasion, he commented to Sam Derry, "They did wrong, but there is good in every man." In 1945, an Italian woman in Rome whose family had fought for the fascists asked the Monsignor to find her son in a German prisoner-of-war camp in England and inform him of the death of his father. The Monsignor found him and spent a day in London consoling the young man. After the war, O'Flaherty became the only regular visitor to Gestapo chief Herbert Kappler, in the Gaeta prison, incarcerated for life for his decisive role in the terrible Ardeatine Massacre. Kappler had tried to capture and kill O'Flaherty on multiple occasions, but the Monsignor himself would eventually baptise the SS officer in prison. When asked why he was helping those on the "other side," O'Flaherty's response was simple: "God has no country."

How did this humble man achieve so much during the dark days of the Nazi occupation when so many others were shackled by fear? During that trip to Rome, we visited the Teutonic College, where O'Flaherty had spent most of his years in Rome. The rector, Dr Fischer, showed us the registry book from the chapel for the war years. As we could see from the entries, the Monsignor began every day with an early-morning celebration of the Eucharist. He continued this even during his last years of illness when he returned to Ireland. Hugh O'Flaherty's life was centred on the sacrificial self-offering of Jesus. Everything else was made possible by this fact. If there is one common thread running through the many testimonies on the Monsignor's character, it is his cheerfulness, heartiness, and general optimism. He was convinced that he was in the safe hands of Providence, that he had been redeemed. For him, every day was a day made by the Lord.

3

A Day Made by the Lord

For he will give his angels charge of you
to guard you in all your ways.
On their hands they will bear you up.

—Psalms 91:11–12

When Pope John Paul II visited Ireland in 1979, over half of the population mobilised to see him at five main venues around the country. A modest enough crowd was expected at the race grounds at Limerick, but in excess of four hundred thousand people showed up. For those who were present that day, the festive nature of the atmosphere made the occasion an unforgettable one. But in the midst of all the festivity, John Paul gave a startling homily whose prophetic nature has become fully apparent only in our own time. Ireland was at a critical moment of decision in her history, the crowds were told. Would she follow other nations in making material possessions and economic development her god? Would she renounce her inner freedom to embrace the way of decadence and fleeting temporal enjoyment? Or would she give priority to the things of the Spirit? If Ireland was to preserve her soul, she would have to look to the inspiration of her forefathers who suffered so much to preserve the faith. "What will it profit Ireland if she gains the whole world and loses her soul?" the pope passionately demanded! Satan, he said, was using all his might and all his deceptions to win Ireland to the ways of the world.

For one young woman, the visit of John Paul II had a special meaning, even though she was unable to be present. She did not experience the atmosphere or hear the homily, but the papal visit to Limerick had a lasting influence on her life. Many years later, in an unexpected way, her moving story came to light.

Already at his funeral in 2005, significant numbers of people were calling for the Polish pope to be recognized as a saint, as the many signs with the words *Santo subito!* attested. No one was surprised when the process for canonisation was fast-tracked by John Paul II's successor. As time went on, the question in Rome on everyone's lips was "When will the canonisation take place?" It was not just the devotees of John Paul who were asking: the hotels and tour operators wanted to know as well. For those in the hotel business, this event would surely be a windfall of epic proportions.

Eventually, on September 30, 2013, the long-awaited announcement came, and the date was set for the first Sunday after Easter, April 27, 2014. The importance of the occasion was raised even higher when the Holy See announced that Pope John XXIII would be canonised in the same ceremony. John XXIII had called the Second Vatican Council and was the most beloved of the Italian popes of the twentieth century.

Canonising the two of them together all seemed very significant and edifying. But for people like us, who eke their living from the travel industry, the decision was met initially with great trepidation. If a parish or a diocese asked us to take them to the event, how could we possibly find suitable accommodation? The canonisation of either one would represent an occasion of historic proportions, but both together would constitute the biggest canonisation event of all time. How could this already-creaking city cope with such multitudes converging towards a single spot on the same day? Would airfares to Rome go through the roof? If our hotel accommodation was not in walking distance of the Vatican, how on earth would we be able to get our group to Saint Peter's Square that morning?

Given that our pilgrimage groups always included a fair proportion of retired or elderly people, this issue of transporting people to the event was my greatest worry. Saint Peter's Basilica is not far from the Tiber. Virtually all routes into that area of the city require doing a stretch on the *Lungotevere* (the thoroughfares that carry traffic along the banks of the river) or arriving from the north along the Via Gregorio VII. Both alternatives are notoriously prone to gridlock on any day of the week. What would these streets be like if hundreds of thousands of people were trying to reach the Vatican at the same time?

A few days after the date was announced, we received a call from a priest in the Killaloe Diocese, in the south of Ireland, asking if we would organise a diocesan pilgrimage to the canonisation. This priest knew Rome particularly well and was aware of the challenging nature of attending an event of this magnitude. I couldn't help but admire his courage for deciding to lead a group to the Eternal City for the occasion.

"I suppose you already have had plenty of requests from groups for the canonisations?" he asked.

"Well, no, actually, you're the first."

As it would turn out, he was also the last. Many individuals and small parties from Ireland made their way to Rome for that April weekend, but the number of large pilgrim groups was relatively few. Apart from Killaloe, no other Irish diocese made a full-scale official pilgrimage to Rome for the ceremony. It was ironic really. The very attractiveness of the occasion was putting people off because they feared that too many people would try to be present. The scale of the event gave rise to too many uncertainties. It would be a journey into the unknown.

The original trepidation that Laura and I felt about organising the pilgrimage soon wore off, and a very different feeling came to replace it. We always felt that we had a special connection with John Paul II. The week after we were married, as couples in Italy do, we dressed up again in our wedding attire and went to the Wednesday Papal Audience. John Paul was already visibly suffering from Parkinson's that week in July 2000, but he still shook our hands firmly and gave us his blessing. Our travel company was set up in 2001, and the tricky initial years were characterised by dozens of groups whose main purpose in visiting Rome was to attend the General Audience with John Paul II. As the winter of 2013 deepened, we began to forget our worries about the scale of the upcoming event and started to realize that it was a privilege to organise a pilgrimage to this canonisation. On a more personal note, I was aware that I probably would not have even attended the event if the Killaloe group had not decided to travel.

There were problems too, but it took a while for them to surface. Killaloe had contacted us just days after the official announcement of the date of the canonisations, which meant that we were able to strike early as far as securing hotel rooms was concerned. Laura managed to book a hotel for the group just a few yards from Saint Peter's Square. The price was on the high side, but it seemed more than worth it. We would be able to walk to the canonisation on the morning of April 27, and the whole transportation nightmare that I had dreaded would be averted. I just couldn't believe our luck that Laura had found a hotel in this position.

Our publicity for the trip made much of the fact that we were staying at Saint Peter's, and the bookings started to come in quickly. The airfare was higher than usual, but not as much as we had feared. Everything seemed to be going extraordinarily well. I decided to book a B and B for myself close to the hotel for the night of April 26. It cost just 55 euros, a lot less than the hotel, and it would mean that I could stay the night preceding the canonisation in the area of Saint Peter's. Normally I would have stayed with my in-laws, but they lived on the other side of the city. It didn't seem wise to risk getting stuck in traffic, or in an impossibly overcrowded metro, on the morning of the big event. It was essential to be at the hotel early that day to lead the group over to the square. I was particularly pleased with myself for finding this good-value B and B in such a perfect location. All these years of working in Rome and getting to know the ins and outs of the city were clearly bearing fruit, I mused, quite satisfied with myself. There was even time to feel a little sorry for other tour operators who didn't know the city so well and were probably struggling to find well-located accommodation.

The first hiccup happened about six weeks after we had begun to publicize the trip and had already received quite a few bookings. The phone rang in the office one morning. It was a girl speaking English with a strong Italian accent.

"We have taken over the bookings for the B and B that you have reserved for April 26," she said in a cheerful tone. "I'm afraid your original booking is no longer valid, but we have a very good alternative for you at the same price!" She gave me the address of the new place. It was quite a few miles from Saint Peter's.

"But I need to be close to Saint Peter's on that night!"
I protested. "And I already paid a deposit! You can't just
cancel my room like that!"

"Oh, no, we're certainly not cancelling your room, sir!"
the girl said in the same chirpy voice. "You can still have that
room if you wish, but the original quotation is no longer
valid. It will now cost 220 euros for that night. We have
found you a suitable alternative at the original price, which
is all we're obliged to do. If you like, however, you can have
a full refund of your deposit. Or you can have the original
room back for 220 euros. You just tell me what you would
prefer!"

"But you can't do that—!" I began to say, but then I became instantly subdued. It was clear that there was no point
at all in protesting. "Okay," I said in a resigned tone. "Just
give me back the deposit."

Worse was to come—much worse. We had asked the
hotel to extend the deadline for the payment of the deposit
until a good number of bookings had been received. Now
the new deadline had arrived, and it was time to pay the initial deposit. But when we received the bill, we saw that we
were being charged vastly more than the original quotation
had seemed to say. We asked the hotel for clarification, and
it transpired that the initial quotation had been worded in
an unusual and very unclear way, or at least so it seemed
to us. The real cost of the rooms was much more than we
had budgeted for. We had no choice but to cancel the hotel
immediately.

Now we were in real trouble. More than two months had
passed since the announcement of the canonisations. Official channels were already forecasting that millions of pilgrims were on their way to Rome for that weekend. Prices
had risen sharply, and the larger tour operators were say-

ing that every affordable bed in the city had long since been snapped up. So much for our quickness off the mark and our "superior" experience in finding accommodation in Rome! The only viable hotel options, from a financial point of view, were miles out. And, more worrisome, we already had a large number of bookings from people who had been promised hotel accommodation "a stone's throw" from Saint Peter's! What were we going to do?

"We'll pray to John Paul!" I would say to Laura, as she trawled the Internet, looking for a solution. Or sometimes I would call over to her, "Leave it all in John Paul's hands! He won't let us down!" But I felt a great uneasiness inside. Every rational fibre of my being was saying that it would be impossible to find hotel rooms in Rome for a group of this size for an event that was already vastly oversubscribed. And then how were we to break the news to the people who had already booked? What an embarrassment it would be to have to return to people and say, "Sorry! We messed up on the hotel booking. You can have your money back, or you can still travel. If you travel, you will be staying in Tivoli, twenty miles from Saint Peter's. Instead of walking to the canonisation, we're going to board a coach at about 2:00 A.M. and hope we make it to the event on time, if we make it at all."

The ones who had already booked would have two options: to travel in such unpredictable and volatile circumstances or to cancel altogether. We had already spent thousands on the flight, so if they cancelled—as they surely would —we stood to lose everything. Not for the first time, financial meltdown was staring us in the face.

But then the problem was resolved almost as quickly as it had cropped up. Laura had contacted dozens, perhaps hundreds, of hotels and religious guesthouses in the city. None had sufficient space available. She also tried the incoming tour operators in Rome in the hope that they might still have unused block bookings in the centre of the city. They had nothing either. Then, in an act of desperation, she wrote an e-mail to an organization whose dodgy-looking website she had happened upon at some point during her epic search. This organization performed the service of finding rooms in Rome. She had little hope that they would come up with anything, but she wrote the letter anyway. To our complete surprise and utter relief, a reply came back stating that a very good three-star superior hotel at the Spanish Steps had sufficient rooms for the entire group! And the price being quoted was within our budget!

I still had the uncomfortable job of phoning everyone to say that a mistake had been made and the original hotel was not actually affordable but that we had found a satis-factory alternative at the Spanish Steps. The location was not as good as far as the canonisation was concerned, but the logistics of attending the event were far from impos-sible. I had often walked from the Spanish Steps to Saint Peter's and knew that it could be done in under half an hour. By walking, the nightmare of traffic gridlock that morning could be avoided. It would just take longer than previously advertised. We would take our time and rest along the way, if necessary. A complete refund would be given if anyone was not satisfied with the new hotel situation.

Phoning everyone was a nerve-wracking prospect. Would they be upset? How many would pull out? How many would complain? I had to steel myself before picking up the phone, but it turned out to be a relatively painless experience. In an hour or so, the job was done. No one had complained, and no one had pulled out. All of them seemed as keen to go as they had been in the beginning. The pilgrimage to the canonisation was still on track.

It was the evening of April 26, 2014, the eve of the ceremony. I had left our group in the hotel at the Spanish Steps and was on my way by metro to the home of Laura's family. Everyone in the group had been advised to go to bed as early as possible. Tomorrow would be a day like no other, and we did not know what to expect. The hotel had agreed to give us breakfast at 5:45, and we planned to leave on foot at 6:15. This was very late to depart for Saint Peter's for an event on this scale that was due to begin at 10:00, but there were some elderly and infirm people in the group, and it seemed wise to shorten the day for them as much as possible.

My in-laws were away, and I had the house to myself. At about 9:00, I went to bed but was up at midnight, unable to sleep. After pacing around the house for a while, I tried going back to sleep and then quickly gave up on the idea. Saint Peter's was exerting a magnetic influence on me! I dressed and went into the city. The metro in Rome normally closes from about midnight to 5:30 A.M., but on this occasion, the trains were running all night. My train was not packed, but still busy. Virtually everyone got off at the stop nearest to the Vatican. There was an almost surreal atmosphere as I walked down Via Ottaviano towards the Vatican walls. Even though it was about 2:00 A.M., the city was filled with life. All the cafés and the occasional restaurant were open for business. People were standing at bars, drinking coffee as if it were breakfast time. Something else, however, made the atmosphere seem peculiar, and it took me a while to realize what it was. Then it struck me: there was an almost total silence. The sidewalks were filled with people, but there were no cars running. When people spoke, it was in virtually hushed tones, as if they were worried about disturbing the people sleeping in the apartments above.

I reached Piazza Risorgimento, which is bordered on one side by the Vatican walls. Via di Porta Angelica, which leads from there to the colonnade of Saint Peter's Square, was completely filled with people, wall to wall, standing still. There was little point in trying to reach the square along that route. It seemed to me that the best strategy was to attempt to get around to the Via della Conciliazione, the broad street that runs from the Tiber to Saint Peter's Square, so I took a route that led to Borgo Pio. From here I tried to reach the broad thoroughfare through the successive narrow alleys leading to Via della Conciliazione, but each one of them was blocked by police. Peering down these alleys, as far as I could discern, Via della Conciliazione seemed to be already filled with people. Eventually I arrived all the way down at Castel Sant'Angelo, the former mausoleum of the emperor Hadrian. This stands on the banks of the Tiber on the spot where pilgrims would traditionally have crossed the river from the city to make their way to the Vatican. It was only at this point that the full scale of the crowd became apparent. Via della Conciliazione was packed with people all the way from Saint Peter's Square to the river! I was no expert on crowd calculation but had often heard that the street and the square between them could easily hold well over half a million people. It was only two o'clock in the morning, eight hours before the Mass was due to begin. Most of these people had probably been here since before midnight.

I walked to the hotel at the Spanish Steps, stopping for a coffee along Via dei Banchi Nuovi, an ancient street where bankers and merchants used to set up their stalls in order to attract business from the pilgrims on the principal route to

Saint Peter's. It was a strange novelty to drink coffee at a bar at three o'clock in the morning. Once back at the hotel, I sat in the dark of the foyer for more than two hours until the first members of our group began to arrive for breakfast just after 5:30. Then we made our way to Saint Peter's. Who could have asked for a more glorious walk to a canonisation on a fine, crisp morning? We walked by the church of Sant'Andrea delle Fratte, where another great Pole, Maximilian Kolbe, had celebrated his first Mass; past the Irish Pallottine church of San Silvestro, which contains the head of John the Baptist; behind the imposing Palazzo Montecitorio, designed by Bernini and now used as the Italian House of Parliament; skirting around the Pantheon and past the French church of San Luigi dei Francesi, adorned with the masterpieces of Caravaggio; glimpsing Piazza Navona before we entered Via dei Coronari and on to the river. We had our fold-up chairs over our shoulders, and we set them up in orderly rows just off the Via della Conciliazione, in sight of one of the big screens. We would sit here for more than three hours until the ceremony began.

Canonisation ceremonies usually last more than two hours. The most significant part happens right at the beginning, and it is very easy to miss it. Invoking the authority of Jesus, and that of Saints Peter and Paul, the Holy Father solemnly declares in Latin that the blessed person is now inscribed in the register of the saints. The whole assembly responds, "Amen!" and the Gloria is begun soon afterwards. It was only a couple of days later that we understood better the significance of that part of the ceremony. While we were driving to Assisi, the then bishop of Killaloe took the microphone on the coach and gave us his reflections on the occasion.

"The Holy Father proclaimed in the name of the Church

that John Paul and John XXIII had been found worthy of being revered as saints," he said. "Okay, you were towards the back of the crowd and a long way from Saint Peter's, but you were still physically part of the congregation. When you responded, 'Amen!' to the pope's declaration, you were really saying that you fully assented to the declaration that these men be recognised as saints."

The bishop paused for a moment. "It was a bit like the part of a wedding ceremony where the priest asks if anyone knows of a reason why this man and woman should not be married. Your 'Amen!' was a public affirmation on your part, in communion with the Church, that you fully supported the decision. So, you know, it wasn't just Pope Francis who canonized John Paul and John XXIII: you joined him in doing that too!"

Soon after the canonisations, the bishop of Limerick contacted us regarding the idea of a diocesan pilgrimage to Rome for that autumn. John Paul had visited Limerick in 1979, and the bishop wanted to organise a return visit from the Limerick Diocese to the tomb of John Paul II, now that the Polish pope had been canonised. Various dates were proposed and then ruled out for different reasons. Eventually, we settled on October 18–22 and began taking bookings. Shortly afterwards, it was announced by the Holy See that Pope Paul VI would be beatified on October 19. We weren't sure if this was a fortuitous coincidence or not. It would be great to be present at this beatification, but surely it would raise the usual difficulty of finding hotel rooms in Rome.

The plans for the pilgrimage went ahead, and the group began to fill. During the summer, we took other groups into Saint Peter's Square, and every time we entered the area, I recalled the unforgettable scene of April 27. October 18 came around quickly, and the Limerick group arrived. The following day, we attended the beatification of Paul VI. The crowd situation was completely unlike the canonisation event. The police had put their barriers down Via della Conciliazione, as if they were expecting a large crowd, but not even the square was full. We arrived as late as 8:00 and still had good seats near one of the corridors. Before the ceremony began, Pope Francis passed directly in front of us on the popemobile, at touching distance, and he did so no fewer than three times. Even though we ended up spending more than four hours in the square, the atmosphere was relatively relaxed, and everyone arrived back at the hotel in good spirits.

On October 21, we celebrated Mass at the tomb of John Paul II. This is situated at the altar of Saint Sebastian, towards the back of Saint Peter's Basilica. Michelangelo's *Pietà* is at the adjoining altar. Originally John Paul was buried in the same earth in the crypt where Pope John XXIII had previously been buried. One of the features of a visit to Saint Peter's Basilica in the years 2005 to 2011 was the huge queue for the crypt on account of the number of the faithful who wished to venerate the tomb of the Polish pope. Upon beatification, his remains were taken up to the chapel of Saint Sebastian, which made veneration much easier. Our Mass at this tomb was one of the high points of the pilgrimage: the return visit of the Limerick Diocese to the mortal remains of the Polish pope—a return made in gratitude for his visit to their city thirty-five years previously.

After our Mass at the tomb and a visit to the major sights in the basilica, we made our way back to the hotel for some rest time. The Limerick group was due to return to Ireland on the evening of the following day, which was Wednesday. The plan for Wednesday morning was to attend the General

Audience with Pope Francis. We would then have a relaxing afternoon before heading to the airport. As we walked towards the hotel at lunchtime on Tuesday, I suggested to the bishop something that had been on my mind for some time. I hadn't mentioned it previously because there were demanding things on the itinerary that needed to be dealt with first, but now the programme was almost completed and the time seemed right to broach the idea.

"On Sunday we spent a good few hours in the square at the beatification of Paul VI. We all got really close to Pope Francis a few times. Maybe there is no real need to go to the audience tomorrow at all?"

"Oh?" replied the bishop. "What did you have in mind?"

"Sometimes the last day can be a real drag when the flight is in the evening. It can help to pass the time if we visit something famous or memorable in the afternoon. Last week, we had the National Saint Columbanus Pilgrimage in Rome. They flew to Dublin on Wednesday evening as well. Before flying home, I took them to Montecassino, and we had Mass at the tomb of Saint Benedict. We saw the abbey, had a good lunch, and then drove directly to the airport."

"That sounds like a nice idea," the bishop began, but then he remembered something. "The only thing is that tomorrow is October 22, the actual feast day of Pope John Paul II. It will be the first time that his feast will be celebrated since he was canonised. Maybe people in the group would want to attend a papal audience on that day?" The bishop gave a smile. He seemed easygoing about whether we should go to the audience or not, but still he added, "Francis is the successor of John Paul. They both stand in the role of Peter. People maybe aren't so interested in theology; they probably haven't heard much about the significance of the Petrine ministry; but they still recognize that there is an invisible link there. What do you think?"

"Yes," I said. "But you know we sat there for hours just a couple of days ago. I'm not sure how enthusiastic the group will be about having to do all of that again."

We were arriving back at our hotel on Borgo Pio, just a couple of hundred yards from Saint Peter's Square. The bishop said, "Let's tell the group about your idea, and we'll see what they think."

So we gathered the group in the foyer of the hotel, and I told them the plan. It was clear that people were generally happy with either option. No one insisted on going to the papal audience, and they seemed very positive about the proposal to visit Montecassino. But it was also evident that they would be more than happy to attend the audience as well, if that was the decision. Only one person in the group expressed strong enthusiasm in either direction. Father Leo had visited Rome only once before, decades ago, and on that occasion, the planned trip to Montecassino had been unexpectedly cancelled. He had always nurtured a desire to fulfil his old intention of visiting the abbey. Now it seemed that the opportunity was providentially presenting itself. He loved the idea of celebrating Mass at the tomb of Saint Benedict—but he also made it clear that he would be happy to attend the audience, if things turned out that way.

It was a sort of stalemate situation, and I wasn't sure how to proceed, so we told everyone that we would make a decision later on and let them know before evening. Then everyone dispersed for lunch, and I sat down in the foyer with the bishop.

My memory is not always the most reliable, but I recall this particular conversation very well. The bishop seemed genuinely entertained, in a good-natured sort of way, about my determination that we go to Montecassino. I think he saw that I was trying to do something positive for the group but that I was a little dazzled by my own wonderful plan. He didn't say anything of this sort in words, of course. He just wanted to present the alternative case, and he did so in a very easygoing way, not insisting that we attend the audience but stating that he could see a great value in doing so for a group of this sort. They had come to Rome to pay their respects to John Paul II, after all. This was the crucial point, he felt. Tomorrow was his feast day and a very appropriate occasion to be in the company of his successor.

I was still attached to my own plan, but I could see the sense behind the bishop's point of view. So, on impulse, I made a proposal.

"I have to go over to the Vatican this afternoon to pick up our tickets for tomorrow's audience. If we are given special tickets close to Pope Francis, then we'll stay. If we get the regular tickets, then we'll go to Montecassino. That way, we'll let the Lord decide. What do you think?"

The bishop laughed in the same good-natured way that he had been doing throughout our conversation.

"It's a deal! You have the experience in these matters, Kieran. Let's do it that way then!"

Group tickets for papal audiences can be picked up on the Tuesday preceding the audience between 3:00 and 7:00. Alternatively they can be picked up on the morning of the audience itself from 7:00. The office for collection is just inside the Portone di Bronzo—the Bronze Door—where the right-hand Bernini colonnade begins. Usually we would aim to pick up the tickets at about 5:00 on Tuesday. The initial queue that begins to build up before the office opens at 3:00 would usually have died down by then.

On this particular Tuesday, however, we had a busy programme. Following lunch, we visited the Basilica of Saint John Lateran, the cathedral of Rome. Afterwards we called in to the Irish College and then made our way back by coach to the hotel. As the coach drove up the Via della Conciliazione, the bishop and I went over the deal that we had made: "good" tickets and we would go to the audience; "bad" tickets and we were on our way to Montecassino. The bishop gave me a smile and seemed genuinely tickled by the situation. Without either of us saying anything, there was no doubt that we each favoured a different outcome.

I hopped off the coach at the top of the street, right at the perimeter of Saint Peter's Square. The coach continued round Via dei Corridori to drop everyone else close to the hotel. Once I had collected the tickets, I would go directly to the hotel to inform the group of the programme for tomorrow. As I walked through the colonnade towards the Bronze Door, I was aware of something that I had felt earlier in the day as well. When I had said to the bishop "We'll let the Lord decide," I was really banking on statistics and not on the Lord. Having attended more than two hundred papal events down the years, I knew that the chances of special tickets were exceedingly slim. On many of these occasions, Irish bishops had made strong pleas on behalf of our groups for special tickets, but we had been granted front-row tickets only about five times. On this reckoning, there was a forty-to-one chance that the Limerick group would end up with ordinary tickets. For one particular multidiocesan group of ours in 2006, no fewer than five Irish bishops sent a request to the Papal Household asking for special tickets, but we ended up with the usual standard admission. Sometimes it is said that the Holy See is a den of intrigue and favouritism, where all procedures are tainted with the partiality that was characteristic of nepotism in bygone ages. But as far as special places at papal events are concerned, our experience is that we have always been treated with the same cool even-handedness. My many efforts to court favourable treatment have all failed miserably.

I fully expected the same outcome for the Limerick application. I had seen the letter the Limerick Diocese had sent to the Prefecture of the Papal Household regarding admission to the audience. It described the nature of the group and their motive in going to Rome—an expression of gratitude for the visit of John Paul II in 1979. There was no plea for special treatment. I felt I knew the form of the people in the Prefecture well enough to be confident that they would not be impressed by talk of a return visit to the mortal remains of John Paul II. The guys in that office had heard it all before and were ice cold. Our bishop would need to be at least a cardinal for a simple letter like that to have any influence. Okay, I felt a little guilt as I walked towards the Bronze Door. When I had said, "We'll let the Lord decide," I was really saying, "We'll let Kieran decide." That *was* a little crooked on my part, I had to admit, but this was a clear case where the courier knew best. The group had done their time in Saint Peter's Square when they attended the beatification just two days ago. Once we were in front of the unforgettable spectacle of Montecassino Abbey, everyone would realize what a great plan it had been all along.

It was already 6:30, and I hurried along, aware that I had never picked up tickets this late before, even though the letter always stated that the collection could be made until 7:00. As I approached the security barrier right at the centre of the colonnade, I could see that there was some sort of problem ahead. Two people were brandishing the same kind of letter that I had, but they weren't being allowed to pass.

A plainclothes security guard was talking in animated fashion. "This barrier closes at 6:30 P.M. every day! From now on, people can make their *exit* through here, but nobody can enter!"

"My letter says that the tickets can be collected up until 7:00 P.M.!" a lady protested.

"That's not my problem!" the security guard snapped, raising his voice. "That's the problem of whoever sent you that letter! Anyway, you can pick up your tickets tomorrow morning from 7:00 A.M. What's the big deal? No one gets by here after 6:30 P.M.! Even if Pope Francis himself came along at this hour, I wouldn't let him pass!"

That seemed to settle the matter fairly decisively, and the two people skulked away. I looked on in dismay. Our group needed to know right *now* whether we would be going to the papal audience or to Montecassino in the morning. The time for breakfast and checkout would be set much earlier if we were going to the audience. And our coach driver needed to know in advance as well. I couldn't wait until tomorrow morning to see if we had "good" tickets or "bad" tickets! I needed to know now! What on earth would I do?

I stood a couple of yards back from the barrier with the letter still in my hand. The security guard looked disdainfully in my direction as if defying me to mention anything about collecting tickets for the audience. But he seemed more relaxed now that he had let off some steam and had asserted his authority even over those who sat on the chair of Saint Peter. He turned around and walked over to one of the nearby columns where another guard was sitting on a chair. As he lit a cigarette from that of his colleague, I took my chance and, with a lump in my throat, walked briskly by. I was expecting to be called back at any moment, but the fact that there were still quite a few people on the other side of the barrier probably saved my bacon. Some people were taking photographs of the Swiss Guard who stood in front of the Bronze Door. Others were heading towards the exit. One or two were propped up by one of the columns, rummaging in backpacks. In the general confusion, I managed to slip by unnoticed, and I turned the corner and ascended the steps to the Bronze Door.

The office was still open even though no one was being allowed to enter the area from outside—one of those anomalies that is par for the course in the Vatican. I handed the letter to the immaculately suited man behind the desk, and he ran through the long line of envelopes arranged in alphabetical order. Dozens of packages had not been collected yet. He found the envelope for Limerick Diocese and handed it to me. When you receive a thick, heavy envelope in this office, you know that you have been assigned the ordinary Joe Soap tickets for the audience. Ordinary admission always involves a separate ticket for each individual member of the group, so if you have a large group, you'll end up with a bulky envelope. I have picked up so many of these thick envelopes that I sometimes expect the officials to greet me with, "Ah, Mr. Soap, how are you today? Still hoping for special tickets, are we?" When special admission has been granted, on the other hand, you receive a slim envelope with a single precious slip of paper inside, covering admission for the entire group. As soon as I took the wafer-thin envelope, I realized that we had been given a special ticket.

Slightly downcast, I made my way back to the hotel. Sure, it would be nice to be up close to Pope Francis, but we had seen him already, and a visit to Montecassino would have been even better. I had no option, though, but to accept the way things had turned out. A deal is a deal. At the hotel, the bishop was sitting in the foyer, the picture of absolute calm and relaxation. He smiled broadly as I gave him the envelope, and he was genuinely surprised that we had been given a special ticket. Word soon spread, and the rest of the group gathered around. The only person to show any slight regret was Father Leo. "That's the second time my trip to Montecassino has been cancelled," he said dolefully. "I'm just not meant to go there!" He was putting on a brave face, but we could sense his disappointment.

Now we had the question of planning what to do for the afternoon after the audience. Check-in for the flight home was not until 6:30 P.M. We would have to vacate our hotel rooms in the morning. and it would be quite a drag for the group to stay around Rome all day.

"Why don't we go to Castel Gandolfo after the audience?" I suggested to the bishop. "It's only a forty-minute drive from the city, and we can celebrate our final Mass in the parish church up there."

Castel Gandolfo is situated in the Alban Hills a few miles to the south of Rome. It is perched above Lake Albano, which lies in an extinct volcanic crater. The little town itself is very picturesque, and the view over the lake is spectacular. The popes have had a summer residence in the centre of the town since the 1600s. The bishop readily agreed, so I got Laura to phone the parish in Castel Gandolfo to arrange a Mass for 4:00 P.M. the following day.

October 22, 2014, the very first feast day of Saint John Paul II, dawned beautiful and sunny. We checked out of the hotel and left our suitcases at reception before making our way to Saint Peter's Square at about 8:30. Our bishop went on ahead by himself since he would be permitted to sit in a line of seats close to Pope Francis. An Irish priest who works in one of the congregations very kindly accompanied us into the square and led us to the foremost section, close to the canopy where Pope Francis would be positioned during the audience. He was holding the special ticket that normally would have guaranteed us immediate entrance to the front section. I was at the rear in order to ensure that none of our members got detached from the group and that no opportunistic "outsiders" tagged along. On these occasions, I always took my guard-dog role very seriously.

When the Irish priest reached the entrance to the section, he showed our ticket to the Swiss guard, but the official shook his head, shrugged his shoulders, and appeared to be apologizing for something. I was called to the front to be told that a clerical error of some sort had been made and too many front-row tickets had been issued for that particular audience. The front section was already filled with people who had shown up and queued outside the square even before the security barriers were opened at 7:30 that morning. Then a security man led us all back down the square and into one of the furthest sections from the front! All the other areas were already full.

Nobody in our group complained, but after we had entered this section, many people stood around with a bewildered look. I raised my voice to get everyone's attention and asked that they take seats as close to one another as possible. The section was already packed with thousands of exuberant Mexicans, but there were just about enough seats left for us. We hadn't got our front-row position, but we were here and would have to make the best of it. Pope Francis would be out in about an hour.

I had no sooner sat down when a lady named Mary from the group came over to me.

"I would really like to get as close to Pope Francis as possible," she said. "It's hard to explain, but it's just something that I feel I have to do today. Where do you think I should place myself?"

"Well, Mary, unfortunately we're a bit late now to get into a good position. The popemobile is going to pass all along these corridors around our section. But as you can see, people are already lined up along every inch of the barrier."

The seating for an audience in Saint Peter's Square is arranged in sections that hold about five thousand people each. As the crowd streams into the square on Wednesday mornings, the areas around the edge of each section fill up first because people know that the popemobile is going to pass along there. We had arrived at the square relatively late that morning because we had expected our special ticket to guarantee us a spot close to Pope Francis.

Mary and I looked around our section. There was a real carnival atmosphere as the Mexicans danced and chanted.

"I'm sorry, Mary, but you won't have a hope of getting over to the barrier," I said, shaking my head despondently, for I could see that she really wished to get close to Pope Francis. "I've been in sections with Mexicans before. They're a lovely, warm people, but they go completely crazy when Pope Francis is driving by. There will be a huge surge when the popemobile comes around."

"All right," said Mary. "But I'll just see how close I can get." She looked with trepidation at the mass of people in front of her and began moving in the direction of the barrier.

"Okay, Mary, but watch out for the elbows!" I called after her. "And keep your feet when Pope Francis is driving by!"

I sat back and began to feel decidedly sorry for myself.

Here we were in a virtual no-man's land in the middle of Saint Peter's Square when we could have been on our way to Montecassino! Okay, a bishop is a bishop, and the bishop of Limerick had been to his fair share of papal events. And I had no doubt that a bishop is given a special charism by the Holy Spirit, but I had been to more than *two hundred* of these events, and this was clearly a situation in which the courier knew best. I could tell when a group had done its share of waiting in Saint Peter's Square, and we had certainly paid our dues with interest at the beatification ceremony a couple of days before.

After considerable time had passed, my thoughts were interrupted by the sound of trumpets over the public-address system. The popemobile was on its way under the Arch of the Bells and into the square. The Mexicans had been jubilant earlier, but now they went into a state of near ecstasy. Members of our group became excited as well, and some of them stood on their chairs, trying to see which corridor the popemobile was in. I sat glumly in my seat, feeling sorry that Mary would not get close to Pope Francis, feeling regret that Father Leo would probably never get to Montecassino. Then the noise in our section rose to fever pitch, and it was clear that Pope Francis was approaching. I found myself standing on my chair now as well and began clapping, barely discerning the figure of Pope Francis fifteen metres away through the waving flags and raised cameras. Glum though I was, it was hard to repress the familiar thrill that arises whenever a pope goes by. It never mattered whether it was John Paul II, Benedict, or Francis; there is something about the office of the successor of Peter that has a unique effect on people. I even found myself involuntarily hollering "*Viva il Papa!*" a few times as the figure in white disappeared towards the adjoining section.

I quickly sat down again, however, and did my best to return to the state of self-absorption that I had been in previously. The drive to Montecassino was so smooth and enjoyable, I always found. And once we started climbing those hairpin bends to the abbey, the feeling of expectancy on the coach would begin to mount. Then, on the way up, there was the impressive Polish cemetery containing the graves of more than a thousand Polish soldiers whose bravery finally led to the end of the Battle of Cassino—by coincidence, on the birthday of John Paul II in 1944. And the restaurant below the abbey where we took all our groups was always a major success, with that homemade fruit-of-the-forest dessert. It would have been the perfect way to end the pilgrimage to Italy. Instead, here we were surrounded by deafening cries of "*Meh*-ico! *Meh*-ico!" and scarcely in sight of the Holy Father.

The audience had begun, and Pope Francis was sitting under the canopy, but I was barely hearing anything that was being said. At one point, I pricked up my ears when Pope Francis made reference to the fact that today was the feast of John Paul II, the first celebration of the feast since his canonisation. Everything else went over my head. Eventually, the audience ended, and the crowd began streaming out. I tried to gather the group together at the fountain to the left of the square. When we had established that everyone was present, we began to make our way across the square and towards Borgo Pio, where we would have some free time for lunch. As we were walking, I noticed that Mary was crying.

"Is Mary okay?" I asked the person beside me.

"Yes, everything is fine," I was told, and then, as we were walking the two hundred yards across the very ground where Saint Peter the apostle was killed, I learned the full story.

In 1979, Mary was expecting a child when Pope John Paul II came to Limerick. She really wanted to attend the papal Mass, but her parents wouldn't allow her to go because she was too far advanced in her pregnancy. She didn't see John Paul on that occasion, but she always associated him with her son, who was born shortly afterwards. In 1999, at the age of nineteen, her son was killed in a completely unprovoked street attack, and Mary entered a period of profound bereavement. She became involved in a bereavement group that had been set up to assist parents like herself who had lost a child.

At the audience that day, Mary had made her way over as close to the barrier as possible. She did not encounter the sharp elbows and pushy people I had predicted; quite the contrary. Before the popemobile entered the square, she was already positioned right at the barrier. But it still seemed unlikely that she would ever manage to touch the pope. There were more than forty thousand people in the square that day, and Pope Francis would touch perhaps only one hundred of these during his journey in the jeep. That is odds of four hundred to one. The vehicle flies along the corridors at a fairly substantial speed, screeching to a halt only at unpredictable times, whenever Pope Francis spots in the crowd a baby he wants to bless. One of those babies was right beside Mary. The vehicle stopped, Pope Francis was given the baby briefly, and just after he handed the baby back to his parents, he caught Mary's hand for a moment.

When Mary touched Pope Francis' hand, she had the sensation that she was also touching the hand of John Paul II, and, even more than that, she felt that she was once again in the presence of the son whom she had always associated with the Polish pope. Later that day, she said, "When I think of my son, I think of John Paul always, and that will never, ever leave me, even more so after today."

When this story had been told to me, I fell into silence. What a narrow perspective I had taken on the day's events! How much more was going on here than I had ever imagined! And it was the very unlikelihood that Mary would touch Pope Francis' hand that made the entire event shine with the grace of God. If our special ticket had given us entrance to the reserved section, then we would all have sat up front, and Mary might well have shaken the pope's hand, but no one would have been too surprised. It would have been the eloquence of the bishop's request and the quality of the ticket that would have taken the credit. But when the ticket fails, when the courier has given up, when you are in the most improbable position imaginable, and yet the events conspire to permit you to touch the hand of the successor of Peter—the rock instituted by Christ—then you cannot help but believe that a greater power is guiding everything from above. And on top of all that, it was the perfect day, October 22, the first feast day of the new saint, John Paul II.

I felt sheepish when I realised that the Lord had also worked through my conceit. The proposal to allow the tickets to decide whether we went to the audience or to Montecassino was a devious way to impose my own will on the situation, but the Lord had used it to direct things in another direction entirely. This feeling of sheepishness would persist for a while, but my glumness had completely evaporated. I realized that the good Lord was at work all around me, even in the things I was doing badly, bringing good in spite of me. My spirits soared. It was clear that even I was playing a role in a wonderful day.

The day was not over yet, however, and other surprises

were on their way. We drove to Castel Gandolfo after lunch and climbed up to the town from the coach park. Before entering the parish church, we walked over to the lookout point and admired the stunning view of Lake Albano below. Father Leo had been chosen as the principal celebrant. He would have been given the honour of celebrating at the tomb of Saint Benedict if we had gone to the Abbey of Monte-cassino. Being the main celebrant in the parish church of Castel Gandolfo didn't seem to be in the same league, even though the beautiful church was designed entirely by the great Bernini, but Father Leo had accepted the honour graciously.

The group seated themselves in the pews, and I went into the sacristy with the priests. Maurizio, the sacristan, was passing the vestments and sacred vessels to Father Leo, giving a commentary in Italian as he did so. I was interpreting while Maurizio spoke matter-of-factly, no doubt repeating what he would have said on many previous occasions.

"This is the ciborium given as a gift to us by Pope Paul VI when he stayed at the papal palace. It was used by Pope Paul on many occasions when he stayed here, so I suppose it could be called a relic of the pope beatified a few days ago." Maurizio was referring to the fact that objects touched by a saint or a blessed are considered second-class relics of that person.

"Oh, my word!" Father Leo replied. "Would you believe it? Isn't it a wonderful privilege to be able to use that?"

"And this is the chalice given to us by Pope John XXIII and used by him," Maurizio continued. "This is certainly the relic of a saint."

"And we are being allowed to use that for Mass today?" Father Leo said in amazement. "That's incredible!"

"Of course you can use it," replied Maurizio, in the most

matter-of-fact way, but he hadn't finished yet. Father Leo was almost vested, and the only thing remaining to put on was the chasuble, the outer garment worn by the priest during Mass.

Maurizio began placing the chasuble over Father Leo's head. "This chasuble was given to us as a gift by Pope John Paul II," the sacristan said. "And he wore it himself when he celebrated Mass here on numerous occasions."

Father Leo was left speechless. On the very first feast of Saint John Paul II, as part of a pilgrimage that had come to Rome to pay its respects to the same pope, he was celebrating Mass wearing the vestment of the Polish saint!

In his homily during the Mass, Father Leo told us how disappointed he had been that we had not gone to Montecassino that day. He had tried to hide it from the group, but he had felt a little disillusioned all the same. Now he was standing there in front of us on the feast of John Paul II, wearing the chasuble of the saint, using sacred vessels donated by the other two principal figures we had honoured during the pilgrimage, and none of it had been planned! It had all happened as a result of an apparently chance sequence of events. "When God appears to be closing one door, he is really opening another," Father Leo said, visibly moved by all that had unfolded.

After Mass, we had enough time for a cappuccino in the village square before heading to the airport. Father Seamus, another member of the group, was in a generous mood and wanted to buy coffee for everyone. The evening temperatures had dropped sharply, as they can do in Castel Gandolfo at that time of year. We sat out in the picturesque square in front of the little fountain, hugging our hot drinks and thinking about everything that had happened that day, the very first feast of the Polish saint. I had hatched my wonderful plans and tried to steer events in my direction, only to discover that the good Lord had matters well in hand right from the beginning.

Our bishop was moved when he heard about Mary's experience, but he didn't seem surprised. "The pope has that special grace of the Holy Spirit, you know, as visible head of the Church," he said. "Things like that are probably happening all the time here."

The Catholic understanding of the Petrine ministry is something that developed theologically over the course of the centuries. The papacy perpetuates the role of Saint Peter as visible head of the Church, guarantor of orthodoxy and anchor of the faith. A significant historical example of the expression of this belief came with the Council of Chalcedon in the year 451. The Church had been assailed for over a century by aberrant views about the nature of Christ. Some, such as Arianism, asserted that Jesus was neither fully human nor fully divine, but a sort of demigod, a halfway house between God and man. Such a belief had great appeal because it seemed to eliminate the mystery of how Jesus could be God and man at the same time. A vast number of bishops and faithful went over to the Arian camp at different stages during the fourth and fifth centuries. In its wake, another equally insidious view, called Monophysitism, became popular. This effectively denied Jesus' full humanity, asserting that he had a single nature that was basically divine.

The Council of Chalcedon was called to resolve these disputes once and for all, but it was racked by controversy until delegates from Rome read out a letter from Pope Leo I. In his letter, Leo explained clearly that Christ has two natures: he is fully human and fully divine, yet both natures are united in a single divine person. According to the official transcript of the council, after the pope's "tome" was read out, the bishops who were present began to cry out in unison, "This is the faith of the fathers, this is the faith of the Apostles. Peter has spoken thus through Leo. This is the true faith."

It is often said that the Church has a Petrine aspect and a Marian aspect. If Peter is the guarantor of the one apostolic faith, Mary is the guarantor that God really became man and lives among us. There has been no great council of the Church that does not emphasize the full incarnation of Christ in the womb of a very special mother. And so it was at Chalcedon when the bishops cried out, "He is Peter!" The Petrine and Marian elements had been working together. Leo's letter could not assert the true nature of Christ without making reference to the dignity of the Virgin Mary. If Christ is to be made fully human, Leo said, then he must be given a body that is real, a body derived from a human mother.

As we descended the hill from Castel Gandolfo with the spectacular view of Rome on the plain beneath us, I recalled the Mexicans we had encountered that morning in Saint Peter's Square. As always, some of them were holding up images of Our Lady of Guadalupe. This image is of a young woman, half Spanish, half Native American, with a ribbon around her waist to indicate that she is pregnant. Mary guarantees the true incarnation of the divinity in human flesh. She is the good ground in which the divine seed is sown, bearing a fruit that is priceless. As I thought back over what had happened to Mary Fitzpatrick that morning, it seemed appropriate that she had experienced her grace-filled moment while surrounded by devotees of the one who was full of grace.

4

Full of Grace

Sing and rejoice, O daughter of Zion; for behold, I come
and I will dwell in the midst of you, says the LORD.

—Zechariah 2:10

It was a matter that had been knocking on the door of my
consciousness for years, but it had never come in. Certainly,
I knew the response that the lady had given to the question
of Saint Bernadette. Anyone who had worked as a courier in
Lourdes could not be unaware of the famous reply from the
vision when Bernadette asked her name. Up until that very
moment, it seems that virtually no one of note believed that
the little shepherdess was really seeing a lady from heaven
down at the city dump. The parish priest was probably the
most sceptical of all. "Ask the lady her name!" he roared at
Bernadette. "Does this woman really expect me to build a
chapel for her when I don't even know her name?"

When the woman finally revealed who she was, her answer came like a bolt out of the blue: *I am the Immaculate Conception*. Bernadette could barely read or write at this point.
She had no knowledge of theology, and little enough of the
basic catechism, but she was given an answer that represents
an authentic high point in Christian doctrine. She had to
repeat the phrase to herself over and over again as she ran

to the parish priest's house. "I am the Immaculate Conception!" she blurted out when the door was opened. "That is the name of the lady!"

That Bernadette had really seen the lady from heaven is not proven by the countless miracles of healing that have taken place at the shrine in the intervening years. Nor is it guaranteed by the fact that Bernadette herself lived a life of heroic sanctity afterwards and that her body—though never embalmed—now lies perfectly preserved for all to see in a convent in the little town of Nevers. The truth of the little shepherdess' testimony is confirmed above all by the fact that the words spoken by the vision—*I am the Immaculate Conception*—were words that an illiterate child could never have imagined or invented.

While working as a courier in Lourdes, I took many groups down to the Cachot, the damp basement where the Soubirous family lived. We visited the grotto of the apparitions as a matter of course and knew the details of the story inside out. How many homilies I listened to on the story of Lourdes! But the significance of this title of Our Lady all but eluded me. Every evening for an entire season, I would join the candlelight procession with the wheelchair pilgrims and thousands of others on its route around the grounds of the sanctuary. My fellow couriers thought I was mad. "Not joining the procession *again*!" they would say when they spotted me with my candle half hidden, heading shiftily down towards the grotto. But even as I lifted my lighted candle to the sound of "Ave Maria!," a good part of the message of Lourdes was going over my head.

Some years passed, and I was teaching English in Rome. It was December 8, the feast of the Immaculate Conception, and someone suggested that we go down to the Spanish Steps to see if we could catch a glimpse of Pope John

Paul II. The custom is for the pope to come to the square on that day, and, in his presence, the youngest fireman in the city drapes a wreath of flowers over the arm of Our Lady on top of the Immaculate Conception column. This column was erected in front of the Spanish Embassy after 1854 to commemorate the Church's definition of the dogma. The Spanish crown had always been great defenders of the Immaculate Conception of the mother of Jesus.

It was the sort of crisp, sunny day that is typical of early December in Rome. In those days, the Via dei Fori Imperiali was still open to traffic, and it was filled with scooters, small cars, and buses, all racing towards Piazza Venezia in the frenetic way that is part of the character of the Eternal City. We diverged from the traffic and took the road leading past the ruins of the Forum of Augustus, dominated by the great columns of the Temple of Mars Ultor, built to mark the victory of the emperor over Mark Antony and Cleopatra. This victory ushered in the Pax Romana, the period of peace and stability in the Roman Empire that just happened to coincide with the birth of the real Prince of Peace.

Our intention was to come at the Spanish embassy from the direction of the Trevi Fountain, but when we had passed the fountain and got as far as Via del Tritone, we found that the street in front of us was completely jammed with people. Not wishing to give up, we walked down towards Piazza San Silvestro, where the head of Saint John the Baptist is conserved by the Irish Pallottines in a church of the same name. From here we tried successive streets leading up to Piazza di Spagna, but all were impassable because of the crowds. In desperation, we walked down Via del Corso almost all the way to Piazza del Popolo, to the church with two Caravaggio masterpieces hanging casually on its walls. We wanted to see if we could come into the square from

the opposite side. But even here, masses of motionless people blocked our way. It was no use. Despite the crowds,
there was an incredible calm in the area, almost a silence.
We stood in the throng for a while until news filtered back
that it was all over. Our Lady had been given her wreath of
flowers, and the pope was gone.

"What was all that about?" I wondered, as I trudged home
wearily. Crowds like that for an event that lasts only a few
minutes? Flowers from the pope? Was this column really
so important? But the mystery of the title really started to
impinge on my consciousness a few months later when I
took a group into Saint Mary Major Basilica. It was hard to
get by just teaching English, and I was relatively new to the
job of taking Irish groups around the city of Rome. The
itineraries were very busy, and we were expected to visit a
large number of monuments and churches every few hours,
which meant that many visits were short and efficient. This
suited me fine, since my knowledge of most places was quite
limited.

We came up the central aisle of Saint Mary Major, and
I pointed out the mosaics in the apse. These were done by
a Franciscan friar called Jacopo Torriti in the late 1200s, I
explained. In the central scene, Jesus and Mary are depicted
sitting on the same throne, with Jesus in the act of crowning
his mother. "And down here," I said, motioning to the area
beneath the high altar, "we have a portion of the crib of
Bethlehem, visible behind the glass of its ornate reliquary."

"Who's the big guy on his knees down there?" someone
asked, referring to the enormous statue of a kneeling figure.

"That's Pope Pius IX," I replied.

"Why is he there?" the same voice asked, with an irritating directness, but the real source of irritation was more
likely the fact that I hadn't a clue as to the answer. The com-

pany that was employing me, no doubt aware of my short-comings, had warned me never to let on to people if I was unsure of something. "Bluff! Change the subject! Make up a story! Do anything to keep them happy, but never reveal how little you know!" they exhorted. It was advice I took very much to heart.

"Pius IX was the pope who defined the dogma of the Immaculate Conception of Mary," I answered. "For that reason, it is entirely appropriate that he should be shown kneeling in front of the crib of Bethlehem."

My interlocutor looked back at me open-mouthed, and I quickly changed the subject, pointing out on the ceiling the Borgia coat of arms, which was said to have been gilded by the first gold that Columbus brought back from the Americas. When the tour was over, I cringed inwardly. "What has the conception of *Mary* got to do with the crib in which *Jesus* was born?" I groaned to myself. "The group will have figured out that I was just bluffing!" However, as time passed and I reflected on my "gaffe," I came to realise that the answer I had plucked out of the air was exactly right, to a theological T. I had spoken a profound truth completely by accident. Pius IX is placed kneeling in front of the crib where Jesus was born because he is the pope who defined the dogma of the Immaculate Conception of Mary. And this dogma tells us even more about the Incarnation of God than it does about Mary. But it took me some time to appreciate the wisdom of my own words. Fortunately, events conspired to assist with my eventual enlightenment.

For a time in those years, it seemed to me that the Immaculate Conception was everywhere, in the stories of the personalities who had shaped the Eternal City, in the works of art, in the background of significant historical events. The most obvious example confronted me when I would take tours into the Vatican Museums. Here the virtual sole objective of every group was to see the Sistine Chapel, the place in which popes are elected and whose ceiling and end wall are covered by the frescoes of Michelangelo. The Sistine Chapel, however, can be visited only as part of the Vatican Museums, and this involves a long trek through many corridors of exhibits before arriving, stressed and weary, at the chapel. The museums are filled with treasures, not least among them the magnificent paintings of Raphael in the papal apartments. But the groups I was working with would have had few enough people interested in high works of art. Their main interest was to "see" the famous ceiling of Michelangelo. Our tour, therefore, was tailored to focus on a few of the highlights of the Sistine Chapel and to get in and out of there with as little hassle as possible.

In those years, before online bookings were possible, the business of queuing up outside could sometimes take hours. When we finally got inside, I would gather the group in front of one of the large reproductions of the ceiling frescoes. These were for the use of guides and were placed in various locations inside the museums. It was a chance to point out things that would be impossible to describe once we were inside the chapel. The central scene on the ceiling shows the creation of Adam. God the Father extends his finger towards the limp finger of Adam, giving him life. As God the Father does this with his right arm, he is holding a number of figures in the embrace of his left. One of them is a beautiful woman. "Who could *she* be?" I wondered sometimes. But when I got to know the other scenes on the ceiling from the Book of Genesis, it became apparent that this woman is Eve. At the moment of the creation of man, God the Father is already holding woman in his embrace! "So God created man in his own image, in the image

of God he created him; male and female he created them"
(Gen 1:27).

We would discuss some of the other scenes on the ceiling
and from *The Last Judgement* on the end wall. One of my own
favourites was the painting of the prophet Jeremiah, found
on the ceiling in the first position on the left from the side
of the high altar. At the right knee of Jeremiah, Michelangelo had painted a scroll with the Greek letters alpha and
omega. This was the artist's official "signature" following
his epic work of four years painting the ceiling. In the Book
of Revelation, Jesus says, "I am the Alpha and the Omega,
the first and the last, the beginning and the end" (22:13). By
using these letters as his signature, Michelangelo was saying
that—whatever merits were in these frescoes—they came
from the Lord alone, the Creator who had inspired him and
given him his artistic ability.

Then we would begin our trek through the museums
and towards the Sistine Chapel. Before moving off, I would
exhort the group to stay close to me, not to become detached in the immense crowds. Above all, they would need
to be ready for the key turning point after the Gallery
of Tapestries and the Gallery of Maps. At this point, we
would be presented with two options: turn left into the
room of the Immaculate Conception or swing down the
stairs to the right. The latter was the short route to the
Sistine Chapel, but it was not always open. If it was open,
then it was essential that we should take it; otherwise our
route to the chapel would be much longer. But that year,
the short route was closed on most of the occasions we
visited the Vatican Museums, so we ended up, time and
again, passing through the room of the Immaculate Conception. This had to do with crowd control. Whenever the Sistine Chapel is critically full, the strategy is to delay people's

arrival there by sending them along a more circuitous museum route.

On a few occasions, I managed to persuade one of the guards on duty to open the rope and allow our group to take the short route to the Sistine. My pleas were based on the advanced-age profile of the group and the stifling heat inside the museums. Before approaching the guard, I would call a few of the more elderly members of the group up alongside me so that he could see for himself the bad state we were in. The worse we looked, the better. On some of the hotter days, I even developed a bit of a limp myself at that point. Mostly, though, my pleas fell on deaf ears, and we were dispatched mercilessly on the longer route. There was nothing for it on those occasions but to shuffle with the crowd through the corridors, keep the group in tow, and try to enjoy the paintings of Raphael and the other exhibits along the way.

Eventually I began to ask myself about the contents of that first room we encountered after being denied access to the shortcut to the Sistine Chapel. What was this room of the Immaculate Conception anyhow? In the centre of the room was a very ornate bookcase. According to the description, this bookcase held gifts from various royal families and dignitaries to Pope Pius IX on the occasion of the definition of the dogma. But these gifts were nothing other than translations into various languages of the pope's own document *Ineffabilis Deus*, in which he defines the dogma! On the wall in front of the bookcase, an enormous Raphael-like fresco depicts the pope standing and proclaiming the definition.

"Shouldn't the pope be sitting down when he proclaims a dogma?" I asked myself, after I had noticed this for the first time, quite proud of my scant knowledge of papal affairs. The expression *ex cathedra*—"from the chair"—is used to describe the action of the pope in authoritatively speaking on an issue of faith or morals from his position as successor to the Chair of Peter. The dogma of the Immaculate Conception would have been proclaimed while the pope was seated in his chair. Later, I read somewhere that Pope Pius IX himself had asked the artist, Francesco Podesti, to depict him in a standing position to increase the dramatic effect of the scene.

And it surely was a dramatic moment! Why was the dogma defined at that moment in time, I wondered, more than eighteen centuries after the time of Christ? Weren't there already enough obstacles to our reunion with the other Christian denominations? If the doctrine was part of the deposit of faith, why did it take so long to be officially formulated? And why was it so important to formulate it at all?

The puzzle increased sometime later when I visited the town of Roccasecca, south of Rome, for the first time. I was with a group of students and teachers from Aquinas College in Belfast. Saint Thomas Aquinas was of noble blood, and his family had a castle above the little town of Roccasecca, not far from the famous Abbey of Montecassino. Father Grant, the ever-enthusiastic chaplain of the group, wanted to take in this rather obscure place at all costs. It wasn't so simple to fit it in because our excursion that day was also to include a tour of the ancient city of Pompeii, beyond Naples, as well as the Abbey of Montecassino. It was an incredibly demanding schedule, and everything needed to go smoothly if our driver was to complete the programme within the maximum number of hours that he was allowed to drive in a day.

The castle of Roccasecca is in ruins, but a corner of it was transformed into a church in the fourteenth century, and it proudly claims to be the first church dedicated to Saint

Thomas Aquinas after he was canonised in 1323. On our many visits to this chapel with the Aquinas College in the intervening years, we have always followed a similar routine. We clamber up the old steps covered in grass and briars and stand inside the chapel, which is otherwise opened only for the occasional wedding. We admire the old fresco of Saint Thomas on the exterior wall and take a group photograph on the steps, which afford a spectacular view of the Liri valley far below.

But on this first occasion, I was not very familiar with the story of Aquinas and had to do some reading in preparation. As the coach went around the hairpin bends towards Roccasecca, I took the microphone and summarized Saint Thomas' immense contribution to Catholic theology, his successful project of using the philosophy of Aristotle to express and defend Christian truths, and his influence on the liturgical life of the Church, principally evidenced in his role in the introduction of the celebration of the great feast of Corpus Christi.

I had chosen the concept of transubstantiation to illustrate the thought of Saint Thomas. Catholics believe that Christ is really present in the bread and wine consecrated in the Eucharist. Aquinas used the philosophical distinction between "accidents" and "substance" to illuminate this article of faith. Objects typically have accidents and substances (or essences). For example, there are many types of table: wooden tables, glass tables, round tables, square tables, and so forth. These can be distinguished from one another because they have different accidents; in other words, their own particular characteristics and properties. But they can all be thought of as having the *same* essence or substance; each of them has the function of being a table. In the case of the bread and wine used for the Eucharist, these elements retain their accidental characteristics. The bread continues to have the smell of bread, the look of bread, the taste of bread. But after the Eucharistic Consecration, its *substance* has changed. It is now the Body of Christ, while retaining the accidental properties of bread. Commonsense philosophical principles such as these were used by Saint Thomas to help us get a grasp on the mysteries of faith. The mystery is not removed by the philosophical treatment. On the contrary, clear thinking only helps to bring the mystery better into focus.

The coach was nearing its destination, and everyone was silent, admiring the breathtaking landscape beneath us.

"Saint Thomas didn't believe in the Immaculate Conception, you know." It was Father Grant, sitting directly behind me, who was speaking. I turned around in surprise. "Really?" Aquinas had such a broad influence on theology that it didn't seem possible that he would diverge from what would later become the official teaching of the Church on a matter so important as this one.

"Well, some scholars think that he may have changed his views on the subject a number of times. But there's no doubt that he had a couple of major questions with regard to the Immaculate Conception."

"Oh? What were they?"

"His main concern was to uphold the teaching that Christ redeemed *all* of mankind. Because of the Fall of Adam, mankind was in a state of Original Sin and needed redemption. If Mary was conceived without Original Sin, then that would seem to say that she didn't need to be redeemed. That was a major stumbling block for Aquinas. He struggled with that."

"Christ as our universal Redeemer! Everyone needs salvation, and only Jesus saves! How did the Church get over
that obstacle?"

"Not so much how but *who*. His name was Duns Scotus.
He solved the riddle, but it took the Church 600 years to
accept his solution—and another 150 years to beatify him!"

Duns Scotus. I had heard about this medieval figure before, but I wasn't sure if the stories were true or just legend. Someone had told me that the name "dunce" derived
from the notoriety of this Franciscan thinker: he was slow in
understanding any given argument, and his reasoning tended
to be convoluted. Elsewhere I had heard that "dunce" was
the derogatory word used by Protestant scholars for the
sort of argumentation employed by followers of Duns Scotus much later, in the sixteenth century. Whatever the truth
of the matter, the friar had left no impressive body of theological work comparable with that of Aquinas. But on the
matter of the Immaculate Conception, he had prevailed over
the great Aquinas, against all the odds. His argument was
deceptively simple. He began from a principle that had been
formulated in the eleventh century by Saint Anselm: *potuit,
decuit, ergo fecit* (it was possible, it was fitting, therefore it was
accomplished). We can see how it was eminently fitting that
the Mother of God should be free from Original Sin, but
how was it *possible*? After all, Christ had not yet redeemed
humanity. Duns Scotus removed this obstacle by arguing
that, instead of being excluded from the redemption of the
Saviour, Mary obtained an even greater redemption by being
preserved from all sin by the future merits of Christ. This,
explained Scotus, attributes to Christ an even more prominent role as Redeemer, because redeeming grace, which *preserves* from Original Sin, is greater than that which purifies
from sin already incurred. Mary benefits from this redeem-

ing grace by virtue of the anticipated merits of Jesus' Passion and death.

The theology underlying the dogma of the Immaculate Conception was provided by Scotus, but the belief was already there among the Christian faithful throughout the centuries. The feast of the Immaculate Conception was being celebrated in the Eastern Church from the earliest times. Throughout the rest of Europe, churches and devotions in honour of this title of Mary were widely diffused. I began to notice this more and more as I trekked around Italy with pilgrim groups, from north to south, from Turin as far as Sicily. Incredibly, the evangelisation of the Americas was also linked to the title. In 1531, Our Lady appeared to a Mexican native, Juan Diego, on the very day that the feast of the Immaculate Conception was being celebrated by the Spanish colonists. Following decades of failed evangelisation, this event would lead to the conversion of millions of Mexican natives in a few short years, one of the most spectacular feats of evangelisation in history.

Much later, when I discussed this subject with Laura, she told me about an online catechesis she had heard by a man called Edward Sri on the chapter in Luke that describes the Annunciation to Mary. When the angel Gabriel greets Mary, he says, "Hail, full of grace! The Lord is with you!" (Lk 1:28). Now, it is unheard of in Scripture for an angel to give honour to a mere man or woman. Usually it is man who bows down in awe before angelic visitations. But what is really unusual about this greeting is the Greek term placed by the evangelist Luke on the lips of Gabriel. The term, *kecharitomene*, was traditionally translated in Latin as "gratia plena" and in English as "full of grace." The difficulty in rendering this term is that it does not appear in this form *anywhere else* in the New Testament or in secular

Greek literature. It seems to be a unique term that has been constructed by Luke to express in Greek the unique words spoken by the angel to a unique lady in her native language. But that is not to say that it does not make sense. It makes perfect sense. The angel uses this term as if it were the proper name—the heavenly name—of Mary. And the word refers to an action that has already been performed on her: she has been made perfect, filled with grace.

But as we travelled home from Roccasecca and the birthplace of Aquinas, the fuller significance of Our Lady's title still hadn't hit home for me. It would take another visit to Saint Mary Major Basilica sometime later before this realisation would take place. A pilgrim group from Saint Patrick's parish, Belfast, arrived in Rome on October 2, 2015. It was a Friday, and we had booked a Mass for the group in Saint Mary Major for the following day, Saturday, as that is the traditional day to honour Our Lady. When the group arrived, however, Father Dominic, the curate, told me that a friend of his was available to give us a tour of Saint John Lateran Basilica the next day. I knew the Sister Emanuela that he was referring to. She was a member of the Sisters of Divine Revelation, and she had given us a very entertaining tour of the Vatican Museums just a few weeks before. Saturday was the only day she was available, so Laura cancelled the Mass in Saint Mary Major and rescheduled it for Monday, October 5.

All seemed well, and the programme looked to be fully arranged, including a Mass on Sunday in the grottoes of Saint Peter's Basilica, close to the tomb of Saint Peter. This would be a highlight for many people. On Saturday, however, we were informed that all private Masses were being cancelled in the basilica on Sunday because the Vatican's Synod on the Family was beginning in Saint Peter's on that day. The only date when there was a chapel available in Saint Peter's for the celebration of Mass was Monday. This meant that Laura had to phone Father Angelo at Saint Mary Major once again and cancel our Monday visit. We rescheduled the Mass there for Tuesday. The coach company was informed again of the change, and all seemed settled once more.

When Tuesday came around, we had a meeting scheduled with the Irish ambassador to the Holy See, who, for a short time, resided in an apartment close to the Pantheon. Ambassador Madigan had very kindly invited the parish to a reception to commemorate the two hundredth anniversary of its foundation. Bishop Patrick Walsh, retired bishop of Down and Connor, was a member of the group, and when he heard that we were visiting the ambassador in a location near the Pantheon, he had a request: Could we celebrate Mass in the German church of Santa Maria dell'Anima nearby? In this church, a friar named Conor O'Devany was consecrated bishop of Down and Connor in 1582. He had gone on to become one of the most heroic martyrs of the anti-Catholic persecutions in Ireland.

Laura was used to my phoning her at all hours of the day to ask her to make changes to our programme, but this was a bit much even for her.

"Father Angelo is going to kill me!" she complained. "How many more times are you going to change this Mass?"

"Don't worry, Laura; this will be the last time! We're leaving Rome the following day, after all. Tell them there's a bishop in the group. That usually helps!"

So the Mass in Santa Maria dell'Anima was arranged for Tuesday, and the visit to Saint Mary Major was rescheduled once again for our final full day in Rome—Wednesday, October 7.

That Wednesday morning, we attended the General Audience with Pope Francis in Saint Peter's Square. As we drove to the audience, the parish priest of St. Patrick's, Father Michael, led morning prayer from the microphone of the coach. He began by referring to the fact that that day was the feast of Our Lady of the Rosary, a detail that had escaped me. As we sat in Saint Peter's Square under a cloudy and foreboding sky, waiting for the pope's jeep to appear, the significance of this date began to sink in. I knew all about the feast of Our Lady of the Rosary because I told its history to every group before we visited Saint Mary Major, but we had never visited the basilica on the feast before. And now, a chain of unexpected events meant that we were going to celebrate the Eucharist there on this great anniversary. But that was not all. Other blessings were in store for us as well.

On the way to Saint Mary Major that afternoon, I told the story of the Battle of Lepanto. In the 1400s, the Ottoman Turks had taken over the lands previously under the control of Byzantium, the eastern Roman Empire, which had endured for centuries after the western empire collapsed. In the sixteenth century, this new empire saw major expansion. Their navy was the most powerful in the world and was making significant incursions into the eastern Mediterranean. Cyprus had already fallen. Christian Europe trembled at the prospect of imminent Ottoman invasion. Pope Pius V summoned a "Holy League" to try to defend Christendom. The motley alliance consisted of Spain, Austria, Venice, Genoa, and the papacy. A fleet was assembled and put under the command of an Austrian leader who is remembered in history with the name given to him by the Spanish, Don Juan. The fleet gathered at the Sicilian port of Messina, and Don Juan was blessed in the cathedral by the local bishop before being sent out to almost certain doom.

Who would have predicted a Christian victory? The Holy League was an uneasy alliance of powers who had a natural distrust of one another. They were sailing against the most successful fleet in the world and were outnumbered.

Pope Pius V was aware of the unlikelihood of victory, so he had decided many weeks earlier that this was a battle that could be won by heaven alone. Being a good Dominican, he did the only thing he knew: he initiated a Rosary crusade. The churches of Rome were left open day and night as people were exhorted to pray the Rosary for a Christian victory. Down upon the seas, on the morning of October 7, 1571, the sailors prayed the Rosary at first light using the beads that had been given to each of them by Don Juan. Holy Communion was distributed to everyone. Curiously, one of the leaders of the Genoese ships was Giovanni Andrea Doria, and his ship carried a banner of Our Lady of Guadalupe, the lady who appeared on the wild hill of Tepeyac on the feast of the Immaculate Conception just a few decades previously, prompting the mass conversion of millions of the Mexican native population.

As the two fleets prepared for battle, the wind favoured the Ottoman side, but, at the crucial moment of engagement, the wind turned. Before nightfall of October 7, the Christian fleet had won the largest naval battle in history since classical antiquity. The scale of the victory was colossal. Virtually all of the Ottoman fleet had been either captured or destroyed. It was a turning point in European history and stopped Turkish expansion in the Mediterranean. When Pope Pius V learned of the outcome, he instituted a new feast, Our Lady of Victory. In time, this would be changed to the feast of Our Lady of the Rosary.

When the group listened to this story, they were moved to think that we were visiting the greatest Marian basilica on this anniversary. As always, it was important to tell them a word about Pope Pius V, the man who had begun the Rosary crusade. Not all of the popes of the fifteenth and sixteenth centuries are well remembered, but Pius V was a formidable character. While still a humble Dominican friar, he rebuked his predecessor, Pope Pius IV, to his face for making a thirteen-year-old nephew a cardinal. When Pius IV died, not many people would have considered—or wanted —this austere friar, Antonio Ghislieri, for the papacy, but Charles Borromeo did. Cardinal Borromeo was the nephew of Pius IV (the pope who had just died) and would have been a front-runner for becoming pope himself. But he recognized the virtues of Ghislieri and persuaded the other electors to choose the Dominican friar. Upon becoming pope, Pius V continued to wear the white habit of his order instead of the papal regalia, and that is why, some say, the pope still wears white today. Pius V abolished many of the extravagant luxuries of the papal court, fought nepotism, and lived a life of great personal asceticism. A severe man, he was a good remedy for the corruption and hedonism of sixteenth-century Rome.

As usual, I had already talked too much, but there was one more thing to be said to the group before entering the basilica. Why was this church built when it was and dedicated to Mary, the Mother of God? The story took us back to the early 400s. A man named Nestorius was trying to answer a mystery that was at the heart of the Christian faith: How can a human creature, Mary, give birth to the Son of God? If this Jesus who was born of Mary really grew, matured, suffered, and died, then he could not *genuinely* be consubstantial with the Father, could he? In other words, Nestorius believed that no true union of the human and the divine was possible. Such a union would be contradictory, since, as Nestorius saw things, it would effectively make Jesus *less* than divine.

Nestorius' "solution" was to detach Christ's humanity from his divinity and place both of these "persons" in the same human body. Mary was the mother of Christ (*Christotokos*—"Christ bearer") but not the mother of the Eternal Word (*Theotokos*—"God bearer"). This theology was very attractive to some people. It seemed to explain how God could reside in flesh that had been contaminated by the Fall. Above all, it avoided the mysterious claim that Jesus was somehow fully human and fully divine in the same person.

When Nestorius found that his view was being condemned by Cyril of Alexandria, he appealed to the papacy, and a great council was held in Ephesus, which now lies in modern-day Turkey. It was a very appropriate location for such a discussion, since the Virgin Mary had ended her earthly life there in the house of John the Apostle. After a tense discussion, the council declared Nestorius' views to be heretical and affirmed that Mary must be given the title *Theotokos*—"God bearer." To mark this important development, Pope Sixtus III built a new basilica in Rome, the first in the West dedicated to Our Lady under the title "Mother of God."

Though I had told this story to every group that I had taken to Saint Mary Major, for some reason on this occasion something sank in that was probably already obvious to most people: the declaration of the Council of Ephesus and the title of this church tell us more about the person of *Jesus* than they do about the person of Mary. Nestorius was probably a good man who was trying to make sense of the Christian faith, but his views were a serious corruption of the truth about Jesus. He was denying the central tenet of the Christian faith: that the Son of God had truly taken on human flesh so that we might become children of the Divine. As we queued for the metal detectors outside the basilica, the well-known passage from Philippians came to mind:

> Have this mind among yourselves, which was in Christ Jesus, who, though he was in the form of God, did not count equality with God a thing to be grasped, but emptied himself, taking the form of a servant, being born in the likeness of men. And being found in human form he humbled himself and became obedient unto death, even death on a cross. Therefore God has highly exalted him and bestowed on him the name which is above every name, that at the name of Jesus every knee should bow, in heaven and on earth and under the earth, and every tongue confess that Jesus Christ is Lord, to the glory of God the Father. (2:5–11)

We gathered on the steps until everyone was through security and then went inside. As was my custom, I first took the group to the side of the altar, where we could view the apse mosaics before the group went down under the altar to visit the relics of the crib of Bethlehem. While the group was paying their respects in front of the crib, Father Dominic, Father Michael, and I went into the sacristy to get things prepared for Mass. The sacristan, Father Angelo, greeted us and told us that we would be celebrating Mass in the Sistine Chapel.

"But aren't we booked in the Cesi Chapel, as is usually the case?" I asked.

"You *were* booked in the Cesi Chapel!" Father Angelo replied with a laugh. "But you have cancelled your booking so many times this week that we have you now in the Sistine Chapel. We left the Cesi Chapel to another group that we were fairly confident would actually show up!"

The Cesi Chapel is the best place in the basilica for a private liturgy. Once the doors are closed and the celebration of the Eucharist begins, you cannot hear much sound from the rest of the building and no stray tourists can wander in. The Sistine Chapel (not to be confused with the more famous chapel of the same name in the Vatican) is not so satisfactory. It is located in the right transept, and, although it does have big gates to keep the tourists at bay, you can hear every noise that is made in the basilica. But I wasn't going to complain about the location on this occasion because Pope Saint Pius V is buried in the Sistine Chapel. In fact, his tomb is opened virtually every day so that pilgrims can venerate his body. And we were going to have the privilege of celebrating Mass on the feast of Our Lady of the Rosary at the tomb of the very saint who had instituted the feast and begun the Rosary crusade that won the Battle of Lepanto.

Our Mass began, and Father Dominic came forward after the Gospel to give his homily. I presume that it was the same homily that he intended to give in Saint Mary Major on Saturday, five days previously, when we originally had booked the Cesi Chapel at the back of the basilica. Father Dominic read an extract from a letter by American journalist James Foley, who began to pray the Rosary while in captivity in Libya in 2011. "I began to pray the Rosary. It was what my mother and grandmother would have prayed." The Rosary as a place of refuge in the storms and battles of life: it was the perfect homily for the feast that was in it.

As I sat there in the Sistine Chapel, something was occurring to me that had not really made it through the fairly thick layers of my skull over the many years in which I had visited this basilica. All of our beliefs about Mary are really designed to shed light on God himself. When we call this lady "Mother of God," we are really making the point that Jesus, while remaining fully divine, emptied himself to the extent of taking on human flesh and was born of a woman. There is a profound mystery there, one that Nestorius wished to eliminate, but Mary's title preserves the mystery and challenges us to enter into it, believing in the creative mercy of God. Our beliefs about Mary have one overriding function: to support that central dizzying belief in the Incarnation of God.

After Mass, there was some free time for the group to visit the basilica on their own. I walked over to the central altar and looked down at the "big fellow," Pius IX, kneeling in front of the crib of Bethlehem. I remembered my "gaffe" of years previously. Now I knew that it was entirely appropriate that he should be placed kneeling in front of the crib of Bethlehem because he was the one who had finally taken the plunge, listened to the Spirit, and defined the dogma of the Immaculate Conception. The vicissitudes of the people of Israel! Their constant difficulties with being faithful to the covenant! The prophets saw the infidelity and desperate condition of the people and cried out, "How long, Lord? How long before you put everything right?" But God prepared a holy remnant, and her name was Mary. He preserved her free from Original Sin so that she might be the worthy mother of God in human flesh. The Immaculate Conception is the culmination of God's work of preparing a people who would bear the Saviour of the world.

As I looked down on the statue of Pius IX, I recalled one of the curious facts of the story of Bernadette. Her parish priest had insisted continually that the lady reveal her name, but it was only on March 25 that she finally responded. March 25 is the feast of the Annunciation, the day when God became flesh in the womb of the Virgin. "*I am the Immaculate Conception. I am the one whom God preserved free* from sin so that the Lord of creation might find a fitting place in which to join himself to the human race. The angel greeted me with the words 'Hail, *Kecharitomene!*' so when you ask me who I am, Bernadette Soubirous, I can do no better than repeat the words of the angel: I am *Kecharitomene*, the one made immaculate by God."

The next day, we drove to Assisi for the last part of the pilgrimage. On the way, I told Bishop Walsh about the repeated deferrals of the visit to Saint Mary Major until we eventually found ourselves celebrating the feast of Our Lady of the Rosary beneath the tomb of Saint Pius V, the man who instituted the feast of the Rosary. Bishop Walsh would not have been a man to jump to wild conclusions, but he agreed that there was something of "the hand of God" in these events.

"And why wouldn't the good Lord shower his blessings on these people?" interjected Father Michael.

I knew what he was referring to. The parish of Saint Patrick's in Donegall Street, Belfast, had seen more than its fair share of suffering during the Troubles in the north of Ireland. Few places had experienced more attacks and incidents of a sectarian nature than they had, often at tragic cost in terms of human lives, but a happier and more devout group I had rarely encountered.

A couple of days later, the pilgrimage was over, and we were saying our goodbyes at Leonardo da Vinci Airport in Rome. One of the ladies, Marie, had told me earlier on the coach that she had something to say to me before leaving. When the bags were all checked in, we made our way to the security checkpoint in front of the metal detectors. This is where I would have to take my leave while they all went through to departures. Marie was hanging back slightly, and I waited expectantly to hear what she had to say. I knew already that—whatever it was—it was going to be short and sweet. Those ladies from Donegall Street didn't mince words.

"Safe journey home, Marie!"

"That was a great trip, Kieran."

"Did you want to tell me something?"

"Yes. You know that thing that happened to us back there?"

"Do you mean the coincidence about Our Lady of the Rosary?"

"Yes. That was no coincidence, you know."

"Don't you think?"

"No." Marie shook her head with an air of certainty. "That was Our Lady sending us all a flower from heaven."

5

A Flower from Heaven

And calling to him a child, he put him in the midst of them, and said, "Truly, I say to you, unless you turn and become like children, you will never enter the kingdom of heaven."

—Matthew 18:2–3

The afternoon sun was sinking in the sky behind me. I had cycled more than a hundred miles through Normandy today, trying to keep off the main roads with their heavy traffic but always maintaining a fairly straight line for Paris. It would take another day's cycling to make it to the French capital, though, and I would need to stop somewhere soon. Ahead, the road seemed to be coming into some sort of town, with a large church on a hill dominating the horizon. I pulled off the road and consulted the map to discover that it was Lisieux. So that was the hometown of Saint Thérèse!

The name of Thérèse was very familiar to me. Her image was to be found in virtually every church in Ireland. One of my friends was very devoted to her, but I knew hardly anything of her story. Surely the big church on the hill was where she was buried?

Upon entering the built-up area, I spotted at a roundabout a sign pointed uphill to La Basilique Sainte-Thérèse de Lisieux. This had to be it! After a stiff climb, I was standing in front of an impressive church with a majestic flight of steps. The basilica was beautiful inside, on two levels, with many interesting altars and works of art. There seemed to be a major relic of Saint Thérèse in an area to the right, but her tomb—wherever it was—certainly wasn't in there.

In the basilica bookshop, I looked through a book on the saint written by a Dominican father named Bernard Bro. The opening paragraph was a quotation from the renowned Jesuit theologian Karl Rahner, and it immediately caught my attention because of its bluntness:

> Many things in this saint and her writings irritate me or quite simply bore me. And if I set out to explain what nearly nauseates me, so that people would understand it, that still would not account for the fact that I took the trouble to do so. There are so many things in the world to deal with that do not necessitate a long exegesis.

I knew that Rahner was one of the most influential theologians of the Church in the twentieth century. Was it possible that he had misunderstood or failed to grasp the point of Saint Thérèse's writings? It seemed unlikely. Was he right, then, about Saint Thérèse? Was she really irritating, boring, and nauseating? The next quotation in the book was almost as startling. Just before Saint Thérèse died, one of her companions was overheard saying:

> My Sister Thérèse of the Child Jesus is going to die soon; and I really wonder what our mother will be able to say after her death. She will be very embarrassed, for this little sister, as likeable as she is, has certainly done nothing worth the trouble of being recounted.

The bookshop was closing soon, and there wasn't time to read more. Needless to say, Father Bro himself did not subscribe to these views, but it would be some years before I would have the chance to read the book in full. Still, I had to admit that these quotations expressed some of the misgivings I had myself. Just what *is* the message of Saint Thérèse? When people talk about how unique she was, why do they end up making her sound so commonplace? What is it that prompts such multitudes of people to be devoted to her? Why are there so many statues and altars to her in churches across Europe?

Later that evening, at the last minute before closing time, I did manage to find the tomb of the little saint, in the beautiful chapel of Carmel at the centre of town, though I completely missed Les Buissonnets, the family home of Saint Thérèse, which by then had become a pilgrimage shrine and could easily have been visited. By the next day, I was back on the road to Paris, and Saint Thérèse was far from my thoughts. It wasn't easy to forget the little saint completely, however, because, over the following years, the groups with which I travelled just kept encountering her in unexpected places.

The years passed, and Laura and I had set up our travel company. Laura organised the trips, and I had become a full-time "tour guide," for want of a better word. The year 2015 was the fourteen hundredth anniversary of the death of Saint Columban, Ireland's greatest missionary. Suddenly a whole host of pilgrim groups was asking us to take them in the footsteps of the Irish missionary. With most groups, we ended up doing limited portions of his travels, confining ourselves to one side of the Alps or the other. On one memorable occasion, we did the full journey from France into Switzerland and Austria, coming over the San Bernardino pass to the saint's final resting place in Bobbio, south of Milan.

Columban had left Bangor in County Down when he was already fifty years of age on a *peregrinatio pro Christo*—making himself a pilgrim for the sake of Christ. His aim was to spread the Gospel in Europe, large tracts of which had reverted to paganism following the collapse of the Roman Empire and the mass migration of peoples from the north and east. After landing in Brittany and travelling southeast-wards, the Irishman was eventually given land on which to build his first monastery. The place was called Annegray. It lay in eastern France at the foothills of the Vosges Moun-tains. This monastery was spectacularly successful and was soon so full of new postulants that Columban had to found a second monastery in nearby Luxeuil and soon a third in Fontaines. The monks took it in turns to enter the chapel for the liturgy of the hours, so great was their number, with the result that a continuous prayer chant could be heard coming from these abbeys day and night. Columban's monks were intrepid in agriculture and the building of mills as well as in studies in Greek and Latin. In a Europe that was still tee-tering after the fall of the Roman Empire, they introduced a work ethic, an approach to education, and a discipline of life that did nothing less than recivilise society.

It wasn't long, however, before the Irishman ran afoul of the royal family of the kingdom in which his monasteries were located, not to mention incurring the rancour of the local bishops. He denounced the multiple adulteries of the queen's son and criticized the pastoral laxity of the bishops who preferred hunting parties to taking care of their flocks. Eventually, Columban was sent packing by royalty and epis-copacy alike. Under armed guard, he was taken to Nantes, where soldiers were ordered to put him on a boat to Ire-land, never to return. Before they got anywhere, however, a storm blew up in the port. The captain became fearful that he might be up against the power of God, so he re-leased Columban and his companions. Then began one of the great missionary journeys in the history of the Church, across France on foot into Germany, up the Rhine by boat into Switzerland, and then on foot to Austria and eventually climbing over the Alps into Italy, founding monasteries along the way. Columban's final resting place is at Bobbio, in the valley of the Trebbia River, which runs between Genoa and Piacenza. The monastery he founded there had an important role in later centuries in defending the correct doctrine of the nature of Christ against a heretical position called Arianism that was rampant in northern Italy at that time (Arius was a fourth-century priest who denied that Jesus was fully divine). At an audience in the Vatican, Pope Benedict XVI said that the monastery at Bobbio and its famous library had a cultural significance on a par with that of the great Benedictine abbey of Montecassino.

On account of the fact that Columban died in A.D. 615, the year 2015 was going to be a major anniversary. In preparation for this event, the Holy See declared a "Year of Saint Columban," which would run from October 2014 to November 2015, culminating in the great anniversary for the feast of the saint on November 23. The dioceses of Ireland organised a national pilgrimage to Rome to coincide with the inauguration of this special year. Many events were planned in Rome, but the big day was to be October 11, 2014, when the relics of Saint Columban were going to be solemnly processed into Saint John Lateran, the cathedral of Rome, and welcomed by the pope's delegate, followed by the celebration of Mass. Columban himself had a great desire to make a pilgrimage to Rome but had never been able to do so. The taking of his bones into the cathedral of Rome would be an emotional event for his many devotees, a kind of final "coming home" for this Irishman who was so fiercely loyal to Rome.

October 11 was a Saturday, and the big Mass for Saint

Columban at the Lateran was scheduled for the evening. As usual, we organised a morning visit to Saint Mary Major Basilica, as Saturday is traditionally a day of Marian devotion. We entered the basilica, and I gave my usual— minimalistic—tour. The group was given free time to visit the manger of Bethlehem below the high altar and to go into the Pauline Chapel to venerate the Salus Populi Romani icon of Mother and Child, the most revered Marian image in Rome. I went into the Pauline Chapel myself to say a prayer, noticing in the back a new glass box with many bones inside. It is not unusual to see bones of saints in Rome, but I wondered whom these belonged to and why they were here in front of the most illustrious image of Our Lady in the city. After kneeling for a minute or two, I spotted Father Gregorio, one of the friars who takes care of the basilica, entering the chapel. I hopped up and went over to him before he could disappear again.

"Excuse me, Father Gregorio," I asked. "Whose bones are those?"

"Saint Thérèse of Lisieux," he answered. "They're only here today and will be gone tomorrow."

Saint Thérèse of Lisieux! I didn't wait to ask him anything else, because I knew that our group would want to see these relics. Saint Thérèse's bones had been taken to Ireland in 2001 and had prompted a surprising response from the public. The organisers estimated that two-thirds of the entire population had turned up to visit the relics in various places throughout the country. People in our group would remember the emotion that this visit had generated and would want to know that her relics were here. I scurried out into the main part of the basilica and began telling every group member in sight that the bones of Saint Thérèse of Lisieux were in the basilica. Soon, most of us had gathered around the glass casket, and one of the priests led us in a prayer.

It was a pleasant surprise to encounter the mortal remains of the little saint in this unexpected way, but the real significance of the encounter passed me by completely until the following day. We attended the recitation of the Angelus with Pope Francis in Saint Peter's Square at midday and then went across the Tiber to visit the Pantheon. There was time for one more visit before lunch—the tomb of Saint Catherine of Siena in the Dominican church of Santa Maria sopra Minerva.

Before entering, the group was given a summary of the life of Saint Catherine of Siena. For much of the fourteenth century, the popes—for purely political motives—were resident in Avignon in France. Catherine knew this to be a scandal. The people of Rome were without a resident bishop, and the pope had abandoned the historical see of his predecessors, many of whom had been martyrs. Through her life of profound prayer and austere penances, and by the force of her intense personality, Catherine convinced the pope to return to Rome. Her letters to prelates and princes were forthright and very influential, though she herself could not write until towards the end of her short life of thirty-three years. It is remarkable to think that this uneducated girl, illiterate for most of her life, was the first layperson, and first woman, to be made a Doctor of the Church. The Holy See gives a person the title "Doctor of the Church" to indicate that his writings have made a significant contribution to theology or doctrine and are of universal relevance and value to everyone who has been baptized.

We had an added motive for visiting Saint Catherine's tomb. A petition had been made from various quarters to name Saint Columban patron of the European Union. In a

letter to Pope Gregory the Great in the year 600, Columban used the term *totius Europae*—"all of Europe"—to speak
of the common cultural bond that ties Europeans together.
It is the first documented usage of the term "Europe" in
this sense. In 1950, the great statesman and co-founder of
the European union, Robert Schuman, gave a speech at the
abbey of Columban at Luxeuil in which he said, "Saint
Columban, this illustrious Irishman who left his own country for voluntary exile, willed and achieved a spiritual union
between the principal European countries of his time. He is
the patron saint of all those who now seek to build a united
Europe." Given the possibility that Saint Columban might
someday be pronounced patron of the European Union, we
were making a special effort to visit the tombs of the patrons
of Europe who were on Italian soil, and Saint Catherine of
Siena was one of these.

After our visit, Father Joe, one of the group leaders, said,
"Columban will be pleased with the way he is being honoured! Yesterday, his pilgrims venerated the bones of the
patroness of the missions; today they visited the tomb of
the patroness of Europe!"

It was true, and I hadn't thought of it before. Here we
were honouring Ireland's greatest missionary and the day
before, quite by accident, we had happened upon the bones
of Saint Thérèse, patroness of the missions. I had completely
forgotten that she had been given this title. The other principal patron of the missions is Saint Francis Xavier, the Jesuit who travelled incredible distances to unknown lands,
built up the Church in the Portuguese colonies, baptised
thousands of converts, learned foreign languages, and then
died as he was poised to embark on a missionary journey
into China. In complete contrast to him, how could a girl
who died at twenty-four and never left the confines of her

convent be named co-patron of the missions? As I learned to appreciate later, however, sometimes the Church gets it exactly right! The Church is not just frenetic activity, missionary outreach, and charitable works. The Church is first and foremost a body of people whose lives are rooted in God. When Mother Teresa and her sisters went out on the streets of Calcutta to work with the poorest of the poor, they did so only after spending a significant part of the early morning in prayer in front of the Blessed Sacrament. Thérèse of Lisieux had a burning desire to go on the missions, but she learned that her vocation was to be love in the heart of the Church and that this vocation of prayer and sacrifice was the real powerhouse of the missions.

I did not appreciate this so well, however, on that occasion in 2014 when our pilgrimage to honour Ireland's greatest missionary encountered in Saint Mary Major Basilica the bones of the little universal patroness of the missions. That trip, with all of its functions and events, was focussed on Saint Columban, his contribution to the evangelisation of Europe, and the idea that he might one day be made patron of the European Union. Having visited the tomb of Saint Catherine of Siena, patroness of Europe, we also made a trip to Montecassino to visit the shrine of that other patron of the continent, Saint Benedict. It was the last day of our trip, and we would have to make it back to Rome that evening for the flight to Dublin. The abbey had given us "extraordinary" permission to celebrate at 2:30 P.M., an hour when Masses were not usually said in those days. The venue for the Mass was to be in the main crypt of the church. I had pleaded that we be allowed to celebrate elsewhere. The crypt had many steps and would not be so easy to access for some of our more elderly pilgrims. No other location was possible, I was told. The chapel of the relics off the sacristy would not hold such a large group as ours, with over sixty people.

"Can't we celebrate Mass from the high altar?" I asked, more in desperation than in the expectation of a positive response.

There was a pause of indignation from the sacristan at the other end of the telephone. "The high altar is reserved for the solemn liturgies of the abbey and for special events," came the frosty reply.

"We *do* have a bishop or two with our group," I pointed out hopefully.

"No, I'm sorry, it just isn't permitted to use the high altar for private events of this sort."

There seemed no point in arguing; the crypt, with its many steps, it would have to be. As we drove from Rome towards Montecassino that morning, October 15, 2014, we could see ahead of us that the day was deteriorating drastically. Angry-looking black clouds filled the horizon, and regular flashes of lightning were visible in the distance. We stopped for lunch about forty-five minutes' drive from the abbey. Incredibly, the day was still dry, but it looked as if a major downpour was on its way. We finished lunch at 1:30 and resumed the coach journey. We were not long back on the motorway when my phone rang. It was the sacristan at the abbey.

"We have a power cut here, and no lights are working," he said.

"Oh?" I replied. "I'm not surprised. We could see the lightning storm ahead of us."

"There is no natural light in the crypt, so it won't be possible for you to celebrate Mass there without electricity."

"Oh no!" I was sure that he was going to tell us that no

Mass would be possible at all that day. The group would be disappointed.

"Actually, the abbot has given you permission to celebrate from the high altar on account of the circumstances, because it is the only place that has sufficient natural light. The only thing is that the microphones won't be working, but we have no alternative location for a group of this size."

"Don't worry! We'll get by without microphones!"

When I told Father Joe that he would be celebrating Mass at the high altar above the tomb of Saint Benedict, patron of Europe, he was pleased!

"See how Saint Columban is looking after his Irish pilgrims!" he said.

A half hour later, we were off the motorway and negotiating the hairpin bends up to the abbey. Montecassino is situated at five hundred metres above sea level in a prominent position overlooking the Liri valley. As we climbed, the magnificent abbey came into sight. It is always hard not to be impressed by its imposing majesty, even if its physical grandeur is dwarfed by its spiritual influence on Western Christendom. Monks from Montecassino built upon the foundations laid by Irish missionaries in the re-evangelisation of Europe in the Middle Ages, contributing enormously to the construction of a thoroughly Christian civilisation.

One of the great examples is that of Saint Boniface, an eighth-century Benedictine of English origin who led a band of monks from Montecassino into the Germanic parts of the Frankish Empire. Their influence in organising and regulating the Church in central Europe was colossal and would have a positive impact for centuries to come. One of the stories about Boniface concerns the origin of the Christmas tree. A great oak tree was being used by one of the Germanic tribes as a place of human sacrifice to one of their gods. Boniface interrupted the sacrificial ritual during the winter solstice and chopped down the tree. The onlookers expected their deity to strike him dead on the spot. When nothing happened, they converted and accepted the God proposed by Boniface. To substitute their worship of the oak tree, Boniface suggested that they place a fir tree in their homes to symbolize the birth of the Christ Child, which was celebrated at that very time of year. It was Christ, after all, who brought all human sacrifice to an end. Candles were placed on the tree's branches, and apples were hung from them. Eventually, the custom of the Christmas tree would spread from Bavaria to the whole world.

The storm had disappeared at this point, and the day had cleared up nicely. We were approaching the last of the hairpin bends to the abbey when my phone rang again. I noticed that it looked like the number of the sacristan. As I answered, I had that all-too-familiar sinking feeling.

"The electric power is back," the sacristan said in his usual monotone.

"Oh?" I replied glumly, unable to disguise the disappointment in my voice.

"However, we don't have time to set up for Mass down in the crypt, so we will continue with the plan to celebrate from the main altar. But the good news is that the microphones are now working."

The high altar *and* microphones! As I put my phone away, I couldn't but marvel at the perfect timing of the storm. Saint Columban really did seem to be looking after his pilgrims!

Three years later, we organised a different pilgrimage to France for the international Saint Columban's Day. In that year, the event was being held in the town of Saint-Coulomb on the Brittany coast because, according to tradition, this is where the little boat of the Irish saint and his companions first made landfall on the continent. In order to make the trip more attractive for people, we really needed to organise a full week's itinerary, but the Saint Columban Day's events lasted only three days. The flight would have to be into Paris from Dublin, so a drive through Normandy to Brittany was inevitable. It was natural, then, to schedule a three-night stop in Lisieux and visit the places associated with Saint Thérèse. Before the group arrived, though, I would need to go back and read Father Bro's book properly.

The fact that it was a translation made the reading a little difficult, but still the book—or rather the young lady it described—was fascinating. This humble and sensitive soul, through dramatic suffering, distilled the message of the Gospel into a formula as pure and simple as it was profound. Born the youngest of five girls who survived into adulthood, she was so thoroughly spoiled by her siblings that she had not learned to dress herself at eleven years of age. Of course, these siblings did not know that they were hampering her development by treating her as their baby doll, but hamper her development they did and thus increased the pain she would feel when maturation was eventually forced upon her.

When Thérèse was just four years of age, her beloved mother died after a twelve-year battle with cancer. Overnight, Thérèse became very shy and timid, and it took very little to make her cry. Following this loss, Thérèse become very attached to her eldest sister, Pauline, who now took up the role as her second mother. Thérèse's connection to Pauline was profound. The little girl was able to bear her very difficult experiences in school in the knowledge that Pauline was waiting for her at home. Everything revolved around her relationship with her big sister.

Then, when Thérèse was nine, Pauline decided to enter the Carmelites. Though the convent was in Lisieux, it was an enclosed order. Visiting times would be limited, and access would be through a grille. This loss of her "second mother" was even more harrowing for Thérèse than the loss of her first. She went into a state of psychological collapse and became bedridden. The doctor declared that nothing could be done for her. Her mental health would be forever damaged. At the climax of this terrible state, Thérèse began to believe that Satan was everywhere, trying to take her soul from God.

In the midst of Thérèse's trembling and moans, her remaining three sisters were filled with fear and began to implore the help of the Blessed Virgin. The sisters thought that the little one was unconscious, but she was awake and was praying with them. Suddenly, she began to sense a deep peace filling her soul. Her eyes turned to the statue of Mary near her bed, and it seemed to her that it was no longer a statue but was real! Our Lady was radiant and was smiling at Thérèse! Deep in her heart, she was convinced that a miracle had taken place.

After this recovery, more difficult days were to come. Thérèse had an extremely sensitive nature. She suffered from terrible scruples and considered herself the vilest of sinners. She was easily upset and could become distraught for minor reasons. All of this suffering was compounded when her sister Marie decided to enter Carmel. Thérèse was thirteen at this point and had become almost as dependent on Marie as she had been on Pauline. By this tender age, she had, in effect, lost three mothers. In an effort to be brave, she began to pray for peace to her four little siblings who had died in infancy. She also prayed for an end to that excessive sensitivity that prompted her to cry over the least disappointment or imagined slight. Her prayer was quickly answered. After receiving Communion at Christmas midnight Mass, she felt herself filled with Christ, who had become a little child in order to fill the human race with his strength.

On the way home from Mass, it seemed to Thérèse that she was a new person. The confidence that had left her when her mother died had returned. The scruples and shyness had disappeared, but this new state of self-possession would soon be put to the test! In those days, it was a tradition for French children to leave their shoes in front of the fireplace on Christmas Eve, to be filled with sweets and presents after midnight Mass. Before opening her presents, as Thérèse was going upstairs to change, she overheard her father saying that he was glad that she would soon be too big for this childishness. Céline, who was present, knew that her little sister had overheard this remark, and she expected Thérèse to fly into one of her customary states of anguish at the most minor of affronts. How amazed Céline was when Thérèse came back down the stairs and cheerfully received her gifts without the slightest complaint and without revealing that she had heard her father's comment! Thérèse would describe this painful moment of self-overcoming as the beginning of her conversion: God had worked a miracle during her Christmas Communion.

At about this time, Thérèse began to have a strong desire to enter Carmel, to live a life of prayer and sacrifice for sinners. She realized, however, that such a course of action would be difficult for her father. He doted on his "Little Queen." Thérèse resolved, therefore, to save souls while she remained at home. She knew that if she completed her daily tasks with joy and fidelity, she could offer them to the Father along with the sufferings of Christ. Thus, at the age of fourteen, Thérèse was already living out her "Little Way," the way that would make her one of the pioneers of what the Second Vatican Council would call the "universal call to holiness"[1] and which would lead her to be declared a Doctor of the Church a century after her death.

Father Bro's book was not easy reading, but it helped me to prepare for the arrival of the Saint Columban pilgrimage in Paris on June 25, 2018. The journey from Charles de Gaulle Airport to Lisieux took more than three hours in the heavy evening traffic. We arrived tired and hungry but looking forward to the events of the coming days. The following morning, our first visit was to Les Buissonnets, the childhood home of Thérèse's family after the death of Zélie Martin, her mother. The tour was conducted very graciously by some ladies from Lisieux who dedicate their lives to showing pilgrims around the Martin family home. We saw the bedroom of Saint Thérèse, where she experienced the smile of the Blessed Virgin and was healed of her psychological illness. Possibly the most moving part of the tour was the visit to the garden in back of the house, where there is a sculpture of Thérèse and her father, representing the moment when she finally asked his permission to enter Carmel. For weeks, Thérèse had been trying to find the right moment to bring up this painful subject. She decided that the feast of Pentecost would be the appropriate day to do it. After dinner, in the evening, Louis was tired and went out into the garden to rest. Thérèse knew that the moment had come to tell her father that God wanted his little daughter to dedicate her life to him. Thérèse trembled as she spoke, tears in her eyes.

---

[1] Second Vatican Council, Dogmatic Constitution on the Church *Lumen Gentium* (November 21, 1964), chap. 5.

"What is it, my Little Queen?" Louis asked, using the pet name by which he always addressed his youngest daughter.

"I want to be a Carmelite," Thérèse said in words barely audible, her head leaning on his shoulder. Both father and daughter broke down and cried bitterly. Louis could easily have refused Thérèse because of her tender age and her ill health, but, after some time, he led her down the garden and picked a white lily.

"This flower is like your heart, Thérèse," he said. "It is white and pure. I won't stop you if you wish to give it to God."

There is a very touching account of the occasion on which Thérèse received the Carmelite habit. She had already been living the life of enclosure in the convent for some time, but for the ceremony she was permitted to join her family in the public chapel of the convent for the last time. When she stepped out of the cloister, her father was waiting for her with tears in his eyes. "My Little Queen!" he said as he drew her close to him. After the Mass, he led her back towards the cloister door. It would be the last time that she would embrace her father. As Thérèse entered the cloister, something remarkable happened. The bishop began to intone the Te Deum, the ancient hymn of thanksgiving traditionally sung at the Easter vigil. Normally, it is not sung on the day a sister receives the habit but only on the day she makes her formal religious profession. The bishop had made a genuine mistake, but no one stopped him, and the Te Deum was sung in full. It would turn out to be prophetic in nature. This humble girl would quickly become a reason for thanksgiving for all associated with the Carmel of Lisieux.

Our group was moved by the story of Thérèse's entry into Carmel and the generosity of her father in encouraging her to go. That afternoon, we had our first visit to Carmel itself and celebrated Mass close to the tomb of the little saint. For a group like this, which had come to France to commemorate Ireland's greatest missionary, it was important to say something about Thérèse's title as patroness of the universal missions. Thankfully, I was a bit better prepared than I had been some years previously when we had encountered her bones in Saint Mary Major Basilica. One of the characteristics of Thérèse's personality was the powerful desires that consumed her. Even before entering Carmel, she felt a strong calling to go on the missions, to tend the sick, to comfort the dying, to carry the gospel to China or Africa. Alongside this desire, however, persisted the thought that more souls can be saved by prayer or sacrifice than by any other means. This thought, she came to realize, was the whispering of God in her heart. She came eventually to the profound realisation that her vocation was to be love in the heart of the Church. This was not love in some abstract sense, but the living out of the pains, sufferings, and drudgery of her daily life with humble faith and abandonment.

One of the first questions that the group asked on this pilgrimage was why everyone refers to Thérèse as the "Little Flower." Her name in religion was Sister Thérèse of the Child Jesus and the Holy Face. The "Little Flower" title arose after her death and comes from a passage towards the beginning of her autobiography, *Story of a Soul*. As she saw it, there are many types of flower in the Lord's garden. Some are beautiful and impressive, such as the lily and the rose. The simple wildflowers of the forests and the fields often go unnoticed by the general population, but they still give glory to God. Thérèse saw herself as one of these wildflowers, simple and hidden, but blooming where God had planted her. Perhaps the most distinctive mark of Thérèse of Lisieux is her passionate conviction that Jesus delighted in his "Little Flower" as much as he delighted in the lily or the rose. In her own words:

> Jesus . . . set before me the book of nature; I understood how all the flowers He has created are beautiful, how the splendor of the rose and the whiteness of the Lily do not take away the perfume of the little violet or the delightful simplicity of the daisy. I understood that if all flowers wanted to be roses, nature would lose her springtime beauty, and the fields would no longer be decked out with little wild flowers.
>
> And so it is in the world of souls, Jesus' garden. He willed to create . . . smaller ones and those must be content to be daisies or violets destined to give joy to God's glances when He looks down at His feet. Perfection consists in doing His will, in being what He wills us to be.[2]

What would quickly become the famous "Little Way" of Thérèse's consisted in humble abandonment to God's will, with a cheerful and generous spirit. It is important to note that it was not self-abandonment for the sake of self-abandonment: it involved tender attachment to the Lord, trusting that he longed for her love. In good times and bad, in sickness and health, Thérèse became the faithful spouse of Christ.

During the pilgrimage of 2018, an unexpected opportunity to put Thérèse's Little Way into practice presented itself. The drive from Charles de Gaulle Airport to Lisieux on the first evening was a long one, and it was a good chance to introduce the group to the distinctive spirituality of the Little Flower. For me, the best illustration of the Little Way

[2] *Story of a Soul: The Autobiography of St. Thérèse of Lisieux*, trans. John Clarke, O.C.D., 3rd ed. (Washington, D.C.: Institute of Carmelite Studies, 1996), 14.

was given by Thérèse herself in her autobiography when she described an experience in the convent laundry room, so I read this passage to the group as we drove into Normandy.

> Another time, I was in the laundry doing the washing in front of a Sister who was throwing dirty water into my face every time she lifted the handkerchiefs to her bench; my first reaction was to draw back and wipe my face to show the Sister who was sprinkling me that she would do me a favor to be more careful. But I immediately thought I would be very foolish to refuse these treasures which were being given to me so generously, and I took care not to show my struggle. I put forth all my efforts to desire receiving very much of this dirty water, and was so successful that in the end I had really taken a liking to this kind of aspersion, and I promised myself to return another time to this nice place where one received so many treasures.[3]

In a religious context, the word "aspersion" refers to the ritual sprinkling of holy water that is performed by a priest on ceremonial occasions, so it was no accident that Thérèse chose such a word to describe this very novel kind of blessing.

On the day after our arrival from Paris, following the morning visit to Les Buissonnets, there was a break for lunch for an hour or so before our visit to the convent of Carmel. I pointed out a few restaurants in the vicinity and asked that everyone be as efficient as possible so as not to be late for our tour of Carmel. As the group dispersed, two ladies approached me. I could see that one of them had a look of discontent on her face. From the previous evening at dinner, when the same lady had made numerous complaints about the food, I knew that her name was Teresa.

[3] Ibid., 250.

"You expect us to find a place for lunch in a strange town, with strange food, speaking a foreign language? Wouldn't it have been better to organise lunch for everyone? That would have been more efficient! Then you'd have all your flock punctually in the chapel for your tour!"

There was quite an aggressive tone in Teresa's voice, and I normally would have given a fairly defensive response of the sort: "If we all went to the same place, lunch for a group of fifty people would take well over an hour in most restaurants! In any case, madam, when you come to a foreign country, part of the charm is to try out the local food and make an effort to order it yourself. Don't you agree? I hope to see you in an hour's time in the chapel, and if you're still having lunch, then please don't hurry, we'll just go on ahead without you!"

But I didn't say that. I had been reading Saint Thérèse since early morning in an effort to prepare for this tour, and my normal defensiveness seemed to have strangely evaporated, at least temporarily.

"Why don't you come with me?" I said cheerfully. "Last time we were here, we found a really nice restaurant with a good menu not too far from the convent."

The ladies seemed surprised by my response, and to tell the truth, I was a little surprised myself. We made our way down the road towards Carmel and then took a right turn along the street that led in the direction of the cathedral. On the way, we passed the tourist office, and Teresa asked if she could call in for a moment to get a map of the town.

"Well, why don't we do that later, Teresa?" I suggested. "We don't have much time for lunch."

"Oh, don't worry!" she replied, "It'll only take a minute." But the other lady and I waited for at least fifteen minutes while Teresa examined every tourist flyer and pamphlet in the place, though she showed no signs of being able to understand a word of French. Eventually we resumed our journey. As we approached the restaurant, I noticed that the place seemed to be in darkness. And when we got to the entrance, we saw a sign hanging on the door: Fermé Mardi (Closed on Tuesdays).

"I don't believe it!" Teresa said, in a tone of great irritation. "We walk all the way down here, and the place isn't even open! And now we don't have time to find another restaurant and order lunch!"

I was on the verge of pointing out that we might have had time to go to another restaurant if we hadn't delayed so long at the tourist office, but again I found that my usual ready rancour in these situations was unusually lacking today.

"I know what we can do!" I said brightly. "There's a place on the next street where we had a quick lunch last year. Come with me!"

We went down an alleyway and on to the next street. At this point, we could see, just a block or so away, the majestic form of the old cathedral where Saint Thérèse had received her First Communion.

"Here we are!" I said. "They do slices of pizza here, but the quality is really good, and the service will be fast."

"You want us to eat pizza in *France*?" Teresa had a look of shocked incredulity on her face. "I am *very* fussy about my pizza," she continued. "There is no way in the world that I am going to try any of the fare on offer here. I'd prefer to starve instead!"

"But this place is pretty good . . ." I began to protest weakly but then realised that it was pointless. Suddenly I had an idea. "There's a Carrefour Express over in front of the cathedral! They certainly do sandwiches there, and there should be a good selection. Let's go and grab a sandwich!"

"Well, we don't have much option now, do we?" Teresa replied as she followed me. "I'm just thinking of the nice lunches that everyone else in the group is probably enjoying while we end up with a humble sandwich! Next time you suggest we join you for lunch, don't take it personally if we decline!"

And, of course, in normal circumstances, I would have been taking all of these comments very personally, but on this day in France, for a limited time only, I was allowing Thérèse of Lisieux to help me accept all of these comments as aspersions from above, blessings that were freely bestowed so that I might draw closer to the God who made me. I received many more aspersions in the Carrefour Express before a suitable sandwich was procured for Teresa, and when we finally gathered in Carmel at 2:00, I noticed only from the rumbling in my stomach that I had forgotten to eat anything myself.

It was a simple experience, hardly the stuff of great sanctity—and the most difficult aspersions are always those administered by one's own family—yet I knew that Thérèse was teaching me something simple and profound. Where in the works of Karl Rahner, I wondered, was there anything so practical for the Christian life? Perhaps the most remarkable thing about Thérèse is that her spirituality can be grasped perfectly by little children. Mary Fabyan Windeatt's classic *The Little Flower*, written for children, is so insightful that adults can also profit by reading it (incidentally, much of the description of Thérèse in this chapter is reliant on that work).

At 2:00 that day, we made our visit to Carmel. The most important place is the tomb of Saint Thérèse, which lies underneath a statue of the saint. There are always abundant roses at the tomb. Above it is placed the original statue of the Madonna that smiled at Thérèse on the occasion of her healing from the psychological illness. In the building adjacent to the convent is a very interesting museum with many original artefacts. For me, the most fascinating was an exhibit on the devotion of French soldiers to Saint Thérèse during the terrible days of the First World War. In fact, we were told, she was the Catholic figure most invoked on the front lines during the conflict, even though she had not even been beatified at that point. Her cause for sainthood was introduced in Rome in 1914 at the exact time of the outbreak of the war. Many soldiers carried with them into action a little booklet on Saint Thérèse. In the museum we saw one of these booklets with a bullet hole in it. A soldier had been carrying the booklet in his breast pocket when he was struck by enemy fire. The booklet, made of flimsy paper, stopped the bullet, and the soldier survived the war. There was also a bent medal of Saint Thérèse that had stopped a bullet destined for the heart of another soldier. Many other depositions from soldiers who attributed their survival to the intercession of Thérèse lined the shelves. The archives of the convent contain a large number of such testimonies, including instances in which Thérèse appeared to soldiers during battle and led them by the hand to safety. It is rare enough for a soldier to give away a medal awarded to him for valour in war, but the Carmel of Lisieux has hundreds of medals donated by soldiers who asserted that the intercession of the little saint had saved their lives.

Before her death, Thérèse had said that she would "spend her heaven doing good upon the earth." In a statement that is startling in its assurance, she promised that she would let fall a shower of roses from heaven upon those who would invoke her. While we were there in the museum of Carmel, one member of the group recounted how these prophetic words were dramatically fulfilled during the exhumation of Thérèse's body on March 26, 1923. A crowd of fifty thousand people, including members of the clergy and the civil authorities, gathered at the town cemetery. History does not record if the mayor of Lisieux was a devotee of Saint Thérèse, but, devoted or not, he had to be present at such an important occasion, not least because the town cemetery was under his jurisdiction. The gravediggers worked from early morning. At one point, a couple pushed a wheelchair through the crowd and brought their twelve-year-old paralysed daughter to the tomb. She was healed instantly and began to walk. It was an emotional scene, but the diggers were ordered to return to their task. By 11:00 A.M., they had uncovered five large stones above the coffin. At the blow of a chisel, one of the stones cracked and the workman stood upright.

"Is one of you wearing a strong perfume?" he asked, looking around. Those in the vicinity responded in the negative, and he resumed his work. But now the sweet scent was undeniable. The workers, policemen, and magistrates all agreed that there was a powerful smell of roses coming from the tomb.

"Mr Mayor, do you not detect a smell of roses?" someone demanded.

It was an almost comical situation, as if the official did not wish to descend to the level of popular piety, with all its talk of the scent of roses and miraculous healings.

"Yes," he replied. "But we placed roses in the vault last time we opened it." He was referring to a prior exhumation of the saint's remains during his long tenure as mayor, but that was thirteen years earlier! And now the unmistakable smell of fresh roses was apparent to all who were present. She may have considered herself no more than a little white flower, but for the Lord, evidently, Thérèse of Lisieux was a fragrant rose.

The procession of Thérèse's remains to her final resting place in the convent was accompanied by other miracles, including the instantaneous healing of a young blind girl as the coffin crossed the threshold into Carmel.

There was only so much of the life of this girl that we could discuss in depth during a pilgrimage that was ultimately focussed on the figure of Saint Columban and his legacy. We spoke little of the great suffering of her final eighteen months and the radical darkness she experienced. During this time, she felt that Jesus was absent, and she was even tormented by doubts about the existence of God. Her sense of desolation was so profound that her sisters felt it necessary to edit her writings after her death so as to expunge these "negative" elements. In total, Pauline made more than seven thousand revisions to Thérèse's manuscript before presenting it for publication. It was many decades before the original, unabridged version of her work found its way into print. To be fair, Thérèse had encouraged Pauline to edit it as she saw fit.

After three nights in Lisieux, we left the area and headed for the great abbey of Mont Saint-Michel. We made our visit to the island monastery, celebrated Mass in the ancient church of Saint Pierre, and continued into Brittany to commemorate, over the following days, the landing of Saint Columban on the European mainland. We left Lisieux far behind us and would end up flying back to Dublin from Nantes, but it seemed that Saint Thérèse was accompanying the group every step of the way. This young lady had made an impression on us all, and people continued to talk about her in those final days:

- The six-year-old who, after her first confession, passed her rosary through the grating for the priest to bless. On her way home afterwards in the dark, she paused under a streetlamp to marvel at the fact that the rosary looked just the same as before, despite the blessing.

- The ten-year-old who, in the depths of a psychological illness, written off by the doctors, was cured by the smile of the Virgin Mary. It was 1883, the thirteenth of May, a coincidence of day and month that would resound through the twentieth century with the message of Fátima.

- The eleven-year-old who cried so much with joy at her First Communion that her classmates thought it was on account of grief for her mother. Her tears, though, were tears of gladness for having the hidden God within her heart.

- The little girl of fourteen who longed to suffer for souls as Christ had done, to stand in spirit at the foot of the Cross and receive his blood so that she could pour it out upon sinners, but who realised that the best way of doing that for the moment was to stay at home and care for her father, being kind and cheerful to all.

- The nineteen-year-old Carmelite who, despite weariness and despondency, invited all the saints and angels to come and sing their songs of love in her heart when she received Communion, convinced that Our Lord would be pleased with such a joyous welcome even if she herself was tired and down.

- The assistant mistress of the novices who began to teach her Little Way with a simplicity and candour that belied the revolutionary character of what she was doing. This unpretentious teacher of the new entrants to the convent had no training in theology or Scripture, but her teaching was nothing less than the truth of the gospel distilled: we are saved if we humbly abandon ourselves daily into the arms of our providential Father.

- The mistress of souls who, when one of her charges complained about how much virtue she still needed to acquire, replied that what she really needed was not to acquire but to *lose*. Instead of climbing a mountain to God, what we really need to do is *descend* into humble and childlike simplicity. This is the sure way that leads directly to God's heart.

- The tender sister who consoled her older sibling for her lack of religious sentiment by saying that pious feelings are of no consequence. God has no need for our feelings or our works. His one desire is that we abandon ourselves with childlike trust into his arms.

- The girl of delicate health, with no consideration for her own well-being or comfort, who was convinced from an early age that her life would be brief, that she was a little white flower who would bloom in her springtime only.

All of this, though, is not intended as a way of giving glory to Thérèse. If there is one thing that this young lady made very clear, it is that God alone makes our lives fruitful. Our task is simply to allow him to work in us. The Lord found in Thérèse of Lisieux a docile spirit, and he was able to achieve great things through her. "You are the light of the world. . . . Let your light so shine before men, that they may see your good works and give glory to your Father who is in heaven" (Mt 5:14, 16).

Ever since that pilgrimage, I sometimes take down Father Bro's book and see if I can understand how someone of the undoubted intelligence of Karl Rahner could have made such a negative evaluation of her. Recall again his words:

> Many things in this saint and her writings irritate me or quite simply bore me. And if I set out to explain what nearly nauseates me, so that people would understand it, that still would not account for the fact that I took the trouble to do so. There are so many things in the world to deal with that do not necessitate a long exegesis.

It seems to me that this is not just a critical evaluation of the impact of Thérèse and her writings. It is dismissive of her very person and borders on the offensive. But it is an effort that ultimately backfires. By seeking to write a sort of obituary for the theological legacy of Thérèse, Rahner was effectively writing an obituary for himself. In one of the ironies that is a hallmark of Christianity, Pope John Paul II named her as a Doctor of the Church in 1997, the centenary of her death. It seems unlikely that the great German Jesuit will ever be honoured in a similar way, despite the vast superiority of his formal education and scholarship to hers. She, as a Doctor of the Church, and her book are held up to us as essential for our spiritual nourishment. Generations of faithful Catholics have discovered more riches and profound spiritual insights in her little book than in the works of many theologians who seek to conform the truths of faith to the spirit of the age.

And so our trip came to an end. We travelled to France to honour Saint Columban but left the country carrying our memories of this flower from heaven. So what was it that she did in the nine short years she spent in Carmel? Did she write great tracts of mystical theology? Did she experience visions, endure the stigmata, stimulate people to conversion, correspond with popes and kings, engage in acts of heroic charity towards the poor? Other saints may have accomplished such things, but Thérèse did none of these. She "only" did more or less what any sister of Carmel was expected to do: she followed the rule of her order and lived an apparently mundane life. For it wasn't what she did but the manner in which she did it that is the key to the revolution that is Thérèse of the Child Jesus and the Holy Face— a life of childlike abandonment, tirelessly seeking the face of God.

6

Seeking the Face of God

For it is the God who said, "Let light shine out of darkness," who has shone in our hearts to give the light of the knowledge of the glory of God in the face of Christ.

—2 Corinthians 4:6

"Your face, Lord, do I seek." Hide not your face from me.

—Psalms 27:8–9

"Is that Sister Blandina?"

"Yes, this is me," came back the reply, in a soft German accent.

"It's Kieran, the guy who comes with the Irish groups. Remember we met last year?"

"Yes, I remember."

"Can you meet another group of ours today in the Church of the Holy Face and tell us about your research on the Veil of Veronica?"

"I'm sorry, I have broken my leg. I am on crutches, and what is more, it is raining! I cannot make it so easily down to the church from my hermitage. The road is steep."

I was disappointed. Our group had just left by coach from San Giovanni Rotondo, the sanctuary of Padre Pio. We were headed for the seaside town of Alba Adriatica, and we wanted to visit the Shrine of the Holy Face in Manoppello on the way. For the past couple of years, I had called in here with different groups, and the previous year, we were fortunate to meet Sister Blandina by accident on a couple of occasions. She had given us a fascinating description of the Veil, and I had asked her mobile number for future visits.

The Veil of Veronica is a mysterious piece of fabric that has been conserved in the Capuchin sanctuary of Manoppello for about four centuries. There is a tradition that a lady named Veronica wiped the face of Jesus as he carried his cross to Calvary and that an impression of Jesus' face remained on the cloth. But this is not the cloth that is conserved in Manoppello. The Veil of Manoppello is called "the Veronica" only because this name signifies "true image" (*vera icona*); it has nothing to do with the lady who went to Jesus on the way of the Cross. Those who have studied the Veil believe that it was one of the cloths that was used for the burial of Jesus after his Crucifixion. A much larger shroud was used to envelop his entire body, and this tea-towel-size cloth was placed on his head. This would accord with Jewish burial custom and is mentioned explicitly in the Resurrection narrative from the Gospel of Saint John:

> They both ran, but the other disciple outran Peter and reached the tomb first; and stooping to look in, he saw the linen cloths lying there, but he did not go in. Then Simon Peter came, following him, and went into the tomb; he saw the linen cloths lying, and the napkin, which had been on his head, not lying with the linen cloths but rolled up in a place by itself. Then the other disciple, who reached the tomb first, also went in, and he saw and believed; for as yet they did not know the Scripture, that he must rise from the dead. (20:4–9)

The "napkin" mentioned in this account is possibly the cloth conserved in Manoppello. The cloth bears a clear representation of the face of a man, bearded, with his eyes open. The first time I saw it, it looked to me like a painted image by an artist who was not so hot on facial anatomy, especially in his rendering of the area around the mouth. But once we met Sister Blandina and heard her account, it was clear that this Veil was something deeply mysterious.

I explained to the group that Sister Blandina had fallen and broken her leg. They would have to make do with my version of the presentation she had given us the previous year. But when we arrived at the shrine and went inside the church, I saw a familiar figure in a Cistercian habit sitting in prayer in the pews in front of us, her crutches propped against the seat beside her.

"Thank you for meeting us, Sister Blandina!"

"Fortunately, I was able to make it after all!"

Her address began as usual in the little presentation room that lies behind the sanctuary of the church. At that time, there were two main sections to the exhibits. The first was a comparison of the Veil of Veronica with the Shroud of Turin; the second was a study of how the image of the face of Christ painted by artists down through the centuries has been influenced by the image on the Veil.

Many years ago, a carbon dating of the Shroud seemed to show that it was medieval in origin, but more recent research has cast serious doubts on these results. The main problem with the carbon dating is that the samples for analysis were taken from a corner of the Shroud, an area that had been extensively handled in previous centuries, part of it being repaired and patched. But apart from the issue of dating, the totality of the evidence indicates powerfully that this shroud was used to bury Jesus of Nazareth. The wounds evidenced by the cloth—the crowning with thorns, the crucifixion, the brutal scourging, the piercing with the spear—all correspond perfectly with the Gospel accounts of the Passion. And the analysis of how the image was made on the Shroud all but rules out the possibility that it could have been created by a skilled forger. It has not been painted or rubbed on by any method, nor can it be replicated by any sort of contact between a body and cloth. Scientists—for example, the Italian Paolo Di Lazzaro—now believe that it was seared on the fabric by a burst of incredibly powerful ultraviolet light, which may have accompanied the moment of resurrection. No natural source for such light seems adequate. According to Di Lazzaro, the ultraviolet burst necessary to reproduce such a subtle image of the crucified man would have to have a duration of less than one-forty-billionth of a second, and its intensity would have to exceed the maximum power released by all ultraviolet light sources available today.

Blandina's main contribution to the presentation in Manoppello is a study of similarities between the Veil of Veronica and the face on the Shroud. There is a striking correspondence between the two images. The size of the face, the distance between the eyes, and the magnitude of facial features, such as the nose, are all in perfect agreement. More remarkably, the wounds on both faces conform with each other in miniscule detail. That these two cloths actually bear images of the same face was convincingly demonstrated to us when Blandina led the group to the exhibit in which a larger-than-life copy of the Veil of Veronica can be slid over a copy of the face on the Shroud. The two images superimpose perfectly, with the only major difference being the fact that the eyes on the Shroud are closed. When Blandina slid the images on top of each other, there was a general murmur of appreciation from the group. What forger could have created such a remarkable correspondence over four hundred years ago, especially containing correlations that are not easily visible to the naked eye?

The surprising connections between the Shroud and the Veil were only part of the presentation, however. There was also the issue of how the image on the Veil was made. The fabric of the Veil is an extremely rare and precious material sometimes called "sea silk," made of the filaments, or byssus, generated by a certain clam in order to attach itself to the seabed. The craft of working byssus is a dying art. Only a handful of women on the island of Sardinia, most notably a lady called Chiara Vigo, are keeping the ancient skill alive. Spinning the thread is just the first challenge, however. Applying colour to it is a whole craft in itself. In order to paint an image on the silk, a primer must first be applied; paint will simply not attach to the fabric unless it is prepared in this way. The mysterious thing is that the Veil of Manoppello is covered neither with a primer nor with pigments of paint. Extremely high-resolution photography of the threads of the material show no pigmentation of any sort. The mystery of how the image was made on the Veil mirrors the question of how the image was made on the Shroud, prompting those who believe in the authenticity of these relics to name them *acheiropoieta*—"images not made by human hands."

The other main section of the museum contained the work of Father Heinrich Pfeiffer, a German scholar of early Christian art. Father Pfeiffer has catalogued the image of the face of Christ as depicted by artists down through the centuries. This catalogue contains mosaics in important churches, countless icons, and paintings on wood, including representations by well-known medieval masters such as Pietro Cavallini. What is remarkable about the catalogue is that it indicates that the face of Christ through the ages has the same characteristics and idiosyncrasies as the Veil of Manoppello! The image on the Veil seems to be the "mother of images," a reference point for the depiction of Jesus both in the East and in the West. The swollen and contorted right cheek, the tuft of hair in the centre of the forehead, the bruise below the mouth: these characteristics and others of the face on the Veil occur again and again. For Father Pfeiffer, there can be no doubt that the Veil was the official template used for depicting Our Lord. How had this happened? For centuries it had been kept in Saint Peter's Basilica before being taken to Manoppello. On certain days, it was displayed in public processions. On other occasions, artists would have been given permission to access the strong room in which it was kept. The preoccupation with being true to this image begins to make more sense when we consider the iconoclastic persecutions that swept the Church in various periods of history.

Iconoclasm—the "breaking of images"—has reared its head at various times in the history of the Church. The rightful suspicion of false images is founded in the Old Testament, with the very first commandment, which forbids worship of any god but the God of Israel. The worship of an image such as a statue made of corruptible material was considered a particularly insidious transgression of the first commandment. However, with the Incarnation of Jesus, it was recognized that material reality could, in some real sense, reflect the face of God. This didn't end iconoclasm, though. The Byzantine Empire, influenced by the rise of Islam, with its unrelenting war on images, in the region, went through periods of fanatical iconoclasm in which sacred images of Christ, the Madonna, and saints were consigned to the flames. The West—at least until the Reformation introduced its own form of iconoclasm—maintained a more balanced approach to the use of sacred images. But there was still a concern that representations of Christ should be faithful to the "true image"—the Veronica. Depicting Jesus was not something that could be done with unbridled artistic freedom.

Now we went outside and ascended the steps to see the Veil with our own eyes. It is conserved between two sheets of glass and exhibited in the area directly behind the altar, corresponding to where the tabernacle would be in many churches. Pilgrims can ascend the flight of steps to the rear and behold the relic from a distance of less than one metre. Sister Blandina remained here on top of the steps, switching on and off the various lights so that we could see how the image on the cloth varies dramatically depending on the illumination. We ascended the steps in groups of five or six, and Blandina repeated the exercise for each group. The way the image on the Veil changes in response to alterations in the lighting is quite remarkable. Not for the first time, I noticed that Sister sometimes seemed to fall into moments of deep contemplation of the image, almost forgetting that anyone else was there.

When the tour was over, the group headed into the souvenir shop, located to the right of the church. One of the pilgrims, Larry, had remarked a few times over the previous days that I seemed to be in multiple places at the same time. "You're in front of the group whenever we're walking to a destination, but then you pop up at the back to drag people out of shops and keep them moving! You're the first down for breakfast and the last to leave! You're everywhere! How do you do it? Are you sure you don't have a twin?"

On this occasion, I wanted to accompany Sister Blandina outside, which meant I would not be going to the souvenir shop. "I won't be with you this time, Larry," I called over in a loud whisper as we walked outside. "And neither will my twin!"

Sister and I stood on top of the steps in front of the shrine. The rain had stopped, but the German nun was looking down the steps with some trepidation, the crutches propped under either arm.

"How will you get home?" I asked.

"I don't know," she replied, with the quiet, matter-of-fact tone with which she usually spoke. It was lunchtime, and there was a man at the bottom of the steps selling food and drinks at a stand.

"Hold on a minute, Sister!" I said and galloped down the steps to the stand.

"Do you know Sister Blandina?" I asked the man who was busy placing sausages on a grill.

"Of course," he replied.

"Would you mind driving her up to her hermitage? It will only take a few minutes."

"Certainly! But you will need to keep an eye on these sausages while I'm away!"

A few minutes later, Sister Blandina had been helped into the front of a tiny Fiat, and they were gone. I went over to the stand and noticed that the sausages seemed to need turning. Conscious that it would be my fault if the food got cremated, I looked around furtively and then went behind the counter. As I turned the sausages, a familiar voice came from behind and made me jump. It was Larry.

"Kieran! I know you're everywhere, but selling hot dogs as well?"

"Well, I'm just helping out," I began. "You see, the owner had to—"

"The courier salary can't be so good if you have to do

that on the side!" Larry cut in, a note of concern in his voice. He looked at the sausages behind me and rubbed his tummy. "Actually, it's been a long time since breakfast. Go on, I'll take one!"

By now, the group had finished their purchases in the shop and were streaming out the front of the church. Maybe it was out of a sense of pity that I apparently had to sell hot dogs to supplement my salary, but soon there was a long queue in front of the stand.

"Ketchup, Larry?"

"Yes, please, and I'll have a beer while you're at it."

I wasn't sure how the owner would normally have presented his hot dogs, but everyone was hungry and seemed more than content to have a sausage in a roll with a squirt of ketchup. Within a matter of minutes, all the sausages and rolls were gone, and I had sold quite an amount of beer and soft drinks as well.

By the time the Fiat came back down the hill, the group had dispersed and I was at the stand by myself. The owner parked the car and strode over to me quickly with an anxious look on his face as he saw the empty grill behind me.

"Where's everything gone?" he said in an alarmed tone. But then he saw the wad of notes protruding from the plastic beer mug, and his eyes bulged. "Anytime you need me to drive Sister Blandina home, just ask!"

Some years later, I arrived back at Manoppello with a group from County Down. On this occasion, we were coming from a different direction, following a visit to Montecassino Abbey. I had long since stopped phoning Sister Blandina before these visits. If she happened to be there when we arrived, well and good. If not, the group would have to make do with my presentation. We couldn't very well disturb a Cistercian contemplative every time we were passing by! It was May 20, which happened to be Pentecost that year. As our coach climbed the hill towards the sanctuary, we noticed that there were cars everywhere, parked on the sides of the narrow roads, taking up every available space.

"I wonder what is going on?" I asked Piero, our driver.

He shrugged his shoulders gruffly. "How would I know? I'm not the courier!"

When we got to the sanctuary, I led the group to the door of the church. A diminutive priest was just coming out the door.

"Why are there so many people around today?" I asked him.

"Don't you know?" he replied. "The third Sunday in May is always the feast of the Holy Face at this shrine. To-day the Holy Veil was taken in procession from the sanc-tuary to the parish church." I learned afterwards that this priest was none other than Father Pfeiffer, the historian who had catalogued the resemblances between the various depic-tions of Christ and the Veil of Manoppello down through the centuries.

The Veil was not in its usual place, though a good copy had been temporarily installed there. We visited the exhi-bition and then took the coach the short drive to town so that we could venerate the real image. The Veil was set up in a stand at the back of the parish church. A funeral was in progress, so our visit was very much curtailed, but the group was happy to be here on such an atmospheric occasion with great crowds in attendance.

After the visit, we went for lunch in a local restaurant. Manoppello is in Abruzzo, an area well known for its dis-tinctive cuisine. We were given a typical meal of the region, a first course of spaghetti alla chitarra—a type of pasta in a ragù sauce—and a second course of roast sausage and potatoes. Afterwards, as I stood near the cash register, waiting to pay, I noticed on the wall a photo of the restaurant owner greeting Pope Francis in Saint Peter's Square. There was also another man in the picture, and I asked the owner who it was.

"That is Paul Badde," he replied.

I knew the name well. Paul Badde is a German journalist who has written extensively on the Veronica, bringing the research of Sister Blandina and Father Pfeiffer to a wider audience. He was also involved in the investigative work that led to the discovery that the Veil was made of marine byssus. Furthermore, he has done extensive historical research on the whereabouts of the Veil at various periods of history and the reasons for its eventual arrival in Manoppello. I had read one of his major books, *The Second Shroud*, the previous year and had been impressed.

"Oh, so you know Paul Badde?" I said.

"Yes! He's a regular customer here!" He pointed to a table behind me. "In fact, he's here right now. Do you see him there?"

A man was sitting at a table with four or five others in animated conversation.

"Is it okay if I go over to greet him?"

"Certainly!"

I went over and introduced myself, complimenting him on his book. He replied to me in perfect English. "I prefer English to Italian," he said. Then he paused, looked me in the eye, and asked a direct question: "Do you believe that the Veil of Manoppello is one of the genuine burial cloths of Jesus?"

I thought for a moment, recalling my encounters with Sister Blandina and her work over the years. "Yes," I said, nodding my head. "Actually, I do."

"Welcome to the club!"

Later that day, as we drove along the coast northwards to Loreto, I thought about the significance of belonging to that club. We live in an age that is preoccupied with images. When people post photos of themselves on social media, those images are often carefully selected, or even digitally doctored, to show them in a particular light, the light that the people wish to be seen in. Every time we do this, we bend our knee in homage to a god who has been created in *our* image and likeness, the worship of a plastic image of oneself. How fixated we are on beauty, on our appearance in the eyes of others! But the beauty that is all the rage on our social media is an empty beauty that is only skin deep.

The image of Christ on the Veronica is different. Its beauty is not one that affects the senses. The face is still distorted by the wounds of the Passion. These wounds destroy beauty on the superficial level, but it is only in the contemplation of these wounds that the deeper beauty of Christ begins to take hold of us. It is a beauty that is apprehended not by the eyes but with the heart.

> He had no form or comeliness that we should look at him, and no beauty that we should desire him. He was despised and rejected by men; a man of sorrows and acquainted with grief; and as one from whom men hide their faces he was despised, and we esteemed him not.
>
> Surely he has borne our griefs and carried our sorrows; yet we esteemed him stricken, struck down by God, and afflicted. But he was wounded for our transgressions, he was bruised for our iniquities; upon him was the chastisement that made us whole, and with his stripes we are healed. (Is 53:2–5)

If there is a "club" of Manoppello, it is not an association that admires the aesthetic aspect of the Veronica. It recognizes the need to look deeper. It acknowledges that the wounds we are contemplating were inflicted by our own transgressions. We have smitten him with our own iniquities, yet he remains merciful. "They shall look on him whom they have pierced" (Jn 19:37).

There is something more happening in this place, however. As is always the case with me, it took a long time for that something even to begin to register. True, I began to go back to Manoppello in order to look upon the face of Christ; that much is to my credit. If a pilgrim group of ours was anywhere along the Adriatic Coast, from Loreto to Bari, I would insert in the programme a visit to the Holy Veil. This had gone on for ten years when it dawned on me that maybe it was the person of the Veil who was seeking me— not just *me*, of course, but all of us who went on pilgrimage there. You see, the most striking thing about the Veil—and you need to go there in order to experience it yourself—is not really what we look upon, but the sensation that the man in the Veil is looking upon *us*. When you climb those stairs and look at the image, you meet the steady gaze of Christ. It is the moment of his Resurrection, when all of creation is being gathered back into the arms of God, a moment that began two thousand years ago but transcends all of history. It is the moment when your sins are forgiven and you are being made into a new creation. I think now that at those times when Blandina seemed to get lost in the image, she was allowing the man in the Veil to gaze upon her.

On these trips, the visit to Manoppello is usually followed or preceded by a visit to one of the most famous and ancient Marian shrines in Europe—Loreto. This is situated about two hours up the coast, and it complements the visit to Manoppello perfectly. I will always remember one of the early groups we took on pilgrimage there. The leader of the group was Canon Brendan, an intrepid pilgrimage organiser who was well known for getting the utmost out of every day. Once, a pilgrim group of his was staying with us at the Irish College in Rome. We had been out late the previous evening, so breakfast was fixed at the relatively late hour of 8:30. That morning, Canon Brendan was first down to the dining room.

"Did you enjoy your lie-in, Canon?" I asked.

"Well, I got up early actually!" he replied in his usual chirpy tone. "I needed to do my daily walk!" Then he proceeded to tell me the route of his walk that morning: it took in Saint Peter's Basilica (three miles away), the Pantheon, Piazza Navona, the Colosseum, the Trevi Fountain, and a host of famous sights. If it had been anyone else, I would have had difficulty believing him. But I knew Canon Brendan well enough at this stage to realize that he had certainly done what he had said, at eighty years of age in the August heat of Rome.

One of the famous (and true) stories regarding Canon Brendan concerned the election of the new pope in 1978. The canon was leading yet another pilgrimage to the Holy Land. There was a flight connection to be made in Rome that involved waiting in the airport for a few hours. Canon Brendan did not want such precious time to be wasted, so he hired a coach that whisked his group over to Saint Peter's as soon as they landed at the airport. They arrived just in time for the Angelus and blessing with the new pope, John Paul I, whose pontificate would last only thirty-three days before his untimely death.

On that first pilgrimage we made with the canon, there were 165 pilgrims, requiring three fifty-five-seater buses. It was the largest group ever for us, before or since. On each coach, we stationed two couriers, and the organisation of a trip with these numbers had to be meticulous. As always, Laura was doing all the work in the background: coach timetables, restaurant bookings, the reservation of churches for Masses. Despite the mad traffic of Rome, the general unpredictability of the Eternal City, and the huge influx of pilgrims that year, the entire programme was fulfilled without a hitch. Canon Brendan had an infectious enthusiasm and was visibly pleased when things were going smoothly. He would always place himself at the front of the group during the guided tours of churches and archaeological sites, completely attentive to every word that was being spoken. When a walking tour was over and our three coaches would come sweeping by perfectly on cue to pick us up, the look of contentment on the canon's face was a pleasure to behold. Never once during that pilgrimage did we have to stand and wait for a coach, in a city where waiting is par for the course. We didn't have a single issue with a Mass booking, an entry time to a museum, or even a restaurant menu for this number of people. Providence smiled on us that entire week. On the strength of this good fortune, Canon Brendan developed such a positive opinion of Laura and me that it was sufficient to launch a series of pilgrimages all over Italy and even into Poland during the following years.

In one of those years, we stayed in Alba Adriatica and visited Loreto and Manoppello. It was the canon's usual practice to read up on a destination before travelling. And he was not too impressed by some of the pious stories he had read about Loreto! The sanctuary consists of an ancient rough stone building encased in a magnificent Renaissance basilica. According to tradition, the rough stone house was originally located in Nazareth and was the place where the angel Gabriel announced to Mary that she would become the mother of Christ. In addition, it is believed that the

Holy Family came to live there after the return from Egypt
and that Jesus grew up within those walls. At some difficult
point in the history of the Holy Land, the house was dismantled, transported, and rebuilt on Italian soil.

The canon would have had no difficulty with any of these
traditions. It was a further embellishment that had been
added to the story that was hard for him to swallow. According to a pious tale, the house was miraculously transported from Nazareth to its current location by the hands
of angels. This legend, which began to appear in historical
documents only from the 1400s onwards, took a great hold
of the popular imagination. As sometimes happens with pious stories, the legend took on a life of its own that began to
overshadow the real significance of the place. In the 1500s,
Donato Bramante designed a stunning marble screen to en-
shrine the simple stone walls of the house. Three sides of
the screen are adorned with sculptures that record significant events, such as the Annunciation to Mary and the birth
of Jesus. The other side has a depiction of the house being
carried through the air by angels! By the early 1500s, the
legend had begun to take on such importance that it was
depicted alongside events of no lesser importance than the
Annunciation itself.

On one of my first visits to the basilica, I was amazed to
discover on the left wall a large slab from the 1600s with a
description in the Irish language of the legendary transportation by angels. On adjacent pillars are corresponding slabs
with the same description in Latin and English. The English and Irish slabs are signed by an English Jesuit, Robert
Corbington. Why on earth, I wondered, would a Jesuit go
to the considerable trouble of inscribing on marble this pious old tale in different languages, and even in Irish?

In those days, information on the Internet was not as

comprehensive as it is nowadays, and it was a few years before I discovered an answer to this question. In the late 1500s, when Catholics began to suffer persecution in England, the Corbington family moved to Ireland, where Robert was born. The situation for Catholics in Ireland would deteriorate very soon afterwards. Along with his two brothers, Robert entered the Jesuit Order. One of the brothers, Ralph, was martyred at Tyburn in 1644. The Jesuits were always known for their policy of "cultural accommodation." This was the strategy of learning the language and customs of the people they were evangelising in order to help sow the seeds of the Gospel more powerfully in that culture. In the 1600s, as a result of the religious persecution in Britain and Ireland, many Catholics from these countries found themselves on the continent, but not always proficient in the local languages. By this time, Loreto had become a major pilgrimage destination. When the earls of Ulster fled Ireland and eventually made for Rome in 1608, they went out of their way to visit Loreto. Robert Corbington felt it important that pilgrims such as these would appreciate being able to read the history of the shrine in their own language. Two Latin slabs describing the miraculous transportation were already present in the basilica, so he undertook to translate the text into Irish and English, erecting slabs in each language on both the left and right sides of the nave. It would be virtually impossible for any pilgrim, whichever door he entered, to miss them.

When I saw the slabs for the first time, I felt a bit uneasy or maybe even a little annoyed. "Evidently the legend of Loreto had already superseded fact by the 1600s," I mused. As the official literature of the sanctuary proclaims, the house of Nazareth is a shrine of the Annunciation to Mary, the shrine of the Incarnation of God among us, the shrine of the action of the Holy Spirit in history, the shrine of the Holy Family, and much else besides. But the text on the slabs in no fewer than three languages is almost entirely dedicated to the story of the angelic transportation from Palestine!

Looking at the slabs, I was reminded of something. Where had I encountered something similar before? Then I realised what it was. In many shrines we visit, there can be a tendency to place the emphasis on the miraculous to the detriment of everything else. In the case of Padre Pio, for example, the fantastic stories that are constantly being told can obscure the spirituality of the man. Sure, every one of those fantastic stories may well be true, but the enduring message of Padre Pio is to be found elsewhere. In Lourdes, there is sometimes such a focus on physical healing that the deeper message of the place is forgotten. When the earls of Ulster came to Loreto, the secretary of Hugh O'Neill, Tadhg O' Cianáin, was with them. He wrote a narrative account of their journey, a unique document in the Irish language from that period. The visit to Loreto is chronicled, but a long and completely disproportional portion of the narrative is dedicated to the story of the angelic transportation! Something about that story captivated the minds of ordinary people, and I felt sure that this took away from the real significance of the shrine.

The problem with pious stories and legendary accounts is that they can damage belief in the historical significance of something. They can bring a place into disrepute. I think that is how it may have been with Canon Brendan. The first part of that pilgrimage had included Rome and San Giovanni Rotondo. We had visited places such as Saint Peter's Basilica and the catacombs. Saint Peter's is built on the bones of the man whom Jesus had called "Rock," and the catacombs were the burial ground of the first Christians, covered in the earliest examples of Christian art and steeped in the blood of the martyrs. More concrete connections with the early Church in Rome would be impossible to find. Now we were on our way to Loreto, to a house that had allegedly been carried to Italy by angels and conveniently deposited on a piece of land then under the control of—guess who— the pope! It was just too much!

We boarded the coach in Alba Adriatica. From there, we had an hour's drive ahead of us to the sanctuary. I turned back in my courier seat and addressed our group leader.

"Canon Brendan, I'm going to give the history of the shrine as we're driving. Just to get everyone ready for what we're going to see."

"Do what you have to do, Kieran! But maybe go easy on that bit about the angels! A house flying through the air like Dorothy's in *The Wizard of Oz*—stop the lights!"

"Stop the lights" was an expression from an old game show on television that Canon Brendan uttered every now and then when he thought that things had gone quite far enough. It was clear that he didn't believe the story, but did he also doubt that the house had any connection at all to Nazareth?

"Don't worry, Canon! I'm going to stick to the facts!"

On that earlier visit to Loreto many years before, I had picked up a booklet in the back of the church. It cost a grand total of two thousand lire—less than one euro in to-day's currency—but threw a lot of light on the entire story. In the early years of the twentieth century, a librarian in the Vatican archives had found a reference to the house of Nazareth in an ancient document from the thirteenth century. According to this record, a family called De Angelis saved the stones of the house of Nazareth from destruction by the Muslims and had them transported to Italy. Decades later, another document was unearthed testifying that the same family gave one of their daughters the stones of the house of Nazareth as a dowry when she married the son of the king of Naples. I was amazed! There it was—a house transported from Palestine by the De Angelis family, the Angels! This powerful family had ruled part of what was once the Byzantine Empire and had been involved in the crusades. Over the centuries, the fertile imagination of pilgrims had surmised that the "Angels" who had transported the house must be the angels of heaven, and how else would angels do anything if not by the power of their wings? In a manner that is typical of legends of this sort, there was a combination of historical facts and myth. The slabs on the wall stated that the angels had completed the transportation on December 10, 1294. The marriage document in which the stones were given as a dowry is from September 1294, a date incredibly similar to that in the legend.

When I told this first part of the story over the microphone, I heard immediate sounds of approval behind me from Canon Brendan.

"That's more like it, Kieran!" he said. "Now it begins to make some sense!"

Then I moved on to summarize the other information that I had found in that same booklet. There were three principal sets of evidence that supported the claim that this house indeed came from Nazareth. The first set of evidence regards the building materials and structure of the edifice. In Nazareth, to this day, there still exists a grotto that is said to be a portion of the house of Our Lady, and the house at Loreto in Italy has only three sides. It seems that this three-sided building was originally built onto the grotto that stands in Nazareth. A comparison of the dimensions of the house in Loreto with those of the cave in the Holy Land, and the stone and the structure of building, indicate that these two entities were once joined to each other. The type of stone and the way it was cut is foreign to the culture and building practice of that part of Italy. The house of Loreto has only three original walls because the eastern side, where the altar now stands, would have opened onto the grotto. The upper part of the walls and the vault are not original and are made out of local stone. Evidently, the portion taken from Nazareth was only the first three metres of wall without any roofing. In addition, investigations have shown that there is no foundation under those three walls. It has been re-erected on an ancient road. This would fit with the story that the house was dismantled down as far as ground level (leaving the foundations where they were at Nazareth) and re-erected from the ground up without foundation. Incidentally, the stretch of road upon which the house was rebuilt was encircled by a laurel wood—*lauretum* in Latin, which explains the origin of the modern name Loreto.

Second, graffiti have been found on the house in Loreto that experts have adjudged to be of Jewish-Christian origin and very similar to other graffiti found in Nazareth. It was commonplace for pilgrims to the Holy Land of the early centuries to leave graffiti on the places that they visited. This often took the form of prayer petitions for loved ones. Graffiti of this precise sort would be completely out of time and place on a thirteenth-century building in Italy. If you visit Loreto today, some of this graffiti can still be seen behind small glass panels on the right-hand interior wall of the building.

Third, during renovation works and the making of entrances to the house, various objects have been found that support the claim that this building was once in the Holy Land. These include five crosses made of red material typical of Crusaders or knights of a military order who defended the sacred relics in the Middle Ages.

By the time I had finished the description, Canon Brendan's attitude had dramatically changed from the scepticism that he had shown earlier. A while later, when we entered the basilica and made our way to the house of Nazareth under the dome, his eyes had their old familiar gleam and his step its characteristic enthusiasm. We celebrated Mass in the crypt, and then people had a couple of hours' free time for lunch and personal devotions. I made my way back into the house of Our Lady and stood there for some time at the back wall. "Am I just naturally gullible?" I wondered. "How come I always end up believing in everything?" And there was no doubt that I did believe. I believed that the angel Gabriel had come within those walls and announced to Mary that the God who transcends everything would become a tiny child in her womb. I believed that Jesus, the second Person of the blessed Trinity, had grown up touching those very stones.

Pilgrims continued to stream through as I stood there. Most stayed for a few minutes and then went on. Virtually everyone raised his hand and touched the walls. After a while, I realised that what I was watching there was a perfect example of popular piety. I was also aware that it would be easy to dismiss gestures such as these as a form of superstition—people rubbing "holy" objects in order to procure some divine help or good fortune. In what way, I wondered, was this different to the practices of pagan religions?

But as I continued to watch the pilgrims passing through and touching the stones, it was clear that there was a big difference between popular piety of this sort and superstition. These pilgrims may not necessarily have been engaged in profound contemplation when they touched the walls, but it was done with reverence, not with a superstitious anxiety. *Reverence* was the litmus test, surely. It showed that what was happening there was based on faith and devotion and was not a meaningless ritual. The attitude of the pilgrims seemed evident to me: Jesus touched those walls; we touch them with reverence as a way of venerating this Jesus, whom we acknowledge to be Our Lord. It struck me that that has been the Catholic way since the beginning. We pray with words because words are a powerful way to express our need of God, our abandonment to God, our praise of God, our petitions for his help. But we also pray with our actions. Touching a wall that was touched by Christ can be a valid way of venerating Christ, praising him, expressing our need for his help.

After a while of watching the pilgrims touch the walls in this way, I gradually became aware of the Latin inscription in gold lettering on the marble behind the altar. There is a beauty, clarity, and elegance about Latin that makes it the ideal language to communicate divine truths with reverence: *Hic Verbum Caro Factum Est*—"Here the Word was made flesh."

When I left the house of Our Lady that day, I felt chastened. Without saying anything much to anyone, I had, for years, in my own mind been disparaging popular piety, the embellishment of stories, the "ritualistic" rubbing of walls. But as I stood in that house, I had been confronted with a valid form of prayer, striking in its simplicity and purity. There could be no doubt that what was happening there was a humble and genuine veneration of Jesus and his mother, a steadfast belief in the Incarnation of God among us. These humble pilgrims bore a silent testimony, but it had power: clearly there was more to popular piety than relics and rituals.

7

Relics and Rituals

She had heard the reports about Jesus, and came up behind
him in the crowd and touched his garment. For she said,
"If I touch even his garments, I shall be made well."

—Mark 5:27–28

Loreto had shown how sincere popular piety can be, but I
was still suspicious of the excess manifestations of it, and
like a latter-day Martin Luther, I was determined to help
stamp it out. In the pilgrimage trade, there is no shortage of
opportunities for this. That same year, we had a parish trip
from Kerry to San Giovanni Rotondo, the shrine of Padre
Pio. The spiritual director cancelled at the last moment and
wasn't able to find a replacement. So it was up to me to
provide the commentary on the spiritual aspects of the trip
as well as tending to the usual matters that a courier looks
after. I didn't need much encouragement.

It was 2003. The following year, the massive new church
of Saint Pio would be opened behind the old sanctuary.
Padre Pio's body would be moved there in 2009, but in
2003, the body was still below a marble slab in the crypt of
the church of Saint Mary of Graces. This was the church
built in 1959 while Padre Pio was still alive. There is an altar set up in the crypt, a few yards from the original resting
place, and the custom was for Masses to be celebrated almost
continuously in front of the tomb. That altar is still used for

Masses, though the tomb is empty. The body of Saint Pio is now on display in the crypt of the new church, surrounded by the stunning mosaics of Father Marko Rupnik.

In the old days, the church of Saint Mary of Graces would close in the evening but would reopen at 9:00 P.M. for a recitation of the Rosary in front of the tomb. After the Rosary, the iron railings at both ends of the tomb would be opened, and pilgrims would have the opportunity to file past, touching the marble slab if they wished. According to Catholic practice, if a religious object, such as a rosary, is touched to the tomb of a saint, it takes on the status of what is called a "third-class" relic of the saint. A first-class relic is a piece of the saint's body, and a second-class relic is a piece of the saint's clothing or an object used by the saint in life.

I had been to San Giovanni Rotondo a number of times that year and had witnessed firsthand the scenes that sometimes ensued after the opening of the iron railing. Some Italian pilgrims of a certain vintage and from certain parts of the country tended, in my opinion, to manifest fanatical behaviour towards Padre Pio. The friars who ran the shrine did their best to keep order, but it wasn't always easy. On one occasion, a fervent Italian pilgrim threw herself on top of the marble slab and had to be removed forcibly by a burly friar. Other pilgrims bore with them sacks of religious objects that they insisted on touching, one by one, to the top of the tomb until eventually a friar would lose patience and hustle them along. The first time I participated in this Rosary, I was so shocked by the frenzied behaviour that I didn't file past the tomb at all, standing aloof outside the railing with—to my mind, at least—a superior sense of restraint.

The group without a spiritual director was the first I had ever travelled with from Kerry. For those not familiar with it, the Kerry accent is very distinctive and musical. Sitting down in my courier seat at the front of the coach, listening to the chatter behind me, I enjoyed hearing it for the first few days. At times, I had difficulty understanding some of the pilgrims, but as the trip went on, their sonorous accents became easier to comprehend. The first few days of the Kerry pilgrimage had been spent in Rome, and I was getting to know the members of the group gradually. One of the pilgrims, whose name was Dickie, a tiny man with a skinny frame and a leather-like, wrinkled face, had immediately stood out. Dickie sat on the front seat of the coach every day and insisted on commenting or asking questions continually as I spoke into the microphone. I tried to be patient at first, but fairly quickly it started to become disconcerting. It was as if Dickie and I were having a conversation that everyone else was party to, whether they liked it or not. Dickie's comments were often of a barbed or cynical sort. He didn't seem convinced by many of the things that I told the group and wasn't slow to offer an alternative account of things. From Roman civilisation to Baroque architecture to the modern history of Italy, Dickie had an opinion on everything.

When the Rome portion of the trip was over, we loaded the coach and began the long journey to San Giovanni Rotondo, a spectacular drive that crosses the Apennines over some of the longest and highest viaducts in Europe. On the way, I had ample time to warn the group about some of the excesses that I thought they would soon be witnessing at Padre Pio's shrine. Having related my experiences of the frantic pilgrims who threw themselves on the tomb of the saint, I went directly to what I intended would be my main point.

"It's all very fine to touch objects to the tomb of Padre

Pio so that they become third-class relics," I said. "But this business of removing objects from their packaging and individually rubbing them on the marble slab smacks of superstition!"

"Superstition, you say?" It was the ever-reliable Dickie who was speaking. "And why would rubbing a whole bag of objects in one go be all right, but rubbing one object by itself be superstition?"

"Because there's no need to be concerned about rubbing each object individually. If we believe in what we're doing, then bringing all the objects close to the tomb in one go is sufficient, surely."

Dickie snorted impatiently. "To me it all sounds a bit like hocus-pocus!"

"No, I'm sorry, Dickie, I can't agree with that," I said, shaking my head emphatically. "Mother Church tells us that the veneration of relics is a legitimate way to honour a person who has allowed the holiness of God to be made manifest in his life. We are really venerating God when we do these things. But we can use relics with genuine faith, or we can treat them as if they were some kind of magical objects."

"Oh, it's *faith* we're talking about now, is it?" replied Dickie with a sarcastic smile. "I didn't realize we were on to such deep matters! A few minutes ago, it was only rosary beads and medals we were discussing!"

By this point, the sing-song Kerry accent was really starting to grate on my nerves. "Oh yes, Dickie! It's precisely faith we're talking about here!" My voice had gotten higher in pitch. "We believe that a religious object takes on the status of a relic when it is brought to the tomb of a saint. So all we need to do is bring it close to the tomb, and that is enough. God's holiness looks after the rest. But if I start removing every religious object out of a bag and begin rubbing it individually on the tomb, then it looks as if I don't really believe that the holiness of God is sufficient. I am behaving as if what *I'm* doing is essential. Rubbing an object in that way certainly smacks of magical or idolatrous behaviour. Don't you agree?"

"Oh, well, if *you* say so!" came the sarcastic reply. "Weren't we lucky to get a courier like you! Someone who can tell if a pilgrim has idolatry in his heart or not! Well, well, how fortunate we all were! The Roman Inquisition could have done with someone as discerning as you!"

There was little point in continuing this conversation. Trembling with exasperation, I sat down in my seat and paused for a few minutes. Why couldn't Dickie just be quiet for once! Luckily for me, the coach was leaving the motor-way at San Severo and beginning the climb up the Gargano plateau towards San Giovanni Rotondo. I had an excuse to change the subject. It was time to speak about the matters that couriers usually occupy themselves with: the layout of the hotel, breakfast and dinner times, how to find the way to the sanctuary, the location of the nearest ATM machine. Dickie could hardly find anything to dispute here, or so I hoped.

By the time we arrived at the hotel and checked in, it was already close to dinnertime. After dinner, people were free to walk up to the sanctuary, but we set no programme for the group. Everyone was tired, and most people had a drink at the bar and then went to bed. The next morning, we celebrated Mass in the old church. This was the place where Padre Pio had said Mass and heard confessions for much of his life. In the choir loft above the church is the crucifix in front of which Padre Pio received the stigmata in 1918. He would bear those marks of the wounds of Christ for fifty years until they disappeared a few days before his death in September 1968.

What were these stigmata all about? According to Pope Paul VI, there were two things that stood out in the life of this friar: the first was that Padre Pio spent his days, from morning to evening, hearing confessions and administering the pardon of Christ. The second was that he bore the marks of the Passion of Jesus. The two are inextricably linked since it is through the sacrifice of Christ that our sins are forgiven. In his Letter to the Colossians, Saint Paul wrote: "Now I rejoice in my sufferings for your sake, and in my flesh I complete what is lacking in Christ's afflictions for the sake of his body, that is, the Church" (Col 1:24). There is nothing lacking in the Passion of Christ, except for our participation in it as members of his Body. It is *we* who are built up by participating in his suffering. If we are to be fully alive, then we must learn to love selflessly. No one else can love selflessly for me; I must do it myself. I must participate in the self-emptying love of Christ; otherwise my part will be lacking, and the Church will be the less for it. Some people are called to participate more and to build up the Church more. Padre Pio's stigmata was a participation to an extraordinary degree in Christ's sacrificial love.

On the afternoon of that first full day in San Giovanni Rotondo, we did the high Stations of the Cross. That too, surely, was a way of participating in the Passion for building up the Church. There are fourteen stations in this popular devotion; they begin with Pilate's condemnation of Jesus, continue through the taking up of the Cross, the three falls under its weight, encounters with various people along the way (including Mary), and end with the Crucifixion and deposition of Christ's body in the tomb. It was an optional exercise, but Dickie was present and insisted on holding the large wooden cross at the head of the group for the entire duration of the Stations. Normally, people take it in turns to carry the cross, with the changeover happening at the end of each station, but Dickie resolutely refused to pass the cross to anyone who offered to take it from him. After the first few stations, no one dared to offer any longer, and Dickie was left to carry the cross by himself until the end.

At dinnertime, I announced that anyone who was interested could come up with me to the tomb for the Rosary at 9:00 P.M. At 8:30, a fair-sized crowd of us gathered at the hotel entrance. A few had gone on ahead by themselves, but there were still about twenty-five of us who made their way up the hill together. I looked around for Dickie but saw that he was missing. I breathed a sigh of relief. This man had become a real source of tension as far as I was concerned. The fact that he was absent was a weight off my shoulders.

It was already dark, and the church was lit in a very low, understated way, which enhanced the atmosphere. We descended the steps into an already-crowded crypt. I had previously told everyone to make their own way back to the hotel once the Rosary and the procession past the tomb were over. The crowds would make it too difficult for us to find one another.

The friars leading the Rosary were seated around the altar, situated a few yards from the tomb. I was propped up against the wall not far from one of the staircases. As the Rosary went on, I realised that the lady standing near me and wearing a mantilla was the owner of the hotel where we were staying. She was accompanied by one of her daughters. The lady, Mirella, was very devout and had known Padre Pio personally. In fact, the famous friar had officiated at her wedding and blessed their hotel in the 1950s when it was opened. It was the first hotel constructed in San Giovanni

Rotondo, and in the beginning, it catered mainly to people who came to Padre Pio for the Sacrament of Reconciliation. On the occasion of their wedding, Padre Pio had told Mirella and her husband that they would one day have a child with a disability. Many years later, Maria Grazia, who has Down syndrome, was born.

The fifth decade of the Rosary had begun when Mirella approached me and spoke into my ear. "Maria Grazia is not well. I need to take her back to the hotel. Would you mind touching these rosary beads to the tomb of Saint Pio?" She handed me a large transparent bag filled with rosaries.

I was a little bit taken aback. Touching rosary beads on the tomb was not something that I wanted to do in front of the group, given what had transpired on the coach between Dickie and me, but I couldn't very well refuse. Then I quickly came around to the idea. It would be a chance for me to walk by the tomb efficiently and touch the bag of rosary beads on the marble slab in a simple way, demonstrating the dignified and reserved manner with which things of this sort should be done.

"Certainly, Mirella! I'll do that."

Mirella and Maria Grazia began to move towards the stairs. Then Mirella turned back and whispered in my ear. "Be sure to open the bag and rub each rosary individually on the tomb. They're gifts for different guests of mine, and I would like each one to touch the tomb directly."

My heart sank. What would I do? There was no chance to protest—Mirella was already climbing the stairs with her daughter. I looked at the bag. The rosary beads were of the simple, plastic sort, and there were at least fifty of them! I steeled myself. Surely this could be done with the minimum of fuss and without anyone in the group knowing. Generally, once pilgrims had processed by the tomb, they continued on up the stairs and returned to their accommodation. The last time I attended, I noticed that the crypt was virtually empty as the last people were filing past the tomb. It was just a matter of waiting patiently, nipping in to the tomb at the end and giving each rosary a friendly rub on the marble slab. No one would be the wiser, and Mirella would be satisfied. She had always been obliging to us over the years, and I couldn't let her down now.

The gates at either end of the tomb were opened, and the procession started. There was a general heave towards the tomb and the shuffling of feet. In the semidarkness, I could see that the Capuchins had chosen well the bearded friar who was in charge of crowd control at the entrance to the tomb. He was a giant of a man. "Golly!" I thought. "Muhammad Ali wouldn't have lasted thirty seconds in the ring with you!"

Unlike on the previous occasion, however, nobody tried to fling himself on the tomb, and I wondered if perhaps I had given the group a slightly exaggerated account of the superstitious fervour that was supposed to be endemic to the event. Indeed, there seemed to be a general sense of reverence among those who were briefly touching religious objects to the top of the marble slab.

After about fifteen or twenty minutes, the crowd had thinned considerably. I had been monitoring closely the other members of our group present in the crypt, but by now they had already climbed the stairs and disappeared. I placed myself at the very back of the dozen or so people who were lining up for the tomb. Eventually it was my turn, and I entered through the open gate and stood by Padre Pio's tomb—the very last person in that night's procession. I was a little nervous and gave the giant friar in front of me a slightly goofy grin before I opened the bag and began to touch the rosaries to the surface of the tomb. I had already planned how I was going to do this efficiently. My anorak had big pockets, so I would pick each rosary out of the bag one at a time, touch it quickly to the tomb, and place it in a pocket before moving on the next one. That way, each rosary would "get done," and there would be no danger of mixing up those already done with those still in the bag.

"*Santo cielo!*" said the friar when he saw the size of my bag, and he waved his hand in a circular motion. "*Dai! Dai!*" ("*Dai!*" is a fairly benign way of saying "Get a move on!")

By the time I had about thirty of the rosaries done, the big friar was beginning to shuffle impatiently and mutter to himself.

"*Quasi finito!* [Almost finished!]" I said breezily and looked up towards him with what I hoped was a reassuring smile. As I was turning back to the task, however, I spotted something that almost gave me a heart attack. In the semidarkness, I could see a figure kneeling outside the metal railing just a few yards from me, hands gripped tightly on the vertical bars. It was Dickie. He was not looking me in the face. His eyes were riveted on the bag of rosary beads in my hand and my action of rubbing the beads on the top of the tomb. There was an almost manic look of jubilancy on his countenance.

All energy left me, and I felt like slumping on top of the tomb myself. I have a vague recollection of wondering what Dickie would think if the giant friar had to drag me and my bag of rosary beads out of the crypt. But now I had no choice but to finish what was started. Lethargically, I touched the last twenty rosaries, one by one, to the marble, stuffed them in my pockets, and staggered away towards the stairs, accompanied by a chorus of grumbles from the giant friar—they could have been swear words for all I knew, or cared, at that moment. I left the basilica in a daze, feeling completely vanquished.

As I walked down the hill towards the hotel, my only thought was how I was going to face Dickie tomorrow. I knew that he would be sitting at the front of the coach in the morning with an infuriating look of triumph on his face. How could I rebut any of his criticisms now? Whatever little credibility I might have had previously had now totally evaporated. And the real source of humiliation was that not a single person in the crypt this evening had shown the slightest display of "superstitious fervour" —except for me.

Amid the humiliation that I would feel over the next few days, however, there was also a benefit, though it would take me a while to appreciate that fact. During the next couple of years, I would take other groups to the recitation of the Rosary at Padre Pio's tomb, but none would have to endure my instructions on the right and wrong way of making third-class relics.

A long time after this event, I came to know something of the life and work of Saint John of Damascus. He lived in eighth-century Syria at a time when there was major controversy in the Church regarding the legitimacy of venerating relics and using sacred images. Islam had just become a major power in the region, and it had a zero-tolerance policy with regard to images. The Byzantine emperor, partially influenced by this policy of his new neighbours, wished to cleanse Christianity of "idolatrous" tendencies. Thus began a number of campaigns of iconoclasm—the destruction of images. The purging of icons, statues, and other works of art was often violent and involved loss of life. What John of Damascus did was to make a clear and systematic distinction, for the first time, between the worship that can be given to God alone and the veneration that can be legitimately given to images for what they represent. He argued that when God became incarnate, the era of the faceless God was ended. For the first time in history, God had a human face and could be represented in pictorial form, overcoming the rightful prohibition on images that was found in the Old Testament. Through the Incarnation, salvation was achieved by means of material creation. Physical objects such as statues and icons could be justly venerated for what they represented, as vehicles of God's grace, just as the physical body of Jesus was the vehicle for grace par excellence. In 787, when John of Damascus was already long dead, the Second Council of Nicaea used his ideas to condemn iconoclasm and rule on the legitimate veneration of images. From then all the way to the Protestant Reformation, Christian art was universally acknowledged as a legitimate way of venerating the God who had become incarnate. In yet another display of how God's sense of timeliness is different to ours, more than a millennium after he died, John of Damascus was made a Doctor of the Church for his vital contribution to a proper Christian understanding of images and relics. His ideas are still relevant today.

There are images, and there are images. There are relics, and there are relics. The Eucharistic miracles of the Church are in a league all of their own. The most celebrated case in Italy is that of Lanciano in Abruzzo, not far from Manoppello. In the tenth century, a monk was having doubts about the Real Presence of Christ in the Eucharist. Day after day, he struggled with this belief as he said the prayers of consecration over the bread and wine. One day, he was shocked to discover that the bread had changed visibly into flesh and the wine into blood in front of his very eyes. The local bishop was informed, and the relics were placed in special glass reliquaries so that they could be displayed to the faithful. To-day, more than one thousand years later, those relics are still on display in the church in Lanciano, and their remarkable state of preservation is not easily explained by science.

Some decades ago, scientific examinations were carried out on the eucharistic elements. It was discovered that the flesh is human heart tissue. All of the chambers of the heart are represented in the sample. In effect, the flesh has all the characteristics of an entire cross section of the human heart. The information displayed in the sanctuary has improved over the years, and the scientific investigations are now de-scribed very well in the room just below the chapel where the miracle is preserved. On one occasion, I was standing there in front of one of the displays with a group from Tip-perary.

"But why is the flesh tissue from the *heart*?" one of the pilgrims asked. "Wouldn't it make more sense if it was flesh from Jesus' hand, or his arm even? He healed with his hands. He touched the sick and raised the dead. His hands were nailed to the Cross."

There was a religious sister named Monica in the group.

"It has to be heart tissue," Sister Monica said quietly, "because God is love." And that was the perfect conclusion to that conversation.

In the seventeenth century, in a vision later approved by the Church, Jesus appeared to Margaret Mary Alacoque in Paray-le-Monial, France. She was asked to spread devotion to Jesus' Sacred Heart, a devotion that emphasizes his un-limited love and mercy for humanity. As you may have gath-ered by now, God's notion of time and timeliness is very different to ours. The Sacred Heart devotion would not be approved until seventy-five years after Margaret Mary's death, and she would not be canonised until 120 years later.

Nevertheless, the devotion was eventually important in countering the severe Jansenist spirituality that would come to dominate France—a view that focussed on human depravity and the supposed need for works of penitence to appease God's wrath.

If Jesus chose to reveal his merciful nature through the devotion to the Sacred Heart, then it is fitting that the flesh of the Eucharist in the miracle of Lanciano should be the flesh of the human heart. Sister Monica was surely right about that. A few years later, this was confirmed to me in a dramatic way. We were visiting the Duomo of Orvieto in central Italy. The cathedral was built to house the relics from a eucharistic miracle that had happened in Bolsena in 1263. Before the miracle happened, a consecrated religious called Juliana of Liège in France had been petitioning for the introduction of the feast of Corpus Christi. She had been doing so, in fact, for more than forty years but without much success. This campaign was inspired by her mystical experiences in which Christ asked her to plead for a feast to venerate the Blessed Sacrament. The archdeacon of Liège, Jacques Pantaléon, was won over to the cause, but it seemed an onerous, if not impossible, task for him to convince the universal Church to adopt such a feast. Providentially, however, Pantaléon was elected Pope Urban IV in 1261 and moved to Italy. He was residing in Orvieto when news arrived of a eucharistic miracle in the nearby town of Bolsena. A priest who was having doubts about the Real Presence of Christ in the Eucharist found that the host he had just consecrated was bleeding onto the white altar cloth known as a "corporal." The corporal was taken to Orvieto and shown to the pope. The occurrence of the miracle was the final confirmation that he needed in order to do what Juliana of Liège had requested: to introduce the feast of Corpus Christi into the calendar of the universal Church.

The great Dominican theologian Saint Thomas Aquinas was commissioned to compose the texts for the Mass for the new feast. The timeless pieces still associated with Holy Thursday and the feast of Corpus Christi, such as "Pange Lingua," were the result. It seems appropriate that the theologian who had formulated the classic expression of the doctrine of *transubstantiation* (the belief that the substance or essence of the bread and wine are changed into the Body and Blood of Christ) should have been the one chosen to write the beautiful liturgy for the feast. A stunning cathedral was built to house the miracle, and the most important part of the cathedral is the Chapel of the Corporal. This is covered from top to bottom with frescoes depicting the occurrence of the miracle to the disbelieving priest, the procession with the corporal to Orvieto, the commissioning of Saint Thomas Aquinas to write the Mass, and other scenes.

Martin Luther and King Henry VIII both believed in the Real Presence of Christ in the Eucharist, but as the Reformation gathered momentum, most of the "reformers" jettisoned the belief as a superstition. Once the interpretation of Scripture is cut loose from legitimate authority in the Church and becomes a matter of subjective taste, then no dogma is ultimately safe. The thirty-nine articles issued by the Church of England under Queen Elizabeth in 1563 denied transubstantiation and banned the Mass. Indeed, for the century and a half preceding Catholic Emancipation in 1829, all aspirants to public office in Britain had to take an oath denying transubstantiation.

The Cathedral in Orvieto may as well have been a million miles away from this controversy. The belief that Jesus is truly present in the eucharistic elements emanates from every stone and piece of mortar. Our group had Mass in the chapel of the miracle, though the corporal itself was not on display. The cabinet in which it is housed was closed, being opened only on special occasions. During the homily, the priest, Father Eugene, told us that he wanted to speak about another eucharistic wonder entirely. I perked up my ears. Why would he talk about another miracle rather than the one hidden behind the doors of the cabinet in front of us, I wondered?

He told how, in 1996, in Buenos Aires, a host was found at the back of a church after Mass. The parish priest, Father Alejandro Pezet, followed the standard practice for discarded hosts that cannot be easily consumed: he placed it in a container of water so that it would dissolve naturally in a matter of days, at which point it would be poured away in a respectful manner. The container of water was placed in the tabernacle of the Blessed Sacrament chapel. Eight days later, when the tabernacle was opened, Father Pezet was surprised to find that the host had not dissolved but had grown larger and taken on the appearance of bloodied flesh. He informed his bishop, who had the relics photographed. The container was placed back in the tabernacle, where it would remain untouched for more than three years.

By this point, the same bishop—Jorge Bergoglio by name —had become a cardinal, and he decided that the host should be subjected to a proper scientific investigation. On October 5, 1999, a sample was removed in the presence of witnesses and sent to New York for examination. In order not to prejudice the analysis, the scientists in New York were not told where it had come from. The team included well-known cardiologist Dr Frederick Zugibe. After the test, he testified that the tissue came from the muscle of the left ventricle of a human heart, the ventricle that pumps blood to the entire body. The sample contained a high number of white blood cells. White blood cells usually die outside a living organism, which indicated that this heart tissue was somehow still alive—a fact that Dr Zugibe found inexplicable. In addition, the white blood cells had penetrated into the heart tissue, which was evidence of severe trauma, as if the owner had been beaten cruelly about the chest.

When Dr Zugibe heard that the sample had been kept for years in water, he was dumbfounded. Even if the heart had been removed from a living human being in 1996, the white blood cells should have ceased to exist in a matter of minutes. A further investigation was then done in which the lab reports from the Buenos Aires miracle were compared with the lab reports from the relics at Lanciano. The experts making the comparison did not know the origin of either report, but they concluded that they must have originated from test samples obtained from the same person, a person with an AB positive blood type, characteristic of a man who was born in the Middle East.

As we sat in front of the cabinet of the eucharistic miracle at Orvieto, we did not need all the dots joined up for us. Lanciano, Orvieto, and Buenos Aires were all part of the same mystery. "The cup of blessing which we bless, is it not a participation in the blood of Christ? The bread which we break, is it not a participation in the body of Christ? Because there is one bread, we who are many are one body, for we all partake of the one bread" (1 Cor 10:16–17). It is not the easiest thing to believe in the Real Presence of Christ in the Eucharist. In fact, chapter 6 of John's Gospel tells us that many people turned away from following Jesus after he taught them that he was offering his body as their true nourishment. Our faith is weak, but the Lord has given

us these great signs to assist us—and not just the signs themselves, but the providential context in which they are given.
A churchman is convinced by Juliana of Liège of the need
to introduce the feast of Corpus Christi, but he is just a
provincial pastor in what is now Belgium and has little influence. Then, out of the blue, he is elected pope and comes
to reside in Orvieto just in time to be presented with a corporal stained in blood that seeped from a piece of unleav-
ened bread. In the Buenos Aires case, a bishop ascertains,
with the help of scientists, that this host has become living
human heart tissue. And then the bishop becomes a cardinal,
and the cardinal becomes Pope Francis, giving the miracle a
profile and a prestige that it would not have had otherwise.

A living human heart traumatised by physical suffering.
God is love. "This is my body, given for you." All of this
was swimming around in our heads that evening as we drove
back to Rome. We were staying at the Irish College, and the
group had free time to go out for dinner. At 9:00, we gathered again at the gate of the college for our evening walk,
which would take in the Colosseum and part of the Forum.
As usual, I led the group to the north side of the Colosseum, where the outer wall is perfectly preserved. Here we
could see the beautiful architectural features: the deliberate
inclusion of the three orders of Greek columns—the Doric,
Ionic, and Corinthian—in the three levels of archways, the
special entrance reserved for the emperor, and the crucifix
set up by John Paul II on the podium where the emperor
would have sat; the emperor was often revered as a god, and
John Paul II wanted the cross of the one true God placed
on that podium once occupied by the leader of Rome.

As was often the case on one of my "tours," I had a
personal hobbyhorse that I was intent on hammering home
above all else.

"Were Christians martyred in the Colosseum?" I asked the group. It was a rhetorical question, but someone replied anyhow before I could continue.

"Sure they were," a lady answered. "They were thrown to the lions here, right?"

"This guidebook here says that we have no documentary evidence that Christians were killed in the Colosseum," I said, waving a copy of a fairly prestigious series in front of the group. "And it really bothers me that books like this take it upon themselves to dismiss some of our most venerable traditions!"

"Oh yes, but the standard history was written by the Christians *after* they had prevailed over the Romans. So why should we believe an account of history that was written from the point of view of the victors?" It was the same lady who was speaking, now turned devil's advocate.

"Because the victors held up truthfulness as a virtue, for starters! But actually, the issue is much easier than that to resolve. We have plenty of documentation from the early centuries that Christians were persecuted. For example, Pliny, writing at the end of the first century, tells us that those who persistently professed the name of Christ were led out to execution. We also know that the Colosseum was used as a place of public execution of criminals on death row. Putting two and two together, we can say confidently that Christians on death row were executed at the Colosseum."

I looked around at the group and waved the guidebook at them again. "But this book is complaining that we have no documentary evidence that Christians died in the Colosseum! Do they think that someone is going to come up with a death certificate saying something like 'Theophilus with an address at Via Appia 64 was killed by the lions at midday in the Colosseum'?"

"Okay, that would be difficult," the lady admitted. "But still you would think we would know the name of *some* Christian who was killed at the Colosseum."

"And we do!" I replied animatedly. "One of the most famous martyrs of the early Church was thrown to the lions here! His name was Saint Ignatius of Antioch. According to tradition, he was a disciple of Saint John the Evangelist and was appointed bishop of Antioch by Saint Peter himself. After his arrest, he was taken in chains to Rome to be publicly executed at the Colosseum."

I paused for a moment and took out the sheet of paper that I usually produced at this point of the tour. It was a summary of some central affirmations from Saint Ignatius. During his journey to Rome, he wrote various letters to Christian communities in different parts of the empire. Seven of these letters have survived, and they contain vital information about the creed and practice of the early Church.

"What Ignatius writes in his letters has all the more power and credibility because it comes from a man who knows he is on his way to imminent martyrdom. Would you like to hear a little summary of his writings here in the place where he was killed for these very beliefs?"

My captive audience didn't have much alternative but to say yes, so I began to go through the three points on the list. Before starting, though, I reminded them of who Ignatius was.

"Don't forget, this is from a man who was a disciple of John the Evangelist! Not only is he very close to the time of Christ; we can also be confident that what he is writing is the authentic teaching of the apostles."

The first point was Ignatius' avowal of the real Incarnation of God as a human being who offered his life for us on the Cross. The second was his description of the Church as being organised under a structure of local bishops who alone could authorize the administration of sacraments such as Baptism or the Eucharist.

Something about the next item on the list made me pause. I had read from this same sheet of paper on many other occasions as I stood in front of the Colosseum, but the fact that we had just visited Orvieto made this last item stand out. It was a quotation from Ignatius on the Real Presence of Christ in the Eucharist. "Consider those who are of a different opinion with respect to the grace of Christ which has come unto us, how opposed they are to the will of God. . . . They abstain from the Eucharist and from prayer, because they confess not the Eucharist to be the flesh of our Saviour Jesus Christ, which suffered for our sins, and which the Father, of His goodness, raised up again. Those, therefore, who speak against this gift of God, incur death in the midst of their disputes."[1]

I was no theologian, but even I could sense there was a profound connection between what we had experienced earlier in Orvieto and the testimony of Ignatius in this place to the very giving of his blood. Jesus offered himself for men in the sacrifice of the Cross. We partake of this one offering in the Eucharist and also through the offering of ourselves for the Church in our daily struggles. How well Saint Ignatius of Antioch participated in the immolation of Christ! Afterwards, as we climbed the Caelian Hill towards the Lateran Basilica, the words from Ignatius' Letter to the Romans came to mind: "Allow me to become food for the wild beasts, through [whom] it will be granted me to attain to God. I am the wheat of God, and let me be ground by the

[1] Letter to the Smyrneans, chs. 6–7, translated in *Ante-Nicene Christian Library*, vol. 1, ed. and trans. Alexander Roberts and James Donaldson (Edinburgh: T&T Clark, 1867).

teeth of the wild beasts, that I may be found the pure bread
of Christ. . . . Then shall I truly be a disciple of Christ. . . .
Entreat Christ for me, that by these instruments I may be
found a sacrifice [to God]."[2] This man who had testified
to the Real Presence of Christ in the bread would himself
become bread for the life of the Church.

The next day, in the afternoon, we were standing in
Santa Maria della Pace near Piazza Navona. This magnificent church is filled with many works of art, the most famous being Raphael's fresco of the Sibyls on the back right
wall. The Sibyls were female oracles of ancient Greece and
Rome who, according to some commentators, were divinely
inspired and foretold the coming of the Saviour. Father Eugene wanted to use this fresco to summarize the things we
had seen in the previous days.

"Everything that we do in the Church is part of God's
plan and has a definite purpose," he said. "The celebration
of the sacrifice of Christ in the Eucharist remains the central
event in the life of the Church. It is this practice that makes
present among us the self-giving of Christ on Calvary."

He looked around, wondering if anyone was following
him.

"Look at these Sibyls! They demonstrate that God's plan
to redeem us was written into the very fabric of history from
the beginning. The Lord was on his way! He was coming
to shepherd us, to feed us with his body, to pardon our
sins, to take flesh in the womb of a virgin. But it would not
happen according to a human conception of when the time
was right. It would happen in God's time, in the fullness of
time."

---

[2] Letter to the Romans, ch. 4, translated in *Ante-Nicene Fathers*, vol. 1.

8

In the Fullness of Time

How long, O LORD? Will you forget me for ever? How long will you hide your face from me?

—Psalms 13:1

Therefore he shall give them up until the time when she who has labor pains has brought forth. . . . And he shall stand and feed his flock in the strength of the LORD, in the majesty of the name of the LORD his God.

—Micah 5:3–4

October 19, 2003. We were on our way to the beatification of Mother Teresa of Calcutta in Saint Peter's Square. More than three hundred thousand people were expected, and we had left our hotel early that morning in the hope of getting into a good position for the ceremony. All of the traffic had been negotiated, and we were almost at our destination, but there was a problem. The attendant wouldn't let us enter the coach park to drop off our group. The parking permit we had was not acceptable, he said. It was only a fax, whereas he needed to see the original.

"But this is how the Missionaries of Charity sent us our permit—by fax! We don't have anything more original!" I protested.

Unusually, all the arrangements for the beatification— parking permits, tickets for the event, ambulance services, and so forth—were being made by Mother Teresa's own order, the Missionaries of Charity, in cooperation with the Vatican and the City of Rome. Our coach had been assigned to a parking area on Via Gregorio VII, not too far from Saint Peter's Square. Regulations were extremely tight, and we had to drop off inside our designated coach park. Any unauthorized drop-offs on the side of the street would have led to a fine. And there were police everywhere.

The attendant refused to be swayed by my protests. Eventually, our coach driver, Mauro, called me aside. "How long have you been working in this city, and you still don't know how things operate?" he rasped in a frustrated tone.

"What do you mean?" I asked, taken aback.

"This guy is obviously trying to earn a little bit of cash on the side. It doesn't matter a damn whether the permit is a fax or an 'original'! Do you really think *that's* the issue here! He'll dig his heels in until you bribe him. Just give him fifty euro, and he'll let us in, no problem!"

I was fuming, but we couldn't afford to lose more time while Saint Peter's Square was already filling rapidly for the ceremony. Mauro understood that I couldn't bring myself to hand the money to the attendant, or even look him in the face, so he took the fifty-euro note from me and slipped it discreetly to the man sitting in the kiosk. The barrier opened instantly, and we drove in and disembarked. We were on our way to the biggest event of the year, but I was shaken. Nowadays, if people ask me what it was like to attend the beatification of Mother Teresa, I have to confess that I don't remember much, apart from bribing my way in.

A couple of years later, I had my second experience of blatant bribery in Rome, and the circumstances were even more sacred than the previous time. In the fourth century, Saint Helen, mother of the emperor Constantine, had ordered excavations in Jerusalem on Mount Calvary. They found what Helen believed were the remains of the true Cross. Nearby, a tomb cut in the rock was identified as the holy sepulchre of Jesus. A church was built over the site of the tomb and, to commemorate its opening, a portion of the Cross was put there for veneration by the public. It was September 14, 335, a date that henceforth would be commemorated as the feast of the Exaltation of the Cross. To mark that feast in 2005, our Padre Pio group wished to visit the Basilica of the Holy Cross in Jerusalem, but it was not available on account of the ceremonies that were taking place there. Instead, I took the group to an alternative church that contained some relics of the Passion. We had a busy day, and we arrived at the church in the evening, only about twenty minutes before its scheduled closing time. That was still more than enough time for the sort of visit we intended. As I approached the entrance with the group in tow behind me, however, I noticed that the door was already being closed. An elegantly dressed man in a suit was peering out.

"Sorry, we're not allowing anyone else in at this point," he said. "Those who are inside already can remain until closing time, but there will be no further admittance." And with that, he began closing the door in my face.

"But your closing time is not for another twenty minutes!" I protested, placing my hand on the door. "We just want to make a short visit. This group is heading to San Giovanni Rotondo tomorrow, and this is our last chance!"

The man looked me up and down. "Where are you from?" he asked.

"Where are we from?" I replied, not sure where this was leading. Then I continued hesitantly. "Ire . . . land, actually. Why?"

The man looked around him furtively, as if to make sure

that none of his colleagues were in earshot. "Can you send me a crate of Black Bush? I love that whiskey, but it's hard to get it over here."

"Black Bush?" I replied slowly. I had no idea how much it would cost to send a crate from Ireland to Italy, but at that moment I was prepared to go along with any proposal that got us access to the church.

"I'm not sure if I can manage that. How . . . how would I send it to you?" I asked, in mock innocence.

Suddenly the door was thrown open wide for us. "You come over here, and I'll give you my details," the man said. "The group can go on ahead and begin their visit."

It was a surreal feeling standing inside the church while the man wrote his address at the little table beside the door. Bribing my way into a church with whiskey was an entirely new experience. I looked around at the scene before me. Our pilgrims were happily doing their spiritual exercises, oblivious to the unholy means used to gain entry. Soon the man had written his details in perfect copperplate on a slip of paper and presented it to me. The door of the church was closed, and our group had a very private and exclusive visit to the place. When I got home later that night and told Laura that I had promised to send a crate of Black Bush to the church custodian, she immediately flew into a temper.

"There is no way that you are obliged to keep a promise of that sort!" she said.

"But we never would have gotten in otherwise."

"It doesn't matter! Over my dead body will we use whiskey as payment for getting into a church!"

It was probably around then that I began to become more aware of the kind of role I often played as the chaperone of these pilgrim groups. People in my job were generally referred to as the "guide" or the "courier," but the job description of "fixer" would have been more apt. It was often a business of solving problems using whatever means were available—threatening, bribing, bluffing, telling half-truths —so that the programme on the brochure would be successfully completed. But by the end of each evening, one might not necessarily be proud of what had transpired during the day.

Back in 2003, even though I had attended the beatification of Mother Teresa and was impressed by what I knew of her, I knew very little about her. Over the next few years, however, her story and spirituality began to emerge almost by accident for me as we took groups around Rome.

Sometimes we did a walking tour that crossed the Caelian Hill from the Church of Saint Stephen in the Round (Santo Stefano Rotondo) to that of Saint Gregory the Great (San Gregorio Magno). On the way we would pass a historic basilica built over the homes of two Roman soldiers, John and Paul, martyred under the emperor Julian in 362. The excavations beneath this basilica of Giovanni and Paolo reveal one of the best-preserved Roman residential complexes in existence. They contain strikingly beautiful frescoes, with both Christian and pre-Christian themes.

During this walk, almost inevitably, we would meet sisters of the order of Mother Teresa, the Missionaries of Charity, along the way. They were always in groups of six or eight, moving much more quickly than our group and often overtaking us with a friendly *"Buongiorno!"* as they walked by. They stood out for their general youthfulness and good humour. It didn't take long to discover that they had a large house right next to the Church of Saint Gregory the Great.

"What do they do in Rome?" I wondered at first, before discovering that they had had houses in the city since 1968 and were very involved in helping the poor and the homeless in various ways. In 1988, Pope John Paul gave Mother Teresa property within Vatican City, and this continues to be used as a soup kitchen. Before 2016, coaches were still allowed to drive up the Via della Conciliazione and around the outside of the left colonnade of Saint Peter's Square. The coach would then emerge in front of the Congregation for the Doctrine of the Faith (the old "Holy Office"), and a courier could point out Mother Teresa's soup kitchen next door, at the corner of Vatican City. Beside a low door, there was a simple marble plaque with the words *Dono di Maria* (Gift of Mary). Our groups were usually generally impressed that this kind of work was taking place within Vatican City, which otherwise had an air of opulence.

Everyone who travelled with us seemed to accept that Mother Teresa was a tireless worker among the underprivileged and specialized in seeking out the poorest among the poor, especially the dying and those who seemed to have no hope left. Considerable damage had been done to her reputation by a British journalist named Christopher Hitchens. For years, he had waged a savage campaign against her, claiming that she did little to alleviate poverty but rather used the misery of the poor to promote a particular brand of religion. Apart from her heroically charitable works, however, no one—including me—seemed to know much about her. Mother Teresa was simply the woman who had given her life to helping the poor. Imagine my surprise, then, when a priest leading one of our groups launched into a description of her character in the most unlikely of places—while visiting a painting by Caravaggio in central Rome.

It was a few weeks before the canonisation of Mother Teresa in 2016, and we were in the French national church, San Luigi dei Francesi. In the top left chapel of this church hang three masterpieces by Michelangelo Merisi, an artist better known as "Caravaggio" to distinguish him from the other, more famous, Michelangelo. Caravaggio had a colourful life. A notorious brawler, he killed a man in a duel and then had to flee Rome with the charge of homicide hanging over him. Though eventually granted a papal pardon, he died of fever on a beach in southern Italy while waiting for a ship to take him back to Rome. He was only thirty-eight years old.

The three paintings in the Contarelli Chapel of San Luigi made Caravaggio the most famous painter of Rome in his day. They depict the call of Saint Matthew, the writing of his Gospel, and his martyrdom, respectively. San Luigi dei Francesi stands halfway between the Pantheon and the beautiful pedestrian square of Piazza Navona, so it has more foot traffic than any other church in the city centre, with the possible exception of Santi Vincenzo e Anastasio at the Trevi Fountain. We call in to San Luigi to see the Caravaggio paintings as a matter of course with virtually every group we take to Rome. On this occasion, I gave my usual description. I was not expecting to hear anyone use the paintings to describe the life of Mother Teresa.

"The painting here on the left shows the call of Saint Matthew," I began. "We see Christ pointing his finger at Matthew, who is sitting at the table surrounded by a motley crew of characters. With one hand, Matthew is pointing to himself, as if to say, 'Who are you calling, Lord? Not me, surely?' but the other hand is still on the pile of money! He was a tax collector, and at this point he hasn't yet made the decision to leave everything and follow Jesus. But does anyone notice anything about Jesus' hand?"

"The hand that is pointing at Matthew?"

"Yes."

There was a pause for a moment. Then a girl in the group, who wasn't much more than eleven years of age, said "It looks like *The Creation of Adam* on the ceiling of the Sistine Chapel."

That was exactly it! Michelangelo's depiction in the Sistine shows God the Father, in the act of creation, extending his hand towards the limp and rather lifeless hand of the first Adam. Caravaggio painted the same hand on Jesus as Adam has on the ceiling of the Sistine Chapel. Why did he do this? To highlight the fact that Jesus is the New Adam, the one in whom the new creation of humanity is accomplished through his Passion, death, and Resurrection. In fact, in the bars of the window above where Jesus is standing, Caravaggio had depicted the Cross.

"God the Father extended his hand towards Adam in the original act of creation," I continued. "Now Jesus extends his hand towards Matthew in a new act of creation. When Jesus calls you and me to follow him, to take up our crosses and go wherever we are led, then we are created anew, made into true children of God.

"On the ceiling of the Sistine, it was God the Father who did everything, making Adam from the dust of the earth. And here it is the Second Adam who is the main actor, making the tax collector into a new man. Matthew only has to follow!"

I had gotten carried away talking about how being called by Jesus is actually an act of being created into something new and had forgotten completely to talk about the famous chiaroscuro technique of the artist. This is the use of strong contrasts between light and dark for dramatic effect, and Caravaggio was a master of it. Just as I was about to launch into a description, however, the steward of the church came over angrily and asked us to leave. Before bringing the group to the Contarelli Chapel, I had asked his permission to speak, but evidently he had had enough.

"Via, via, via! Everyone out! Too much noise! This is a church, not a marketplace!"

Not for the first time, I made my way out of a church in Rome with my tail between my legs. As we gathered outside on the steps, Father Sean indicated that he wanted to say a word to the group.

"Did you notice the chiaroscuro effect used by Caravaggio?" he asked. "The contrast between light and dark is used to bring things into sharp relief and give them more body. And did you know that the life of Mother Teresa, who is going to be canonised in two weeks' time, was also characterised by light and dark?"

I had no idea what Father Sean was referring to. He went on. "Mother Teresa was a shining light in the world. She brought peace and consolation to untold thousands, but she herself went through fifty years of darkness, a spiritual desert in which she felt forsaken and abandoned by God."

All of this was news to most of us, but we could see the point that Father Sean wished to make with regard to the work of Caravaggio. It is the darkness in the paintings that makes the rest stand out so dramatically. Without the dark areas, the figures would have neither form nor depth.

"If Mother Teresa's life had all been consolation, joy, and plain sailing, then it would already have been a remarkable existence," Father Sean continued. "But she persisted in serving the poor in the manner she did despite the spiritual darkness she was feeling inside. That made that service all the more astonishing."

These words stirred my curiosity, and that night, I found an article on the Internet describing the protracted dark night of the soul that Mother Teresa experienced. The article described how the nun had received "a call within a call" while on a train journey to Darjeeling. For a period of several months, she experienced interior locutions in which Christ spoke to her and called her out of her current situation as a sister of Loreto to found a new congregation dedicated to the poorest of the poor. As soon as the Vatican approved the new congregation, however, the locutions stopped, and the nun was plunged into decades of darkness, in which she constantly struggled with feelings of being rejected and abandoned by God. This experience she kept largely to herself; it made general headlines only when her personal correspondence was published posthumously in 2007 in the book *Come Be My Light.*

I had never heard of this book, but the Internet article revealed that its publication caused consternation in some quarters. Many people were bewildered by the extreme spiritual desert in which Mother Teresa had existed. Did she suffer from depression? Had she lost faith? Such an experience of distance from God was surely incompatible with sanctity, some people felt. Predictably, Christopher Hitchens wasted no time in declaring that the correspondence revealed that Mother Teresa was a "confused old lady" who had "ceased to believe."[1]

It was the week before the canonisation, and I was with a different group in Rome. They were being subjected to my "standard" tour of Saint John Lateran Basilica. The tour would begin outside at the great obelisk in the Lateran Square. This four-hundred-tonne stone, the largest of its kind in the world, originally stood in Egypt and was transported to Rome in the fourth century and placed in

[1] "Hitchens Takes on Mother Teresa," *Newsweek,* August 28, 2007, newsweek.com/hitchens-takes-mother-teresa-99721.

the Circus Maximus. In the late sixteenth century, the excavations ordered by Pope Sixtus V rediscovered it in three pieces. It was then erected in front of the Lateran Basilica.

It was a good spot to recount the story of how the emperor Constantine had permitted Christianity to be practiced freely after the Battle of the Milvian Bridge. Before the battle, the future emperor had seen a cross in the sky and had heard the words "In this sign you will conquer." According to the legend, he had his soldiers paint the cross on their shields before entering into battle. The battle was won, and the emperor legalised Christianity and gave the very land on which we were standing to the pope for the construction of the first Christian basilica in Rome. Thus, the Lateran bears the title "Mother and Head" of all the churches in the city and the world. I showed the group the inscription on the base of the obelisk: *Constantinus per crucem victor a Silvestro hic baptizatus crucis gloriam propagavit* (Constantine, victorious through the cross, was here baptized by Sylvester, spreading the glory of the Cross). Historians are agreed that Constantine was actually baptized outside Rome towards the end of his life, and not by the hand of Pope Sylvester, but the general message of the inscription is to link the victory in battle with his eventual Baptism. What is sometimes left out of this story is the crucial role played by Constantine's mother, Helen, in bringing the persecutions to a halt. She was a fervent believer and had prayed constantly for the conversion of her son.

As we walked around to the main entrance of the basilica, I noticed on the street many of Mother Teresa's sisters, in their distinctive blue and white habits. The Missionaries of Charity were everywhere on account of the impending canonisation in a few days' time. In fact, all of Rome was a sea of blue and white during those days. Our tour then moved inside the basilica, and we discussed the many vicissitudes of the story of this building through the Middle Ages up until the mid-1600s. Again, there were dozens of sisters in their characteristic habits in the basilica at that moment. The words of accusation that Christopher Hitchens had directed at Mother Teresa came back to me momentarily as we took up a position at the back of the church, just inside the enormous bronze door that had once hung in the Senate building in the Forum. This was my favourite part of the tour. The stewards had already asked me to keep my voice down, so I asked the forty-strong group to gather as tightly as they could around me while we considered the "poor man's Bible" on the upper walls of the nave. These panels in plaster (stucco) were designed about 1650 by Alessandro Algardi. The panels on the left side of the nave have scenes from the Old Testament, and the panels on the right have a corresponding panel from the New Testament. They are a great illustration of how the New Testament is prefigured in the Old, and how the Old is fulfilled in the New.

We began by looking at the two panels closest to the great bronze door.

"What do you think is represented there?" I asked, pointing to the one on the left. Some wild interpretations have been proposed to me over the years, not all of them biblical in nature.

"Is it Daniel getting eaten by lions?" someone asked.

"Well, Daniel doesn't actually get eaten by lions in the Bible," I replied drily. "Anyone else?"

"Oh, *I* know what it is!" said a woman, with a look of enlightenment on her face. "It's the beast in the Book of Revelation!"

"Sorry to disappoint you, madam, but it's not the beast.

Look a bit closer. Do you see how the man seems to be coming out of the mouth of a sea creature of some sort?"

"Oh!" said someone else. "It must be Jonah coming out of the belly of the whale!"

There were murmurs of agreement all around. Then we looked at the panel on the opposite side, and most people recognized immediately that it showed Christ emerging from the tomb at the Resurrection. We discussed then how Jesus had foretold his Resurrection by describing it in terms of what had happened to Jonah: "Then some of the scribes and Pharisees said to him, 'Teacher, we wish to see a sign from you.' But he answered them, 'An evil and adulterous generation seeks for a sign; but no sign shall be given to it except the sign of the prophet Jonah. For as Jonah was three days and three nights in the belly of the whale, so will the Son of man be three days and three nights in the heart of the earth'" (Mt 12:38-40).

Of course, there was great irony in these words. This sign that Jesus eventually gives is unexpected and not welcomed by many, but it is not a minor sign. The Resurrection is the most significant event in history. The great value of Algardi's panels is that they place together these two signs—the deliverance of Jonah from the jaws of the whale and the deliverance of man from the jaws of death—and they challenge us to heed Jesus' words that foretold his Resurrection. Evil and adulterous race that we are, how indifferent and unbelieving we are before the sign of Jonah!

We moved up the basilica to my favourite panel in the entire series. Again, I asked the group if they recognized the scene.

"Is it Joan of Arc about to be burned?" suggested someone, shielding his eyes from the glare of the midday sun pouring through the window high up in the nave.

"No, these are biblical scenes, remember? It's the 'poor man's Bible.' We're looking for correspondences between the Old and New Testaments. Can you see a man with a knife about to slay a boy who is tied above a pyre of wood?"

"It's the sacrifice of Isaac!"

"Exactly!" Even though it was already familiar to most people, I recounted the story from Genesis 22.

God promised Abraham that he would be the father of a great nation. Though he and his wife had no children at the time and were greatly advanced in age, Abraham trusted in the Lord. His faith was rewarded when Sara gave birth to Isaac. How happy Abraham must have been finally to have a son! But then the Lord speaks to Abraham again: "Take your son, your only-begotten son Isaac, whom you love, and go to the land of Moriah, and offer him there as a burnt offering upon one of the mountains of which I shall tell you."

Abraham sets out to do as he is bid. As they journey to the mountain, the old man places the wood for the sacrifice on the shoulders of Isaac. The boy looks around him and says, "Daddy, I see the wood for the burnt offering, but where is the lamb?"

"Don't worry, my son!" his father replies. "God himself will provide a lamb." Abraham's heart must be breaking! He believes that the lamb who God intends to be sacrificed is this very son that he loves. Yet Abraham does as he is commanded, abandoning himself into the hands of the Lord, despite the utter darkness of the situation. Isaac is bound and placed on top of the pyre of wood. Abraham takes out the knife, but at the last moment God relents. "Do not lay your hand on the boy or do anything to him, for now I know that you fear God, seeing you have not withheld your son, your only son, from me."

We looked up at the expression of fear and submission on the face of Isaac. He too shares in the obedience and trust of Abraham. He could easily have run away, but he submits himself to the will of the Lord. Then we turned and looked across at the corresponding panel on the other side of the nave. There was an audible gasp from the group. Everyone appreciated its significance instantly. Christ has fallen beneath the weight of the Cross. Like Isaac, he carries the wood of the sacrifice on his shoulders. But in this case God does not relent. The only son, the beloved, is led to the sacrifice on a mountain that the Lord indicates, a mountain called Calvary. What Abraham had believed from the beginning we now discover: God is the ultimate provider; God gives, even to the annihilation of himself.

I am not a great public speaker. Someone once described my commentary on the coach as being akin to a mouse squeaking into the microphone. My knowledge and appreciation of art is poor, maybe because I grew up in the country and spent most of my teenage years playing sports (mediocrely). Anything I ever say to our groups is just material regurgitated from someone else. In spite of this, over many years, when pointing out to people the correspondences between these two panels, I have rarely failed to notice tears in some pilgrims' eyes. There is something in these biblical works of art that touches people's hearts, transcending the deficiencies of any guide.

I was pleased that a couple of Mother Teresa's sisters had joined our tour some time previously and were listening intently at the back. They were not aware of the honour they were doing us. Suddenly it struck me that these panels were relevant to the feeling of abandonment that Mother Teresa had suffered during her dark night of the soul. That journey of darkness and doubt that Abraham made with Isaac to the land of Moriah was the journey that she had made for fifty years. It was the journey to Calvary and Resurrection. And, like Abraham, she had never stopped trusting.

On September 3, 2016, Laura, the children, and I boarded a plane in Rome and flew to Dublin. Our pilgrimage was over, and the new school year was about to begin. Mother Teresa was canonised in Saint Peter's Square the following day. The trip had been organised before the canonisation date was announced; otherwise, the plans would probably have been made differently. It was disappointing not to attend, especially after these new details (for me) about Mother Teresa's life were beginning to emerge. As we watched the ceremony on the Internet, the revelation of the fifty years of darkness often came to my mind. Certainly, I could see how a great saint could have been "afflicted" by God in this way. In the Letter to the Hebrews we read that God disciplines the one whom he loves. But *fifty* years of discipline? Wasn't that a bit much, even for a saint? Was there something more to this story?

A week or two later, I was back in Italy with a new pilgrim group from Ireland. Now, when I saw Mother Teresa's sisters happily crossing the Caelian Hill, something about them seemed different. Then I realised that it was something in my mind that had begun to change: it was that their founder had been vindicated by what had happened on September 4 in Saint Peter's Square. She needed to be vindicated in my way of looking at things because I had subconsciously given credence to the accusations that had been made against her. By the end of that week, however, any lingering doubts in my mind regarding the faithfulness of Mother Teresa had faded.

One of the days of the pilgrimage was dedicated to the figure of Saint Paul. He had been imprisoned in Rome for some years and had written letters from his cell, organised meetings, and built up the Church during that time. Eventually, probably during the persecution of Nero after the great fire of A.D. 64, he was taken out to the place now known as "Tre Fontane" (Three Fountains) and beheaded. The fact that he was a Roman citizen entitled him to this form of execution, considered more civilized than the crucifixion suffered by Saint Peter. According to the legend, Saint Paul's head rolled down the side of the slope after his execution, and three fountains sprang up at different points on the hill. A beautiful church stands on the spot, with the fountains inside at different levels, accessible by steps. It is rare now to find water in all three fountains except for sometimes in the winter.

There are two other churches on the site. One is the abbey church used by the Trappist community. Opposite this stands another church called Santa Maria Scala Coeli. According to tradition, this church was built on the spot where Saint Paul was imprisoned and where thousands of Christians were martyred two centuries later, during the persecution of Diocletian. The Christians had been used as slaves to build the enormous baths of Diocletian (near Rome's central railway station) before being executed. They are still commemorated in the liturgical calendar as Saint Zeno and companions.

Inside the little Three Fountains church, we recalled Paul's execution and read extracts from some of the letters he wrote during his imprisonment in Rome. One of these was the Letter to the Philippians and referred to Jesus as one "who, though he was in the form of God, did not count equality with God a thing to be grasped, but emptied himself, taking the form of a servant" (Phil 2:6–7). I immediately pricked up my ears when I heard the reference to being emptied.

Could this shed some light on what Mother Teresa had gone through?

The priest's reflection was exactly on this theme. It is easy to be generous, he said, when we live in abundance, but if someone is generous in the midst of a famine, then that is generosity indeed. It is easy to be peaceful when all is tranquil around you, but peacefulness amid violence and aggression is peacefulness indeed. The measure of what we give depends on the circumstances in which we give it. Christ emptied himself and then emptied himself some more, until he had poured himself out completely for us. On the Cross, in the darkness and despair of being rejected by men, he never stopped loving us utterly. It was not an easy love, and to the extent that it was a difficult love, it was also a deeper and truer love.

"It may not be a popular message nowadays," Father Michael said, "but love has little to do with nice feelings and warm sentiments. True love is proven through suffering. Suffering is the measure of love. A person who continues to love through immense suffering is someone who loves immensely."

The pathway between the church of the Three Fountains and the abbey church is lined with eucalyptus trees. These were sown in previous centuries to deter the mosquitos that bred in the malaria-infested swamps in the area. There is always something soothing about the scent of these trees in the heat of a Roman afternoon. As I walked back towards the coach, my mind, too, was beginning to feel some ease. I had been disturbed by the accusations that had been made against Mother Teresa, but now I was starting to understand just why it was that they were unfounded.

Why had she been afflicted with such spiritual suffering? When life is comfortable and easy, we do not grow. But when we are faced with tribulation, then we are given the opportunity and the means to mature and develop into something greater. God loved Mother Teresa and wanted to make her into something special. Fifty years of isolation and abandonment could do a lot of damage to some people, but to one who accepts it all with trust and humility, to one who continues to love despite the suffering, it can lead to something remarkable. By means of this darkness, had the Lord made Mother Teresa into one of the saints of the century?

The words of Christopher Hitchens came back to me. When Mother Teresa's experience of spiritual darkness was made public, he immediately dismissed her as an "unbelieving old woman." But what kind of superficial notion of faith was that? Who thinks that faith is something easy and natural, requiring no effort, as if it were merely intellectual assent to the truths of logic? Christians know from the inside that faith is not easy intellectual assent!

I recalled Father Michael's reflection. If true generosity is most clearly manifested in times of famine, then, by the same token, true faith is called upon when our reasons for believing are sparse. And if true peace is shown best in times of violence and aggression, then the peace that Mother Teresa maintained in her soul when assailed by the most violent of doubts was truly heroic. As someone who experienced little of suffering, I knew that faith in moments of tranquillity and comfort can be easy and possibly superficial. Faith in times of darkness is surely all the deeper as the darkness itself is deeper. As our coach left Tre Fontane, I had a radical thought: Was fifty years of unrelenting darkness an indicator of faith so profound as to put Mother Teresa on a level similar to that of Abraham himself?

It is funny how, when something is on your mind, everything you encounter seems to speak about that thing. Rome is full of works of religious art, and when your job involves showing people those works, it is inevitable that you will happen upon themes that seem critically relevant at any given time. We were visiting the church of Santa Maria Sopra Minerva behind the Pantheon. One of our group members was a Dominican friar, and he was very keen to visit what was one of most important churches in the care of his order in the city centre. Before entering, we took time outside to admire Bernini's beautiful sculpture of the elephant holding up the Egyptian obelisk. Once inside, I made my usual bee-line for the top chapel on the right-hand side, the Carafa Chapel.

This chapel contains the tomb of Pope Paul IV, who was a member of the Carafa family. The chapel has some of the most beautiful frescoes in Rome from the late 1400s, done by the great Filippino Lippi of Florence. Although Thomas Aquinas figures prominently in two of the scenes, the main theme is a Marian one. The highest part of the main wall of the chapel has the Assumption of Mary, and the central area over the altar has the Annunciation.

I showed the group how Lippi had incorporated Saint Thomas Aquinas and Cardinal Carafa into the scene of the Annunciation, even though neither would be born for many centuries afterwards. Thomas Aquinas is shown presenting Cardinal Carafa to the Virgin. When the fresco was painted, Carafa was still alive but Thomas had already been canonised. What is the painter trying to express? On the face of it, he is depicting Saint Thomas as introducing Carafa to Mary, which is a nice illustration of the intercession of the saints. These holy people are closer to God than we are, and so they can put in a good word for us in heavenly places. It was common enough over many centuries to depict the donor of a chapel or the patron of a work of art in biblical scenes.

However, it is hard not to imagine that there is more than this going on here. Thomas is not just presenting the cardinal to the Virgin. It is the very moment of the Annunciation. The angel Gabriel is in a dynamic pose, making his announcement to Mary, while the Holy Spirit is descending from above. Mary is attentively looking at the angel but manages to bless the cardinal at the same time! This moment is the fulcrum of history, in which all future generations are blessed through the response of the Virgin. The artist depicts the blessing that comes the way of Cardinal Carafa, but it equally comes our way if we are but open to it.

As usual, I read the passage from Zephaniah 3 that foretells the Incarnation:

> Sing aloud, O daughter of Zion;
>> shout, O Israel!
> Rejoice and exult with all your heart,
>> O daughter of Jerusalem!
> The LORD has taken away the judgments against you,
>> he has cast out your enemies.
> The King of Israel, the LORD, is in your midst;
>> you shall fear evil no more.
> On that day it shall be said to Jerusalem:
> Do not fear, O Zion;
>> let not your hands grow weak.
> The LORD, your God, is in your midst,
>> a warrior who gives victory;
> he will rejoice over you with gladness,
>> he will renew you in his love.

As I read it, something reminded me of the situation of Mother Teresa, but I couldn't work it out at that moment. We went to the main altar to pay our respects at the tomb of Saint Catherine of Siena, the mystic who brought the papacy back to Rome after the scandal of Avignon. We then visited, on the left side, the tomb of Fra Angelico, the Dominican friar who never painted without praying first and who wept whenever he depicted a Crucifixion. Later, while the group had some free time to explore the Pantheon, I went for a coffee in a bar up a side street, but I really wanted a moment to reflect on something. What was it that reminded me of Mother Teresa and her fifty years of darkness when we were standing in front of the scene of the Annunciation?

When I thought about it for a moment, I realised that it was the words of the prophet Zephaniah. On the one hand, his words are consoling; they foretell that God himself will dwell in the midst of his people and will save us. On the other hand, Zephaniah was writing about six hundred years before Christ! How God's sense of timeliness is different to ours! Israel must suffer the pain of the exile, the destruction of Jerusalem and the Temple, centuries of war and unrest, and the eventual conquest by Rome. Then, when all might seem lost, in the fullness of time God sends his angel to Israel. Israel may not have been very faithful during those long centuries, but a daughter of Zion living in Nazareth is perfectly faithful. In herself, she embodies the pure and perfect faith of her nation, permitting God to come and dwell with his people.

As with Abraham, God makes us wait for the fulfilment of his promises, not because he takes pleasure in seeing us doubt but because the overcoming of doubt and clinging to hope is what makes us grow into his children, children who entrust themselves into his hands. The more I thought about it, the more the accusations that had been thrown at Mother Teresa seemed unjust. Her years of spiritual desert had led people to consider her an "atheist," a "fraud," and an "unbelieving old woman." The accusers did not allow that real faith is fully compatible with long periods of darkness. Indeed, how else can real faith emerge if not through uncertainty and darkness? To think that she was assailed by such doubt yet never stopped believing, all the while expending her energies sacrificially to serve the poorest of the poor in the most extreme circumstances! And now her faith was being questioned by those who didn't seem to have faith themselves in the first place, while her charitable works were being criticized by people who hadn't even a minimal record of helping the poor.

The last part of the trip was spent in San Giovanni Rotondo at the shrine of Padre Pio. I do not recall much about the long drive across Italy and down the Adriatic coast. The two days in the town were filled with the usual pilgrim practices: Mass in the old church, where Padre Pio heard confessions, the high Stations of the Cross, the visit to the cell of Padre Pio and to the choir loft where he received the stigmata.

Our first visit was to the crypt of the new church to venerate the body of Padre Pio. The building is adorned with the beautiful mosaics of Jesuit father Marko Rupnik. On the ramp that descends into the crypt is a fascinating cycle showing parallel events in the lives of Padre Pio and Saint Francis of Assisi. The crypt itself is devoted to scenes from the life of Christ. The group had paid their respects, and everyone was free to make his way back to the hotel in his own time. As I walked around the back wall of the crypt, surveying the mosaics, my attention became fixed on the scene showing Christ in the Garden of Gethsemane. Evidently, I was still in my "Mother Teresa" frame of mind. Padre Pio had borne the stigmata—the visible wounds of the Crucifixion—for fifty years. What Mother Teresa had borne for fifty years: Was it not the interior spiritual wounds of the Passion of Christ? It has always been recognized by the spiritual giants of our faith that the mental and spiritual suffering of Christ in the Garden of Gethsemane was at least equal to, if not far greater than, the physical wounds of the Passion. It was surely no coincidence that Padre Pio had borne the physical marks for fifty years and Mother Teresa had borne the invisible interior marks for a similar length of time. As this thought struck me, I felt that I was having an original insight.

During the agony in the garden, Jesus approached his sleeping disciples and asked them if they could keep watch with him for one hour. He asked the same of Mother Teresa, and she responded by remaining with him in this state for more than fifty years—440,000 hours. If we conclude that she was an atheist or a fraud for remaining in this state for so long, then we have understood little of the meaning of faith. I looked at the mosaic more closely. Christ is shown on his knees with his head and arms bent over a great rock. Above him is positioned *another* rock jutting out from the mountainside. Jesus is being ground into bread for the world by the two stones of the mill! Was not Mother Teresa also ground into the most perfect bread by her endurance of the spiritual darkness? Did she not also, like Padre Pio, participate in the suffering of Christ to a remarkable degree?

I recalled a passage that Father Michael had read to us in the previous days when he was reflecting on the presentation of Jesus in the Temple:

> Behold, I send my messenger to prepare the way before me, and the LORD whom you seek will suddenly come to his temple; the messenger of the covenant in whom you delight, behold, he is coming, says the LORD of hosts. But who can endure the day of his coming, and who can stand when he appears?

For he is like a refiner's fire and like fullers' soap; he will
sit as a refiner and purifier of silver, and he will purify the
sons of Levi and refine them like gold and silver, till they
present right offerings to the LORD. Then the offering of
Judah and Jerusalem will be pleasing to the LORD as in the
days of old and as in former years. (Mal 3:1–4)

How well refined and purified Mother Teresa must have
been by the time the Lord was done with her! And how
pleasing an offering she must have become! As I stood there,
with Padre Pio's tomb behind me and the mosaic of Jesus
in Gethsemane in front of me, it seemed clear that Mother
Teresa has been given to us as a gift from God to help in
moments of tribulation. We all encounter challenges and
little moments of darkness, virtually every day. At difficult
times, we can look to Mother Teresa as a supreme model
of how to endure. If she could keep the faith for fifty years,
then surely I can keep it through my moments of doubt or
anxiety?

Sometimes it can seem a long trek up from the crypt,
across the plaza dotted with twenty-four ancient olive trees,
and around to the front of the old sanctuary. This is com-
posed of two buildings standing side by side. On the left
is the old Franciscan convent and church where Padre Pio
spent most of his life. Directly adjacent to it on the right
is the larger church of Saint Mary of Graces, completed
in 1959 while Padre Pio was still alive. Our pilgrim groups
rarely spent much time in this larger church. The old church
with the cross of the stigmata and the enormous new church
of 2004 with Rupnik's mosaics tended to occupy most of
our attention.

On this occasion, however, I went inside the church of
Saint Mary of Graces and sat towards the back. The place

was almost empty and in semidarkness. After a while, I received a tap on the shoulder. It was one of our pilgrims.

"Did you see the mosaics?" she asked in a coarse whisper.

I tried to fight a feeling of annoyance. Could I never sit for a moment in peace without one of these pilgrims bothering me? "Which ones?" I replied grumpily, thinking that she was referring to what we had seen earlier in the crypt of the other church.

"Mother Teresa and John Paul II!"

These two new mosaics had been erected a few years before in the church where we were now sitting, but I had hardly bothered to look at them on previous visits. These were completed in 2013 to commemorate the fact that in 1987, twenty-five years previously, both John Paul and Mother Teresa had visited the tomb of Padre Pio to pay their respects.

I had calmed down now and was feeling ashamed of my irritability. The woman and I walked over to view the full-length depiction of Mother Teresa. No doubt my "original" insight that Mother Teresa had borne in an interior way for fifty years what Padre Pio had borne in the flesh for fifty years had probably been noted many times before, for here she was in the church of the Italian friar. As we looked at the smiling image of the little Albanian sister, I felt again that helpless sense of injustice of the previous days. Padre Pio's afflictions were so clearly the wounds of Christ that few people could doubt them, though he himself was mortified by the fame that came with the stigmata. In the case of Mother Teresa, it was not so unambiguous that her anguish was a sharing in the spiritual affliction of Christ. No one called Padre Pio an "atheist" or a "disbelieving old man." His wounds, by their graphic physical aspect, left few people in any doubt that he was united to Christ. *Her* wounds, by their shocking spiritual nature, caused people to think that she must be *separated* from Christ. Yet Mother Teresa had, no less than Padre Pio, participated in the Passion of the Saviour. In his Letter to the Colossians, Saint Paul has a phrase that can seem mysterious: "I rejoice in my sufferings for your sake, and in my flesh I complete what is lacking in Christ's afflictions for the sake of his body, that is, the Church" (1:24). Padre Pio and Mother Teresa had both partaken of the Passion of Christ. By so doing, they had built up the Church and had also been made holy themselves.

We crossed the church to the mosaic of John Paul II. It was fitting that he was here too. Mother Teresa's life had been one of complete conformity to the teachings of the Church and fidelity to the popes. This was not an extra for her but was absolutely essential to her spirituality. It was some time later that I discovered something that probably should have been obvious from the beginning: if we examine the identity of Mother Teresa's critics, it becomes apparent that much of the antagonism against her was motivated by the fact that she refused to toe the majority line with regard to matters such as population control, abortion, and euthanasia. These critics wanted the Catholic Church to endorse things that she had never endorsed before. And so they attacked Mother Teresa because she fed the poor instead of tackling what they considered to be the causes of poverty; because she gave solace to the dying instead of changing the political structures that made living difficult. Mother Teresa was unapologetically disinterested in politics. Her most quoted line from Scripture was, "As you did it to one of the least of these . . . you did it to me" (Mt 25:40).

She worked person to person, heart to heart, one human being at a time. Social teachings, doctrines, and the organisation of the Church she left to others. She had been given her mission; others had been given theirs. On one occasion, when she was asked what she thought of the pope's view on a certain matter, she looked her interlocutor in the eyes and answered simply, "He is Peter."

9

He Is Peter

When they had finished breakfast, Jesus said to Simon Peter, "Simon, son of John, do you love me more than these?" He said to him, "Yes, Lord; you know that I love you." He said to him, "Feed my lambs."

—John 21:15

When you spend your working life travelling to holy places, even if your eyes are half shut, you sometimes get privileged perspectives on the people and events associated with those places. After repeated visits to Rome, Kraków, and Fátima, certain aspects of the shooting of John Paul II on May 13, 1981, impressed themselves on me in a more personal way than any simple reading about the assassination attempt could have done. Eventually, I came to appreciate that this event was filled with remarkable meaning. Alongside the terrible evil that was perpetrated that day, extraordinary grace abounded.

The day begins with a self-offering. He celebrates early-morning Mass in the Vatican with pilgrims who have come all the way from his previous parish in Kraków and then bestows on them the only gifts that he can think of: the objects used for the Holy Sacrifice itself—his vestments and chalice. He has lunch with a brilliant scientist and defender of the most vulnerable in society, a scientist who is ostracised by his peers and reportedly denied candidature for the Nobel Prize in medicine on account of his pro-life views. The meeting between pope and scientist that day would eventually lead to the foundation of the Pontifical Academy for Life, a prophetic institution that would shine like a beacon amid the shady relativism at the turn of the twenty-first century. He goes out in the square where Saint Peter was killed two thousand years previously and is shot on the anniversary of the first apparition at Fátima, a series of visions that included a "secret" regarding a figure in white who is mortally wounded as he ascends towards the cross. Though shot by an expert gunman at close range, he does not suffer fatal wounds, and the gunman himself will later interrogate the pope as to how and why he didn't die. The bullet follows a path within his abdomen that seems not to conform to the laws of physics and narrowly misses all major organs. He is taken to the hospital in an ambulance that he himself had blessed the previous day, and he is its first patient. Every minute is a matter of life and death, but the ambulance arrives at the clinic through desperate rush-hour traffic many minutes earlier than even the most wildly optimistic of forecasts. At the hospital, his life is saved by the rapid intervention of a brilliant surgeon, a surgeon who should not have been at the hospital at all that day but began to drive there earlier "impelled by a mysterious force." During the operation, the doctors believe that their work is futile, that no one can survive injuries and blood loss on this scale, but they continue nevertheless to fight for life, as all good doctors do. They prevail, but it is really the providence of God that has been prevailing all along.

Before recounting the meaning of those details and how they came to impress themselves more forcefully on this author's consciousness, it is useful to consider the story of Poland, a nation whose history can be understood almost entirely from the point of view of its self-abandonment into the maternal arms of Mary.

On the occasion of that concert in Santa Lucia del Gonfalone, I had prayed to Mary, "They have no water!" and my prayer was answered. Some prayers to Our Lady, even if they come from the heart, concern matters, like mine, that are not very grave. On other prayers the fate of an entire continent can depend. In August 1683, the Polish king Jan Sobieski prayed in front of an image of Our Lady and the Christ Child in the old Carmelite church of Kraków. The image is known as Our Lady of Piasek and is considered the most important shrine of the Madonna in the city. Sobieski had responded to a plea for help from Pope Innocent XI to assist the city of Vienna, which had been surrounded by the troops of the Ottoman Empire. The background to the conflict is complex and involved most of the ruling powers in Europe, but there can be no doubt that if the Ottomans had taken Vienna, the history of Turkish expansion in Europe would have been much different.

Sobieski prayed also at the Marian shrine of Częstochowa before marching on Vienna, taking with him virtually every available soldier in Poland and leaving their national frontiers unprotected. By the time they neared Vienna, the situation of the city was critical. The siege had already been going on for more than two months. The Turks had made extensive progress in digging tunnels with the intention of setting explosives under the city walls. If any of these explosions were successful, the city defences would be breached quickly and Vienna would be taken. Despite the high tension and the air of impending doom, the population was being greatly heartened by the efforts of a saintly Capuchin called Marco D'Aviano. Appointed by the pope as advisor to the Holy Roman Emperor, Father D'Aviano called the people of Vienna to repent and to pray the Rosary in the days leading up to the battle.

A week's march away from Vienna, Sobieski's forces met with those of his new ally, Duke Charles of Lorraine, head of the Imperial Army of the Holy Roman Emperor. They had a difference of opinion. Charles wished to take the easiest route to Vienna along the Danube so as to reach the beleaguered city as soon as possible. Sobieski, however, had studied military history and did not want to repeat the error that the Romans made when they were defeated by Hannibal at Lake Trasimeno many centuries earlier. He chose to take the difficult and arduous route through the hills into the woods above Vienna. The journey was demanding and fraught with danger, but it would put Sobieski and his cavalry in a superior position above the Ottoman army.

The battle began on the morning of September 12, 1683. Having taken the easier route, the Austrian and German forces began to engage with the Turks from early morning but without much success. By the afternoon, the Poles had taken the wooded hills above the city and began preparing for a charge. At about 4:00, Sobieski and his eighteen-thousand-strong calvary—spearheaded by the famed "winged hussars"—emerged from the forest above Vienna. For the eyewitnesses who later recounted the experience, it was an incredible sight. What followed was history's largest cavalry charge, led by the Polish king with his fifteen-year-old son by his side. As was their custom, the hussars were singing the Bogurodzica (Mother of God), the most ancient of national anthems. The Turkish army could not stand in the face of such an onslaught, and Vienna was saved. In the following years, the Habsburg army under Charles of Lorraine recaptured large areas of Hungary. The centuries-long Ottoman expansionism in central Europe was at an end.

Famously, after one of his military victories, Julius Caesar wrote a letter to the Roman Senate with the words *Veni, vidi, vici* (I came, I saw, I conquered). In a letter written to the pope from the captured tents of the Turkish forces, Sobieski paraphrased Caesar but left out the egoism: *Venimus, vidimus, Deus vincit* (We came, we saw, God conquered). It was a reference to the prayers he had addressed to Our Lady before undertaking the journey to Vienna. This crucial fact was not lost on Pope Innocent XI. A year later, the pontiff instituted the feast of the Holy Name of Mary, to be celebrated henceforth on the Sunday following the feast of the Nativity of Mary (which is commemorated on September 8). Previously, the feast had been celebrated only in Spain and by the Carmelite Order. The pope now ordered that it be extended to the universal Church. After the Second Vatican Council, the feast was removed from the calendar, but it was restored to September 12 by Pope John Paul II in 2002, following the events of 9/11.

Sobieski is buried in Wawel Cathedral, the most significant place in Poland for the identity of the nation. The central tomb in the cathedral is that of Saint Stanislaus, patron of Poland. Like Saint Thomas Becket, Stanislaus was assassinated by the soldiers of the king, who did not want to be brought to moral order by a troublesome priest. Directly adjacent to the church is Wawel Castle, seat of the Polish monarch for centuries. Even when the capital was moved to Warsaw about 1600, the coronations, royal weddings, and funerals continued to be held in Wawel.

The visit to Wawel Cathedral with a big group is difficult because the church has relatively little open space. The largest area is in front of the tomb of Saint Stanislaus inside the entrance. Afterwards you are confined to walking along narrow areas dotted with royal funerary monuments.

It was a bitterly cold week in February 2017. Kraków was covered in snow following a blizzard of the previous evening. Our coach had been returning to Kraków from Auschwitz with a group of fifty Salesian boys and girls from England in the afternoon when the snowstorm started. A journey that would normally take an hour and a half took more than three. The next day, however, was calm, if desperately cold, and the medieval cityscape of Kraków looked magical under its white winter blanket. We entered Wawel Cathedral, and I showed the group the tomb of Saint Stanislaus. They had already heard the story of his martyrdom. We looked at the first-class relic of John Paul II on the altar in the metal reliquary that looks like an open Bible.

From here, we passed to the left of the tomb and walked into the choir area and up to the top left corner of the church. Here is the casket containing the remains of Saint Hedwig, the young queen who gave all her money to establish the famous Jagiellonian University, one of the oldest universities in central Europe. We had already discussed her life as well, so there was no need to say anything to the group apart from pointing out her tomb and the famous crucifix in front of which she prayed.

The next part of the visit would be trickier. We were right at the end of the cathedral, in front of the Blessed Sacrament chapel, where perpetual exposition goes on. Outside this chapel is the final resting place of King Jan Sobieski. It was important for the students to see this tomb and realise its significance, but I hadn't yet had the chance to tell the story of the Battle of Vienna. There were always stewards standing in this area, and I knew from previous visits that they didn't allow people to stand there and talk for very long.

As we turned away from the altar of Saint Hedwig, two stewards were speaking to each other in low tones outside the entrance to the Blessed Sacrament chapel. I approached them and asked, "Is it okay if I say a few words to my group in front of the tomb of King Jan III?"

The younger one shook his head. "I'm sorry. There is no standing or talking to groups allowed in this area. There isn't enough space, and the cathedral is already very crowded."

I looked at him plaintively. "The students haven't heard the story of the Battle of Vienna. It would be a pity to walk by this tomb and not know its significance!"

The older steward motioned to his colleague and said something to him in Polish before turning back to me. "Go ahead and tell the story," he said simply. So we gathered in front of the tomb for five minutes or so, and the kids were given a very summarized account of how Sobieski had saved Europe, finishing with the words *Venimus, vidimus, Deus vincit.* While speaking, I noticed that the older steward had joined us and was listening at the back, nodding his head in assent every now and then. It was good to see that the Poles still appreciated Jan Sobieski.

By the mid-twentieth century, Poland had gone through a protracted ordeal that Sobieski could never have foreseen. If you look at an eighteenth-century map of Europe, you will find that Poland as a political entity did not exist. The country was divided up between Prussia, Russia, and Austria for well over one hundred years. Each of these powers, to different degrees, supressed Polish identity and culture. Yet the Poles managed to keep their national aspirations alive. Their Catholic faith made a very important contribution to this. Shrines such as Częstochowa had a vital role in grounding and fostering national unity and identity.

After the First World War, Poland finally regained its independence, but it was quickly threatened. Lenin and Trotsky wished to export the communist revolution from

Russia into Western Europe. Their primary aim was to bring the revolution to Germany. High unemployment and social unrest after the war made Germany seem a prime candidate for the communist message of hope and rebirth. Only one country stood in the Red Army's way—the newly independent Poland. The Russians could be forgiven for not considering Poland to be much of an obstacle to their plans. The country had been partitioned and ravaged for 123 years. Its new army had only just been thrown together by General Józef Piłsudski. The Russians, by contrast, had a fearsome two-hundred-thousand-strong "Army of the West" that they intended to unleash upon Europe. In July 1920, the Russian general declared: "The fate of the world revolution is being decided in the West; the way leads over the corpse of Poland to a universal conflagration. . . . To Vilna! Minsk! Warsaw!"[1]

On August 5, Pope Benedict XV made a plea to all the bishops of the world to pray for Poland and Europe. Ten days later, on August 15—the feast of the Assumption—a ramshackle Polish army turned the tide on the most powerful standing army in the world. To say that her victory over Russia was against the odds is an understatement of monumental proportions. Not surprisingly, it is referred to as "the Miracle on the Vistula." Following this most stunning of victories, Poland retained its independence for only nineteen years, but they were important years for galvanising national confidence and identity, qualities that would be needed in abundant proportions before the end of the century.

By the late 1930s, Poland found herself sandwiched be-

---

[1] Quoted in Zdzisław Musialik, *General Weygand and the Battle of the Vistula 1920*, trans. Józef Bohdanowicz (London: Józef Pilsudski Institute of Research, 1987), 20.

tween two of the most evil regimes in history: Hitler's Germany and Stalin's Russia. In August 1939, these powers signed a nonaggression treaty whereby both sides promised not to assist any enemy of the other party. The pact also contained a secret protocol in which Russia and Germany agreed to share between them the territories belonging to Poland and other countries in the region. The savage motivation for this pact would soon become clear. Just one week later, on September 1, Hitler invaded Poland from the west. A couple of weeks later, Stalin did the same from the east. By October 6, Poland had been partitioned between its enemies and once again wiped off the map. The most terrible war of history began with a pact between two evil regimes to invade and divide Poland.

In April and May of 1940, the Soviets rounded up twenty-two thousand Polish army officers, intellectuals, and academics, and massacred them in the Russian forest of Katyn near the border with Belarus. The intention was to eliminate any potential future leaders of Polish resistance. The Nazis had a chillingly similar policy. They executed about sixty thousand army officers, clergy, and academics in the period between September 1939 and January 1940. Hitler's animosity towards the Poles was scarcely less than his hatred for the Jews. Just before the invasion of Poland, he gave explicit permission to his commanders to kill "without pity or mercy all men, women, and children of Polish descent or language."[2]

It is often said that Poland lost the Second World War twice. After the liberation of Poland by the Soviets, a communist regime that was supported and maintained by

---

[2] Quoted in Catherine S. Leach, translator's introduction to *Values and Violence in Auschwitz: A Sociological Analysis*, by Anna Pawełczyńska (Berkeley: University of California Press, 1979), xvi.

Moscow came to power. This led to four decades of repression, economic difficulties, and lack of religious and other freedoms. Of course, the same situation prevailed in all of the countries that were victims of Soviet repression both before and after the war. Many millions of people died of starvation in Ukraine in a famine that scholars believe was man-made and facilitated by Stalin in order to wipe out the Ukrainian nation. Millions died in the Gulag, in the shooting operations of Stalin's "Great Terror," in reprisal killings, purges, and ethnic cleansings. In China, Mao followed the Stalinist model of collectivisation with disastrous results. A famine began in 1958 that would become one of the greatest human disasters in history, claiming thirty-six million victims.

The incredible thing about the tragedy of communism is that it was foretold to three little children in Portugal in 1917, just weeks before the October Revolution that took the Bolsheviks to power. During the apparition, Our Lady said, "Russia will spread her errors throughout the world, causing wars and persecutions of the Church. . . . Various nations will be annihilated." To three uneducated children, "Russia" seemed to be the name of an unknown woman. They noted what Our Lady told them about this "Russia" but wondered who she might be.

There are remarkable connections between the apparitions at Fátima and the unfolding drama of the twentieth century. The Russian Revolution, the end of the First World War, the rapid onset of a more terrible conflict, famine, and genocide on a scale never before seen—all were prophesied to three illiterate shepherd children. The end of communism and the means by which it will be defeated were also foretold. The association between Fátima and communism was probably familiar enough to many Catholics in recent decades. What may have been less evident at first—to our pilgrims who trekked the continent between Portugal, Poland, and Italy—was that Pope John Paul II had been a central figure in the entire story.

We organised our first pilgrimage to Poland in 2011. The main focus of these trips was the Kraków area, but one extended day trip was generally undertaken to the shrine of Częstochowa. The Madonna of Częstochowa in the monastery of Jasna Góra is the most important Marian shrine in the country. During the Swedish invasion of 1655, the entire country had more or less capitulated before the invaders. The damage to churches and to the artistic patrimony of the country was colossal. Every single Polish stronghold had fallen to the Swedes—with the exception of the fortified sanctuary of Częstochowa. Defended by a small number of monks and soldiers, the monastery managed to endure a siege that lasted forty days. The news that Jasna Góra was holding firm spread throughout the country, boosting morale until the tide of war began to turn in Poland's favour. Once the Swedes had been expelled, King Jan II Casimir declared Our Lady of Częstochowa "Queen of Poland" on April 1, 1656. Over the following centuries, the shrine was to have a central place in the hearts of the Polish people as their country was repeatedly subjected to invasion, oppression, and terror.

It was August 26, 2012, and our coach was arriving in Częstochowa from Kraków. I had been to the shrine the previous year and remembered the impossibly heavy traffic on the final approach. It was a pleasant surprise to find that the streets were almost deserted. I wanted to ask the driver if he knew the reason why, but after numerous failed attempts to communicate with him earlier in the journey, there seemed little point. My Polish was worse than hopeless, and my ability to communicate by sign language little better.

We could see the impressive bell tower of the sanctuary through the trees as we swung off the main road and crossed in front of the beautiful public gardens in front of the monastery. At one point, as you head for the coach park, the road traverses the long Avenue of the Virgin Mary, which leads from the shrine towards the centre of town. As we crossed the avenue, the open area in front of the monastery suddenly came into view on our right. We were greeted with a spectacular sight. An enormous crowd of at least one hundred thousand people was gathered in front of an open-air altar set up on top of the bastions of the monastery.

What on earth was going on today, I wondered? Then I overheard someone talking a few rows back. He had been looking up the shrine on his smartphone and had noticed that the feast of Our Lady of Częstochowa was August 26— that day! Not for the first time, I winced inwardly. A major event was in progress, and the courier hadn't known a thing about it—how embarrassing!

I took up the microphone quickly. "Today, of course, is the feast of the Madonna of Częstochowa. That is why they have this large open-air Mass celebration going on." I began to cough nervously before continuing; it was not the first time that waffling or bluffing had prompted in me a strange itchy throat. "Did I not mention this feast to you previously? Oh, apologies for the oversight!" This was followed by another bout of spluttering, and I could see the driver looking over at me, concerned at the sudden deterioration in my health.

On our arrival, we were met by one of the Paulist monks who look after the shrine. Before beginning our tour, he addressed the group with a huge smile: "My compliments!

This is the most special day of the year for visiting the shrine —the feast of the Madonna of Częstochowa!" I was making sure to avoid making eye contact with anyone and was studying the tile patterns on the floor. Out of the corner of my eye, I noticed our guide looking around earnestly at everyone. "Well done to your travel agent for organising your visit to coincide with today's feast! What wonderful foresight!" By this time, I was examining the stuccos on the ceiling and hoping that he would just get on with the tour.

One of the benefits of taking groups regularly to Poland was that the historic significance of the figure of John Paul II inevitably started to become more apparent.[3] Born in 1920, just a few weeks before the "Miracle on the Vistula," Karol Józef Wojtyła was a talented actor and playwright. He dreamed of a future in the world of theatre, believing that the most effective way of protecting and fostering what was best in the Polish psyche was through the healthy development of culture. The events of the war changed all that. By the time his father died in 1941, Karol was thinking seriously about the priesthood and soon entered the illegal seminary in Kraków. Ordained in 1946, Wojtyła became noted for the intensity of his pastoral work in the parishes where he was assigned while lecturing on ethics in the university. At the age of thirty-eight, he became the youngest bishop in Poland when he was named an auxiliary in the Diocese of Kraków.

When Pope Paul VI died in 1978, Cardinal Wojtyła travelled to Rome for the papal conclave. He may have feared that he might be elected pope because Padre Pio had told him in confession many years previously that he would rise "to the highest position in the Church." Upon the election

[3] See George Weigel, *Witness to Hope* (New York: Harper Perennial, 2020).

of the patriarch of Venice as Pope John Paul I, Cardinal Wojtyła breathed a sigh of relief: Padre Pio's "highest position" was evidently a reference to becoming a cardinal, or so he thought. Testimonies from friends and acquaintances indicate that he was overjoyed to be able to return to Kraków and continue with the extensive preparations for the nine hundredth anniversary of the martyrdom of Saint Stanislaus, which was to be commemorated in 1979. This was a project very close to his heart. Just thirty-three days later, however, John Paul I was dead, and the cardinals had to reassemble in Rome. The conclave was deadlocked between two strong candidates, Cardinal Siri and Cardinal Benelli. Eventually, to break the impasse, Wojtyła's candidature was broached. He was elected on the eighth ballot and chose the name John Paul II. His papal motto was a prayer addressed to Mary, Mother of God, entrusting his ministry into her hands: Totus tuus—"totally yours."

Perhaps, on a future occasion, there will be a chance to tell you about John Paul II's defence of the dignity of life from conception to natural death. For this, without exaggeration, he has no equal in world history. It is a story that is easily misunderstood because it has to do with proclaiming the truth with love. But his connection with Fátima and the fall of communism was possibly the most fascinating aspect of his dramatic pontificate. Soon after his election, John Paul began to make plans to visit Poland. The communist authorities were fearful of his potential effect on the nation, but they could not refuse his request. The first visit was for nine days and began in Warsaw on June 2, 1979. In his address during Mass in Victory Square, he did not discuss politics or economics and did not criticize the communist system. Instead—as he would do for the rest of his long papacy— he held up a vision of man that completely transcended any limited ideological view: it is only with reference to Christ that we can understand who we are and where we are going; any system that does not look to Christ to inform itself on the nature of man is fatally deficient. The pope's address ended with these words: "And I cry—I who am a Son of the land of Poland and who am also Pope John Paul II— I cry from all the depths of this Millennium, I cry on the vigil of Pentecost: Let your Spirit descend. Let your Spirit descend and renew the face of the earth, the face of this land!"

The government had made a concerted effort for more than thirty years to remove all public mention of the Divine, but before the Mass had ended, the crowd was chanting, "We want God! We want God!" Over the following nine days, John Paul travelled through Poland, never once mentioning communism or politics but, in every speech, challenging the Polish people to rediscover their true identity as being made in the image and likeness of God. It was like a wind of the Spirit blowing through Poland, awakening people's longing for religious expression, enlivening their courage, giving them the confidence to throw off the shackles of oppression.

The consequences of this visit were enormous for the future of communism, not only in Poland but in all of Eastern Europe. Most commentators are in agreement on this. Professor J. L. Gaddis of Yale university is not a Catholic, but he is one of the most distinguished historians of the Cold War. In his book *The Cold War: A New History*, he writes: "When Pope John Paul II kissed the ground at Warsaw airport he began the process by which Communism in Poland—and ultimately elsewhere in Europe—would come to an end." The 1979 visit prompted the foundation of the Solidarity trade union, which was at the heart of the largely peaceful movement that brought an end to communism in Poland. When the other Eastern European countries under the heel of Russia saw what had been achieved in Poland, they too rose up (relatively peacefully), and the communist bloc fell like a house of cards in a matter of months.

The collapse did not happen immediately after the 1979 visit, however, and there can be little doubt that the communists tried to eliminate John Paul in the meantime. On May 13, 1981, the pope was entering Saint Peter's Square for an audience when he was shot by a Turkish gunman, Mehmet Ali Ağca. Many commentators believe that the former Soviet Union was ultimately behind the attack, possibly using the Bulgarian secret police as an intermediary to hire and facilitate Ağca. After the shooting, the pope was rushed to the hospital by ambulance. He lost nearly three quarters of his blood and was given the last rites as he lay in the operating theatre of the Gemelli Clinic. It took five hours for the surgeons to get him into a stable condition. After he regained consciousness, John Paul asked his surgeon, Francesco Crucitti, to describe his injuries. Dr Crucitti replied by saying that he had discovered something inexplicable. The bullet seemed to zigzag its way through the pope's abdomen in such a way as to avoid all major organs. It missed the aorta by a matter of millimetres. If it had struck this vessel, the pope would have bled to death long before arriving at the hospital. It also narrowly missed the pope's spine and other major nerves, as if it had been mysteriously guided so as not to cause permanent damage. In 1983, when John Paul went to meet Ağca in prison and forgive him in person, the Turkish gunman continually asked, "Why are you not dead? My aim was true. The bullet I shot was a deadly one."

In May 1981, as he lay recovering, he was struck by a singular coincidence. Some weeks later, he declared: "Could I forget that the event in St. Peter's Square took place on the day and at the hour when the first appearance of the Mother of Christ to the poor little peasants has been remembered for over sixty years at Fátima, Portugal? For in everything that happened to me on that very day, I felt that extraordinary motherly protection and care, which turned out to be stronger than the deadly bullet."[4]

Since 1960, the mysterious third secret of Fátima had lain in an envelope in a drawer in the Vatican. John Paul II now asked that it be brought to him at the hospital. He read it and discovered that it described the shooting of a figure dressed in white as he ascended a mountain towards a great cross. Sister Lucia of Fátima, the principal visionary, said on many occasions that she and her cousins always understood this figure in white to be the pope.

From the late nineties until 2005, we took many groups to papal audiences with John Paul II. In the final years, his speech and movement were severely affected by Parkinson's disease. Many people called for his resignation on that account. We know now from the testimony of his secretary, Cardinal Dziwisz, that John Paul did consider retirement because of the grave difficulties in carrying out his ministry. But he was torn between that and the wish to witness to the value of human life even in the midst of infirmity. On one occasion, he said, "Christ did not come down from the Cross!"

My own clearest memory of him comes from a General Audience in Saint Peter's Square, possibly in the summer of 2002 or 2003. There were thirty to forty thousand people in

[4] John Paul II, General Audience (October 7, 1981), quoted in *The Mother of the Church*, ed. Seamus O'Byrne (Dublin: Mercier Press, 1987).

the square. After the initial drive around in the popemobile, John Paul took his seat under the canopy in front of the basilica, and the audience started. As always, it consisted of a short reading from Scripture in six or seven languages, followed by a brief catechesis, followed by greetings from the Holy Father to pilgrims of that particular language group. In those years, John Paul's speech was very difficult to understand because of his illness, yet he insisted on delivering the catechesis himself in various languages. Many people were critical of this apparent stubbornness of his. Sometimes I had to wonder myself if it might not be better to get someone else to do the readings for him.

We were seated in the third large section from the front. Each section holds about five thousand people, and from where we sat, the pope looked like little more than a dot on the horizon. We were in front of one of the big screens, however, so we had a very good view of the entire proceedings. John Paul was in the middle of reading his catechesis in Italian. It was a hot day, and people were fanning themselves with caps, sheets of paper, or anything else that could be used for that purpose. It was a veritable sea of fans in front of us. I remember wondering how many people were actually listening to the Holy Father. He was having difficulty speaking, and it wasn't easy to make out his words as he bent over the microphone with the sheets of paper on his lap. The paper was waving constantly as a result of the tremor in his hand, a classic symptom of Parkinson's. At one point, he seemed to get stuck pronouncing a particular word. He tried a second time to say it, but then looked up from the microphone and, very deliberately, left the sheets to one side. I have no idea what he had been saying just before that, but the next words were as clear as crystal, though said in that husky, slurred voice that had now become normal for him.

It was a five-word sentence, uttered with every bit of force that he could muster, a significant pause between each word: "IO . . . CREDO . . . FERVENTEMENTE . . . NEL . . . VANGELO" (I . . . believe . . . fervently . . . in the . . . Gospel). The crowd did not respond immediately. It seemed to take a moment for the people to grasp that John Paul had just borne witness to his faith in the most heartfelt way. Then a ripple of applause began among the Italian speakers in the audience, which soon became a loud crescendo of clapping that lasted some minutes. I think many of us in the audience that day had been paying little enough attention up to that moment, but now it was as if a bolt of electricity had passed through the crowd. A line from the Gospel came to mind —the one in which Jesus says, "Simon, . . . I have prayed for you that your faith may not fail; and when you have turned again, strengthen your brethren" (Lk 22:32). The Church's understanding of the ministry of the successor of Peter emphasises his role in confirming and strengthening the faith of Catholics, especially at times of confusion and doubt. A personal testimony to faith in the Gospel by the successor of Peter, despite hardships—wasn't that what we had just experienced?

Following the death of John Paul II in April 2005 and his unforgettable funeral, attended by four million people, he was buried in the crypt of the Vatican basilica. Then began a number of years of difficulties for those of us who made a living by taking groups into Saint Peter's. Every pilgrim to Rome wished to visit the tomb of this momentous figure, but access to the crypt was tight. During those six years, up until John Paul II's beatification in 2011 (and the transferral of his tomb into the basilica), protracted queuing outside the crypt was the order of the day for every visit.

As the years went on, I began to hear more and more fascinating details surrounding the events of the day of the shooting. Someone discovered that the ambulance that took the stricken pope to the hospital had never been used before. It was brand new and was waiting just outside Saint Peter's Square for its first commission. Remarkably, it had been blessed the previous day by John Paul himself. During the little ceremony of benediction, he had said, "I bless this ambulance's first patient." That patient would be himself. Its first journey from the Vatican to the Gemelli Clinic was more than forty kilometres, which would normally require much more than forty minutes in rush-hour traffic, but the driver managed to get to the clinic in a fraction of that time.

In the spring of 2012, while at an audience in the Vatican, I was seated behind our pilgrim group in my usual zombie-like state, waiting for the proceedings to end, when something Pope Benedict said made me prick up my ears. A French doctor named Jérôme Lejeune from Paris had just had his cause for canonisation submitted. Pope Benedict mentioned that this geneticist was part of a team that discovered the chromosomal basis of various conditions but was profoundly saddened afterwards when their work was used for early diagnosis in the womb and the termination of pregnancies. Lejeune was shunned by the press, the academic world, and his colleagues for his public pro-life stance. His career was obstructed and funding for his work discontinued, but he did not waver from his conviction that human life begins at conception and that a human being can never be a commodity, even if the child has a condition such as Down syndrome. It was interesting to hear the additional detail that Professor Lejeune, this courageous defender of life—even life that is challenged or disabled—had been to lunch in the Vatican with John Paul II on May 13, 1981, the fateful day of the shooting.

In 2018, during a pilgrimage to Kraków, we discovered another surprising piece of information about that day. Our group was the diocesan choir of Meath. We had asked permission to sing in the church of Saint Florian, where John Paul had served as a priest while continuing to lecture at the university. I went into the sacristy to inform the priest that we had arrived and were ready to sing. There was a religious sister inside preparing everything for the Mass. I noticed that there was a priest's vestment on display in a glass case.

"Did that belong to Father Wojtyła when he was a priest here?" I asked, confident that I had guessed correctly.

"No," she replied. "That was the chasuble he wore at Mass on the morning of May 13, 1981, the day he was shot."

"Wow!" I exclaimed, not expecting that answer. "How did you manage to get possession of *that*?"

The sister laughed. "He gave it to us! *Before* he was shot! Our parish was on pilgrimage to Rome that week. Back then, under communism, times were hard. We had nothing. It was a struggle to get the money together for the trip to Rome. Pope Wojtyła welcomed us into the apostolic palace, and we celebrated Mass with him on the very morning of May 13. After the Mass, he knew that he might not see us again for a long time, and he wanted to offer us a gift of some sort, but I don't believe he ever had any money or personal possessions. So, as we were leaving, he gave us the only things he could: the chasuble he was wearing and also the chalice used in the Mass. He knew that these would be useful to us in the parish because finances were tight."

I was amazed. These objects were a gift from the pope

to his former parish in Poland on that most dramatic of days, objects used in the sacrificial offering of the Mass and then offered freely to the parish. A few days later, we visited the new Pope John Paul II Centre on the outskirts of Kraków. Our main motive was to see the spectacular mosaics of Father Marko Rupnik that covered the walls of the recently opened church. As we moved around the church, viewing biblical scenes such as the crossing of the Red Sea, the Transfiguration, and the Resurrection, another glass case came into view in a side chapel. In the case was a cassock covered in blood, the very cassock that John Paul had been wearing on May 13, 1981. We were able to view the cassock at very close range and could even see the small aperture where the bullet, in obedience to the laws of physics, entered his abdomen, only to begin then flouting those same laws. The next day, while visiting the paternal home of John Paul in the beautiful village of Wadowice, we saw the gun that shot the bullet, on loan from the Italian police, under a glass panel in the floor.

That evening, stimulated by all we had seen, I looked up the shooting on the Internet. The first article I found was an address given by Cardinal Dziwisz, the pope's secretary, in 2001. The cardinal recounted how Professor Francesco Crucitti, the surgeon, confided to him later that he had not been on duty that day, but a "mysterious force" had impelled him to go to the hospital. While still on his way, he had heard on the radio the news of the assassination attempt. He raced to the hospital, fearful that the ground-floor lifts would be occupied, as they always were. On arrival, he found that they were all free and waiting to whisk him to the upper-floor operating theatre, where the ailing pope was waiting. Another interesting detail from the secretary's account concerns the aftermath of the mammoth surgery. When John

Paul eventually regained consciousness that evening, Father Dziwisz went in to see him. The pope's first words were "Have we said night prayer?" His desire was to return to normality as soon as possible, and that meant a return to his customary life of prayer.

Apart from the terrible event of the shooting itself, it really seemed like a day that was especially marked by the providence of God. Permit me to repeat the sequence of events as described at the beginning of this chapter. This son of Poland, successor to Saint Stanislaus, celebrates Mass with pilgrims from his former parish in Kraków and then bestows on them the only gifts that he can think of, the chalice and vestments used for the sacrificial offering itself. He has lunch with an eminent scientist and defender of the most vulnerable in society, a scientist who is ostracised by his peers on account of his pro-life views. The meeting that day would eventually lead to the foundation of the Pontifical Academy for Life, a prophetic institution that would witness to inalienable rights amid the shady relativism of the age. He goes out to the place where Saint Peter was killed and is shot on the feast of Our Lady of Fátima, whose apparitions included a secret revelation of a figure in white who falls under a hail of fire as he ascends towards the cross. Though shot by an expert gunman from close range, he does not suffer fatal injuries, and the gunman himself will eventually interrogate the pope as to why he didn't die. The bullet follows a path within his abdomen that defies the laws of physics, but it is a path that will ultimately preserve his life. He is taken to the hospital in a brand-new ambulance that he himself had blessed the previous day, and he is its first patient. Every minute is a matter of life and death, and the ambulance arrives at the clinic through rush-hour traffic many minutes earlier than the most hopeful of forecasts. At the hospital, his life is saved by the brilliant work of an exceptional surgeon—a surgeon who had not intended to go to the clinic that day at all but began to drive there "impelled by a mysterious force." During the operation, the doctors believe that their work is futile, that no one can survive injuries and blood loss on this scale, but they continue nevertheless to fight for life, as all good doctors do. They prevail, but it is really the grace of God that has been prevailing all along, since early that morning, since the beginning of time, in all of our lives, if only we were aware of it.

When John Paul II died in 2005, after one of the longest pontificates in history, the timing of his death was as marked by "coincidence," as the day of his shooting had been twenty-four years earlier. Among others, a Canadian priest called Raymond de Souza has brought attention to these correlations of times and dates. It is a fact that many saints die on days that are significant, as if the Lord chooses to call them home on those days as a sign of special favour. As John Paul neared the end of his life, some wondered if his death would occur on a particular feast. Given that he had such a devotion to Mary, many people would have bet on a Marian feast day, or maybe any day in the month of May, which is traditionally dedicated to the Virgin.

Another possibility was Divine Mercy Sunday, the first Sunday after Easter. This feast was inserted into the universal calendar of the Church by John Paul himself. The Divine Mercy devotion had been revealed to a Polish nun called Faustina Kowalska. She died just before the Second World War, at the age of thirty-three, but the devotion was suppressed by the Church for decades afterwards on account of misunderstandings regarding some material in Sister Faustina's diary. During his tenure as archbishop of Kraków, John Paul had worked to set the record straight by carrying out a rigorous study of Sister Faustina and her writings. As a result, the Divine Mercy devotion was approved by the Church and diffused throughout the world. In 2000, the Polish pope instituted the new feast of Divine Mercy and canonised Faustina, the first saint of the third millennium. After the ceremony, the pope declared that he had now completed one of the most important actions of his entire ministry. This declaration surprised some and mystified others, demonstrating how misunderstood the spirit of his papacy had been to many.

John Paul lay dying in his apartment on the evening of April 2. It was the Saturday after Easter Sunday, and the following day would be Divine Mercy Sunday. As night fell, his secretary began to pray the Vespers for the feast. This is normal in the Church's liturgy and is also perfectly in accord with the Jewish tradition. The celebration of a feast begins as darkness falls the evening before, with the recitation of first Vespers. Sometime after Vespers, the Mass for the feast was celebrated at the sick pope's bedside, and he was able to receive a drop of the Precious Blood for the last time. Liturgically speaking—and that is the only way of speaking that matters to a pope—John Paul died on the feast of Divine Mercy.

Incredibly, it was also a day full of Marian significance. The message of Fátima involved special devotion to the Immaculate Heart of Mary on the first Saturday of each month. That Saturday in April 2005 was a first Saturday. As Father de Souza points out, it is not possible for any of the Marian feasts to fall within eight days of Easter Sunday, but a first Saturday can naturally occur. In fact, the first Saturday of April occurs within the Octave of Easter about once every four years on average. There are nearly thirty-six thousand hours in four years. To die on the feast of Divine Mercy and on a first Saturday means dying within a window of about six hours—odds of six thousand to one—but that is exactly what happened. John Paul's last words, spoken in Polish on the evening of April 2, were "Let me go to the house of the Father." The Pope of Divine Mercy and the Pope of Fátima had gone to the Father's house on the feast of Divine Mercy and on a special day of devotion to Our Lady of Fátima.

Laura and I had left Rome to fly to Dublin on the evening of April 1. It was clear that we were leaving the city at an emotional time, but we never imagined that the funeral would develop into a happening of such global significance. Some people at the funeral had makeshift placards with the words *Santo subito!* (Sainthood now!), expressing their conviction that this man should be declared a saint quickly. Other voices were critical. In many ways, the public perception of Pope John Paul II had been polarised almost from the beginning. There were those who put him on an impossible pedestal. Others accused him of traditionalism, conservatism, and misogyny. To be declared a saint by the Church, however, does not demand that a person be perfect, not by a long shot. It requires that a person display heroic sanctity, which is a different thing altogether. There can be no doubt that John Paul II had certain blind spots and made errors of judgement, some of them grave. He was easily swayed by any display of evangelical zeal, and (sometimes) naïvely expected such zeal to be genuine, as he himself was genuine. In the case of the Legionaries of Christ, he was so taken in by the energy and outward zeal of their founder that he was blinded to the real character of this corrupt and immoral man (though it should be pointed out that sincere people in the Legionaries were also taken in completely by their founder). Such failures of judgement, though remarkably few in a pontificate that lasted twenty-seven years, tarnished the Polish pope's reputation in some eyes. Is it fair, though, to judge a person's integrity on the basis of errors of judgement? It is upon *actions* that our moral integrity should be evaluated, surely? Occasional errors of judgement and defects of character were obvious enough in Karol Wojtyła, and they were certainly given prominence by his critics. In the New Testament, who is the single figure with the greatest catalogue of gaffes, blunders, and failures? It is Peter, who was nevertheless chosen to be head of the Church and who died a martyr. Apart from Karol Wojtyła's much-publicized imperfections, did he still exhibit heroic sanctity?

The process of canonisation involves different stages. Since the early centuries of Christianity, the Church has required that a detailed investigation of the life of a person be conducted before that person can be added to the list of recognized saints (called the "canon"; hence the term "canonisation"). Once a person is canonised, the faithful have the right to venerate that person publicly in the liturgy. The investigation of Karol Wojtyła's life was an onerous task. It involved minute analysis of every page of his extensive writings, personal correspondence, and speeches; the compilation of a detailed biography; and hearing accounts from a truly enormous array of eyewitnesses. This material was not received uncritically by the Church. A fundamental figure in every such process is the "promoter of the faith," whose task it is to question the material that is presented. Popularly, he is known as the "devil's advocate."

At the end of this initial stage, the Church may decide to acknowledge the heroic virtue of the candidate, at which point he can be given the title "Venerable." But in order to arrive at the point of declaring the candidate a saint, the Church leaves the final word to God. If, as a result of praying to the candidate, a miracle occurs, this is taken as a sign that the candidate is certainly in heaven, since only a saint in heaven would be in a position to intercede with the Lord and procure a miracle. Two miracles are normally required for canonisation. These nearly always involve cures from serious illnesses. A committee of medical experts evaluates each case, and the cure must be found to be instantaneous, complete, and enduring. It is not so common to find cures—even natural ones—that have all of these characteristics! Moreover, no natural explanation of any sort for the healing must be available. The medical commissions appointed by the Vatican to investigate such cures have a reputation for scientific rigour and professionalism. It is fair to say that no other religious body in the world has a comparable discipline for the evaluation of miracles.

Diagnosed with Parkinson's disease in 2001, a French religious sister called Marie-Simon-Pierre could not write legibly, drive, or move around easily. Constant pain made sleep very difficult. She knew that further degeneration was inevitable, and she dreaded watching John Paul, also a Parkinson's sufferer, on television, because it reminded her of what she was likely to become. Her disease deteriorated after the pope's death, and her entire congregation prayed for his assistance to ease her suffering. One night, she scrawled his name on a scrap of paper with her trembling hand and went to bed. The next morning, she woke up at 4:00 and walked to the chapel with none of her usual mobility difficulties. Her hands had stopped shaking, and the stiffness and pain in her body had gone. She realised that she was fully cured. That same day, she went back to work as a nurse in the maternity ward.

The Church initially kept the case quiet, conducting a private investigation in which it interviewed more than a dozen witnesses, including neurologists, medical professors, and a psychiatrist. Satisfied that the recovery was medically inexplicable, the Vatican commission gave Pope Benedict XVI the go-ahead to issue the decree for John Paul II's beatification, the penultimate stage before sainthood.

Those who carried the *Santo subito!* placards at the funeral of the Polish pope meant business. On the very day of the beatification, the miracle that would eventually lead to the canonisation took place. Floribeth Mora Diaz, of Costa Rica, suffered a brain aneurysm in April 2011. After a series of tests, including a brain scan, the doctors told her that her condition was inoperable and that she would have only one month to live. A wife and mother, she had a strong desire to survive and serve her family. She turned to John Paul II to plead for his intercession.

On May 1, she was lying in bed watching the beatification ceremony live from Rome. On her lap was a magazine whose cover had a photograph of John Paul II with his arms outstretched. After the ceremony, Floribeth fell asleep but was awakened by the unmistakable sound of the Polish pope's voice saying, "Get up! Don't be afraid!" To the complete surprise of her husband, she got out of bed and told him that she felt well. Floribeth afterwards underwent rigorous medical tests, including new brain scans, which left her neurologists dumbfounded. They declared her instantaneous cure to be scientifically inexplicable. Later, a commission of medical physicians was assembled by the Vatican. They brought Floribeth to Rome for more tests and concluded that her cure could not be explained by any natural agency.

During a canonisation—the ceremony in which someone is formally proclaimed a saint—one of the most moving parts of the liturgy involves the solemn presentation of a relic of the new saint to the Holy Father. On May 27, 2014, Floribeth Mora Diaz, a mother of four, a woman who should have died in May 2011, presented the relic of John Paul II to Pope Francis. Behind her stood a sea of people reaching all the way to the Tiber, people from every nation on earth, the largest crowd ever assembled at one moment in the long and storied history of the Vatican.

THE PILGRIMAGE TO ROME AND LORETO is now over, and the coach is speeding along the highway to Leonardo da Vinci Airport. Drivers never go so fast as when they know they're on the last run of the day. As we get nearer to the coast, seagulls swoop over the frenetic lines of traffic. On the side of the road stands the occasional stone structure dating back to the time of Trajan's port, located near here at the very dawn of Christianity. But it is all becoming a blur to me now because I have another group arriving on the inbound flight, and my concentration is already faltering. How many people have to be picked up—is it forty-eight or forty-nine? Did Laura inform the hotel of our estimated time of arrival? Where the heck did I leave the mobile number of the new driver?

All of that will have to wait until later because we have arrived at the terminal, and it is time to say goodbye. This is the part of public speaking that I dislike the most. Just when I am starting to know these people, and they are finally getting used to their courier, it is time to leave. Most of them I will never see again.

"Thank you for joining us. I know it is hard to take in everything in this great city, but hopefully some of what we have seen and heard will be spiritual food and drink for you in the months ahead."

There are other things that could have been said, but when

you're just the courier, people expect you to talk about practical things only—baggage allowances, the best queue through passport control, the quickest route to duty-free shopping. So you end up not saying what—in this place—even the seagulls and the rocks by the wayside would cry aloud if they were able:

We have walked in the footsteps of saints and treaded the ground that once ran with the blood of martyrs.

We have stood in the presence of the successor of Peter, the rock on which Christ founded the Church, the primary witness to the Resurrection, guarantor of the truths of faith and the transmission of the Holy Spirit.

We have brushed our hands against the very stones touched by Jesus, the only-begotten Son of the Father.

We have lifted our gaze and glimpsed, in painting and sculpture, in the lives of martyrs and saints—through the scales that dim our vision—the beauty of God, who took on a human face.

But when you're only the courier, you can't really say any of that, unless you write it down in a book. The most uplifting thing you can muster is "Hope to see you all again. Don't forget to take everything from the overhead compartments. Thanks for travelling with us."

And thanks to all of you—for your company on the journey, for joining us along the way with Our Lady of the Skies!

—K. Troy
Feast of the Holy Name of Mary, 2020